THE STORM

—BEFORE

THE STORM

THE BEGINNING
OF THE END OF THE
ROMAN REPUBLIC

MIKE DUNCAN

THE
STORM
BEFORE THE
STORM

THE
STORM
BEFORE THE
STORM

The Beginning of the End of the Roman Republic

MIKE DUNCAN

PUBLICAFFAIRS
NEW YORK

PublicAffairs
Hachette Book Group
1290 Avenue of the Americas, New York, NY 10104
www.publicaffairsbooks.com
@Public_Affairs

Printed in the United States of America

Originally published in hardcover and ebook by PublicAffairs in October 2017
First Trade Paperback Edition: October 2018

Published by PublicAffairs, an imprint of Perseus Books, LLC, a subsidiary of Hachette Book Group, Inc. The PublicAffairs name and logo is a trademark of the Hachette Book Group.

The Hachette Speakers Bureau provides a wide range of authors for speaking events. To find out more, go to www.hachettespeakersbureau.com or call (866) 376-6591.

The publisher is not responsible for websites (or their content) that are not owned by the publisher.

Book Design by Linda Mark

Library of Congress Control Number: 2016962748

ISBNs: 978-1-61039-721-6 (hardcover); 978-1-61039-722-3 (ebook); 978-1-5417-2403-7 (paperback)

10 9 8

For Brandi
for everything

CONTENTS

viii   CONTENTS

TIMELINE

146–78 BC

146 Aemilianus sacks Carthage
     Mummius sacks Corinth
     Senate annexes Greece and Africa

139 Secret ballot for electoral assemblies

137 Numantine Affair
     Secret ballot for judicial assemblies

135 Beginning of First Servile War in Sicily

134 Aemilianus departs for Numantia
     Death of King Attalus of Pergamum

133 Tribunate of Tiberius Gracchus
     Passage of *Lex Agraria*
     Fall of Numantia
     Beginning of Aristonicus's revolt
     Death of Tiberius Gracchus

132 Anti-Gracchan tribunal
     End of First Servile War

131   Secret ballot for legislative assemblies

130   End of Aristonicus's revolt

129   Death of Scipio Aemilianus

125   Fulvius Flaccus proposes Italian citizenship
       Revolt of Fregellae

124   Lucius Opimius sacks Fregellae

123   First tribunate of Gaius Gracchus

122   Second tribunate of Gaius Gracchus
       Founding of Aquae Sextiae

121   Senate issues first *senatus consultum ultimum*
       Suicide of Gaius Gracchus
       Battle of Isère River in Gaul

119   Prosecution and suicide of Gaius Carbo
       Tribunate of Gaius Marius

118   Founding of city of Narbo

117   Marius fails to win aedileship
       Death of King Micipsa of Numidia
       Jugurtha assassinates Hiempsal

116   Adherbal appeals to Senate for aid
       Opimius leads Roman delegation to Numidia
       Marius elected praetor in possibly fraudulent election

115   Praetorship of Marius

114   Scordisci defeat Cato
       Marius curbs banditry in Spain

113   Jugurtha attacks Adherbal
       Cimbri arrive from north
       Cimbri defeat Gnaeus Carbo at Noreia

112   Jugurtha besieges Cirta
       Jugurtha kills Adherbal
       Jugurtha's soldiers massacre Italians
       Rome declares war on Jugurtha

111   Lucius Bestia leads legions to Numidia
      Bestia and Scaurus conclude peace with Jugurtha
      Memmius calls Jugurtha to Rome
      Prosecution and suicide of Gnaeus Carbo

110   Jugurtha assassinates Massiva

109   Jugurtha defeats Romans and forces legions to pass under
          the yoke
      Mamilian Commission established
      Metellus's first campaign in Numidia
      Cimbri return and demand land in Italy
      Cimbri defeat legions led by Silanus

108   Marius elected consul
      Sulla elected quaestor
      Marius recruits soldiers from all classes
      Jugurtha and King Bocchus of Mauretania forge alliance

107   First consulship of Marius
      Marius campaigns in Numidia
      Tigurini defeat legions in Gaul

106   Caepio restores control of courts to the Senate
      Caepio "loses" the Tolosa gold
      Marius defeats Jugurtha and Bocchus near Cirta
      Birth of Cicero
      Birth of Pompey the Great

105   Sulla induces Bocchus to hand Jugurtha over to the Romans
      Cimbri wipe out legions at Battle of Arausio
      Marius elected to second consulship

104   Second consulship of Marius
      Triumph of Marius over Jugurtha
      Marius reforms legions in Gaul
      Beginning of Second Servile War in Sicily
      Senate relieves Saturninus of his duties

103   Third consulship of Marius
      Saturninus secures land for Marius's veterans
      Mallius and Caepio exiled
      Lucullus defeats slave army in Sicily

102 Fourth consulship of Marius
Lucullus demobilizes legions in Sicily
Cimbri, Teutones, and Ambrones migrate south
Marius defeats Teutones and Ambrones at Battle
  of Aquae Sextiae
Cimbri successfully invade Italy

101 Fifth consulship of Marius
Marius defeats Cimbri at Battle of Raudian Plain
Aquillius defeats slave army in Sicily
Supporters of Saturninus murder Nonius

100 Sixth consulship of Marius
Second tribunate of Saturninus
Metellus exiled
Supporters of Saturninus murder Memmius
Senate issues second *senatus consultum ultimum*
Death of Saturninus and Glaucia
Birth of Julius Caesar

98 Marius meets King Mithridates VI of Pontus
Metellus recalled from exile
Sulla elected praetor

95 Sulla installs King Ariobarzanes on throne of Cappadocia
Mithridates and King Tigranes of Armenia forge alliance
Birth of Cato the Younger

94 Scaevola and Rutilius reform administration of Asia
Sulla meets Parthian ambassador

92 Trial and banishment of Rutilius

91 Tribunate of Marcus Drusus the Younger
Mithridates invades Bithynia, Tigranes invades Cappadocia
Drusus proposes Italian citizenship
Drusus murdered
Beginning of Social War

90 Rebel Italians establish capital at Corfinium
Varian Commission prosecutes those accused of
  inciting Italians

Gaius Marius takes command of legions in northern Italy
Aquillius escorts Nicomedes and Ariobarzanes back to
    their kingdoms
Lex Julia extends citizenship to Italians not under arms

89   *Lex Plautia Papiria* extends citizenship to all Italians
     Nicomedes of Bithynia invades Pontus
     Mithridates invades Cappadocia
     Pompey Strabo captures Asculum
     Sulla wages successful campaign in southern Italy
     Sulla and Pompeius elected consuls

88   Death of Poppaedius Silo
     End of Social War
     Sulpicius proposes equal suffrage for the Italians
     Sulpicius gives eastern command to Marius
     Sulla's march on Rome
     Marius flees to Africa
     Mithridates invades Asia
     Mithridates orders massacre of Italians

87   First consulship of Cinna
     Sulla departs for east and besieges Athens
     Cinna pushed out of Rome after proposing equal suffrage
         for the Italians
     Cinnan army surrounds Rome
     Death of Pompey Strabo
     Cinnan army enters Rome
     Marian reign of terror

86   Seventh consulship of Marius
     Second consulship of Cinna
     Death of Gaius Marius
     Sulla sacks Athens
     Sulla defeats Pontic army at Chaeronea
     Flaccus and Asiaticus lead legions east
     Sulla defeats Pontic army at Orchomenus

85   Third consulship of Cinna
     Fimbria kills Flaccus
     Lucullus lets Mithridates escape

Sulla and Mithridates conclude peace
Sulla forces Fimbria to commit suicide

84   Fourth consulship of Cinna
Cinna killed by mutinous soldiers
Sulla imposes settlement on Asia
Senate and Sulla negotiate his return

83   Sulla returns to Italy
Metellus Pius, Pompey, and Crassus join Sulla
Beginning of Civil War

82   Beginning of siege of Praeneste
Sulla addresses the Romans
Sulla wins Battle of Colline Gate
End of Civil War
Sulla appointed dictator

81   Sullan proscriptions
Sulla reforms the Republican constitution

80   Sulla resigns dictatorship and becomes consul

79   Sulla retires

78   Death of Sulla

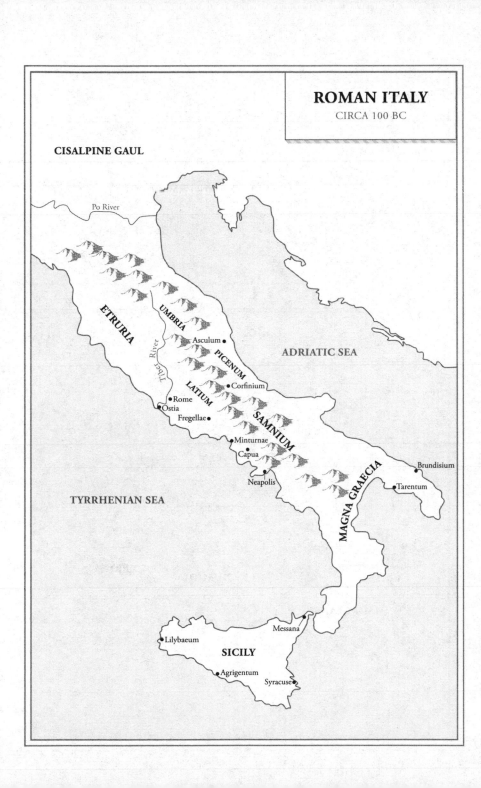

ROMAN ITALY
CIRCA 100 BC

CISALPINE GAUL

Po River

ETRURIA

UMBRIA

Tiber River

PICENUM

Asculum

ADRIATIC SEA

LATIUM

Corfinium

Rome
Ostia
Fregellae

SAMNIUM

Minturnae

Capua

Neapolis

MAGNA GRAECIA

Brundisium

Tarentum

TYRRHENIAN SEA

Messana

Lilybaeum

SICILY

Agrigentum

Syracuse

THE REPUBLICAN EMPIRE
CIRCA 100 BC

BLACK SEA

Sinope

PONTUS

BITHYNIA

CAPPADOCIA

MACEDONIA

Pergamum

ASIA

SYRIA

Athens

MEDITERRANEAN SEA

EGYPT

AUTHOR'S NOTE

No period in history has been more thoroughly studied than the fall of the Roman Republic. The names Caesar, Pompey, Cicero, Octavian, Mark Antony, and Cleopatra are among the most well known names not just in Roman history, but in human history. Each year we are treated to a new book, movie, or TV show depicting the lives of this vaunted last generation of the Roman Republic. There are good reasons for their continued predominance: it is a period alive with fascinating personalities and earth-shattering events. It is especially riveting for those of us in the modern world who, suspecting the fragility of our own republican institutions, look to the rise of the Caesars as a cautionary tale. Ben Franklin's famous remark that the Constitutional Convention had produced "a Republic . . . if you can keep it" rings all these generations later as a warning bell.

Surprisingly, there has been much less written about how the Roman Republic came to the brink of disaster in the first place—a question that is perhaps more relevant today than ever. A raging fire naturally commands attention, but to prevent future fires, one must ask how the fire started. No revolution springs out of thin air, and the political system

Julius Caesar destroyed through sheer force of ambition certainly wasn't healthy to begin with. Much of the fuel that ignited in the 40s and 30s BC had been poured a century earlier. The critical generation that preceded that of Caesar, Cicero, and Antony—that of the revolutionary Gracchi brothers, the stubbornly ambitious Marius, and the infamously brash Sulla—is neglected. We have long been denied a story that is as equally thrilling, chaotic, frightening, hilarious, and riveting as that of the final generation of the Republic. This book tells that story.

But this book does not serve simply as a way to fill in a hole in our knowledge of Roman history. While producing *The History of Rome* I was asked the same set of questions over and over again: "Is America Rome? Is the United States following a similar historical trajectory? If so, where does the US stand on the Roman timeline?" Attempting to make a direct comparison between Rome and the United States is always fraught with danger, but that does not mean there is no value to entertaining the question. It at least behooves us to identify where in the thousand-year history of the Roman Empire we might find an analogous historical setting.

In that vein, let's explore this. We are not in the origin phase, where a collection of exiles, dissidents, and vagabonds migrate to a new territory and establish a permanent settlement. That would correspond to the early colonial days. Nor are we in the revolutionary phase, where a group of disgruntled aristocrats overthrow the monarchy and create a republic. That corresponds to the days of the Founding Fathers. And we aren't in the global conquest phase, where a series of wars against other great powers establishes international military, political, and economic hegemony. That would be the twentieth-century global conflicts of World War I, World War II, and the Cold War. Finally—despite what some hysterical commentators may claim—the Republic has not collapsed and been taken over by a dictator. That hasn't happened yet. This means that *if* the United States is anywhere on the Roman timeline, it must be somewhere between the great wars of conquest and the rise of the Caesars.

Further investigation into this period reveals an era full of historical echoes that will sound eerily familiar to the modern reader. The final victory over Carthage in the Punic Wars led to rising economic inequality, dislocation of traditional ways of life, increasing political polarization, the breakdown of unspoken rules of political conduct, the privatization of the military, rampant corruption, endemic social and ethnic prejudice, battles over access to citizenship and voting rights, ongoing military quagmires, the introduction of violence as a political tool, and a set of elites so obsessed with their own privileges that they refused to reform the system in time to save it.

These echoes could be mere coincidence, of course, but the great Greek biographer Plutarch certainly believed it possible that "if, on the other hand, there is a limited number of elements from which events are interwoven, the same things must happen many times, being brought to pass by the same agencies." If history is to have any active meaning there must be a place for identifying those interwoven elements, studying the recurring agencies, and learning from those who came before us. The Roman Empire has always been, and will always be, fascinating in its own right—and this book is most especially a narrative history of a particular epoch of Roman history. But if our own age carries with it many of those limited number of elements being brought to pass by the same agencies, then this particular period of Roman history is well worth deep investigation, contemplation, and reflection.

Mike Duncan
Madison, Wisconsin
October 2017

THE TRIUMPH OF
THE ROMAN REPUBLIC

> Who is there so feeble-minded or idle that he
> would not wish to know how and with what
> constitution almost all the inhabited world was
> conquered and fell under the single dominion
> of Rome within fifty-three years?
>
> POLYBIUS[1]

PROCONSUL PUBLIUS SCIPIO AEMILIANUS STOOD BEFORE the walls of Carthage watching the city burn. After a long, bloody siege, the Romans had breached the walls and pierced the heart of their greatest enemy. The Carthaginians had put up a fight, forcing the Romans to conquer the city street by street, but at the end of a week's fighting the Romans prevailed. After systematically looting the city, Aemilianus ordered Carthage destroyed and its remaining inhabitants either sold into slavery or resettled further inland—far away from their lucrative harbor on the coast of North Africa. Long one of the great cities of the Mediterranean, Carthage was no more.[2]

Meanwhile, seven hundred miles to the east, consul Lucius Mummius stood before the walls of the Greek city of Corinth. For fifty years, Rome had attempted to control Greek political life without ruling Greece directly. But persistent unrest, disorder, and rebellion had forced the

Romans to intervene repeatedly. Finally, in 146 BC, the Senate dispatched Mummius to end these rebellions once and for all. When he breached the walls of Corinth he made an example of the rebellious city. As with Carthage, the legions stripped the city of its wealth, tore down buildings, and sold its inhabitants into slavery.[3]

By simultaneously destroying Carthage and Corinth in 146, the Roman Republic took a final decisive step toward its imperial destiny. No longer one power among many, Rome now asserted itself as *the* power in the Mediterranean world. But as Rome's imperial power reached maturity, the Republic itself started to rot from within. The triumph of the Roman Republic was also the beginning of the end of the Roman Republic.[4]

THE ROAD TO Rome's triumph began in central Italy six centuries earlier. According to the official legend, twin babies Romulus and Remus were found abandoned beside the Tiber River by a she-wolf who suckled them back to life. When they came of age the twins resolved to found a city on the spot where they had been discovered. But an argument over where to place the city's boundary markers led to a quarrel; Romulus killed Remus and became the sole founder of the new city of Rome. The legendary founding date is April 21, 753 BC.[5]

The oft-told story of Romulus and Remus is obviously a myth, but that does not mean the story is pure invention. There is archeological evidence that shows human habitation dates back to the 1200s BC with permanent settlements by early 900—roughly corresponding to the legendary timeline. Contrary to the myth, however, the location of Rome has nothing to do with fortuitous encounters with friendly wolves, but rather strategic economics. Rome sits nestled in a cluster of seven hills commanding one of the few stable crossings of the Tiber. Most of the early Romans were farmers, but the location allowed them to control the river, establish a marketplace, and defend themselves in case of attack. Their small community was soon stable and prosperous.[6]

Rome spent its first 250 years as just another minor kingdom in Italy. As records from these early days were nonexistent, later Roman historians relied on the oral tradition of "The Seven Kings of Rome" to explain the early evolution of their city. Though the evidence was slim, the Romans believed that most of their core public institutions traced their roots to this semimythical monarchy. The first king, Romulus, organized the legions, the Senate, and the popular Assembly. The second king, Numa, introduced priesthoods and religious rituals. The sixth king, Servius Tullius, reformed the Assemblies, conducted the first census, and organized the citizens into regional tribes for voting. But though the later Romans credited the kings with laying the political and social foundations of the city, they also believed that kings were anathema to the Roman character. The Roman Kingdom ended abruptly in 509 when a group of senators chased the last king out of the city and replaced the monarchy with a kingless republic.[7]

The new Roman Republic was not a freewheeling democracy. Families that could trace their lineage back to the original senators appointed by Romulus were known as the *patricians* and by both custom and law these families monopolized all political and religious offices. Anyone outside this small aristocratic clique was called *plebeian*. All plebeians—whether poor farmer, prosperous merchant, or rich landowner—were shut out of power. It did not take long for the plebs to agitate for equal rights. As the historian Appian says: "The plebeians and Senate of Rome were often at strife with each other concerning the enactment of laws, the cancelling of debts, the division of lands, or the election of magistrates." The running battle between patrician and pleb became known as the Conflict of the Orders.[8]

About fifteen years after the founding of the Republic, a debt crisis among the lower-class plebeians finally led to a great showdown. Incensed at arbitrary patrician abuse, the plebs refused to muster for military service when called to face a looming foreign threat. Instead the plebs withdrew en masse to a hill outside the city and swore to remain there until they were allowed to elect magistrates of their own. The Senate yielded and created the Plebeian Assembly, a popular assembly closed to patricians. This Assembly would elect tribunes who acted as guardians against patrician abuse. Any citizen could seek sanctuary with a tribune, at any time, for any reason. By sacred oath the tribunes were declared *sacrosanct*—within the city limits of Rome not even a consul could lay a hand on them. They became sentinels against the tyranny of the senatorial aristocracy.[9]

But though tension between patrician and pleb helped define the early Republic, Roman politics was not a class affair. Roman families organized themselves into complex client-patron networks that worked down from the elite patrician patrons through an array of interconnected plebeian clients. Patrons could expect political and military support from their clients, and clients could expect financial and legal assistance from their patrons. So though the conflict between patricians and plebs occasionally led to explosive clashes, the client-patron bonds meant Roman politics was more a clash of rival clans than a class war.

What truly bound all Romans together, though, were unspoken rules of social and political conduct. The Romans never had a written constitution or extensive body of written law—they needed neither. Instead the Romans surrounded themselves with unwritten rules, traditions, and mutual expectations collectively known as *mos maiorum*, which meant "the way of the elders." Even as political rivals competed for wealth and power, their shared respect for the strength of the client-patron relationship, the sovereignty of the Assemblies, and wisdom of the Senate kept them from going too far. When the Republic began to break down in the late second century it was not the letter of Roman law that eroded, but respect for the mutually accepted bonds of mos maiorum.[10]

THOUGH SOMETIMES DIVIDED internally, the Romans always fought as one when faced with a foreign threat. Romulus stamped the Romans early with a martial spirit and rarely did a year go by without some kind of conflict with a neighbor. Occasionally these seasonal skirmishes erupted into full-blown wars. Starting in 343, the Romans became locked in a long war with the Samnites, a nomadic people who populated the hills and mountains of central Italy. Waged over the next fifty years, the Samnite Wars eventually sucked the rest of Italy into an anti-Roman coalition. When Rome defeated this coalition in 295 they became undisputed masters of the peninsula.[11]

But that victory only led to an even greater conflict: the Punic Wars. As Rome grew in strength during the 300s, the prosperous merchant city of Carthage had been rising in North Africa. By the time the Romans conquered Italy, the Carthaginians had pushed their way onto the island of Sicily and would soon be moving over to Spain. The two budding empires inevitably clashed, and for the next hundred years Rome and Carthage battled for control of the western Mediterranean.[12]

Rome was nearly defeated in 218 when the great Carthaginian general Hannibal invaded Italy, but the stubborn Romans refused to surrender. In fact, they were soon able to spread the conflict throughout the Mediterranean. In an attempt to shut down Hannibal's supply lines, the Senate sent legions to attack Carthaginian lands in Spain. When they discovered Hannibal sought an alliance with King Philip V of Macedon, the Senate ordered a fleet to Greece. Finally the great hero of the war, Scipio Africanus, led an invasion of the Carthaginian homeland in North Africa. There he defeated Hannibal at the Battle of Zama in 202. Carthage surrendered.[13]

Emerging from the crucible of the Punic Wars, Rome was no longer merely a regional power—it had become *the* dominant power in the Mediterranean. But the Senate resisted taking direct imperial control over the territories they now commanded. The final treaty with Carthage was surprisingly lenient. It stipulated a number of punitive clauses—the Carthaginians owed an annual cash indemnity and were forbidden from fielding an army or a navy—but other than that, Carthage retained its traditional domains in Africa and was free to govern itself.[14]

The Senate also wanted no part of ruling the Greeks and Macedonians. Having successfully kept Macedon out of the war, the Roman fleet withdrew back across the Adriatic. The plan was to leave Greece to the Greeks but, much to the Senate's consternation, King Philip V of Macedon intentionally violated a treaty obligation and Rome was obliged to send legions east again. In 197, Philip paid for his provocative miscalculation when the legions crushed him at the decisive Battle of Cynoscephalae. Philip agreed to confine himself to Macedon and not make further trouble. But though Greece was now at their mercy, the victorious Romans declared in 196:

"The Senate of Rome and T. Quinctius, their general, having conquered King Philip and the Macedonians do now decree and ordain that these states shall be free, shall be released from the payment of tribute, and shall live under their own laws." The Romans had not come to conquer the Greeks, but to set them free.[15]

But though the Senate eschewed direct imperial rule over the "civilized" Carthaginians and Greeks, they showed little hesitation annexing "uncivilized" Spain. Attracted by lucrative silver mines, Rome kept its legions in Spain after the Punic Wars to ensure Spanish silver made its way into Roman temples. Roman conduct in Spain was riddled with double-dealing, extortion, and periodic atrocities. This led to rapid cycles of insurrection and pacification that in turn led the Senate to formally organize the Spanish coast into two permanent provinces: Nearer Spain and Further Spain. In 197, they joined Sicily and Corsica as some of the earliest overseas provinces of the Roman Empire.[16]

THIS WAS THE world into which Publius Scipio Aemilianus was born in 185 BC. The son of an ancient patrician family, Aemilianus was adopted by the childless head of the Scipione family—making him legally the grandson of the great Scipio Africanus. Adoptions like this were a common way to cement alliances inside the Roman aristocracy, and Aemilianus grew up inside the most powerful family in the most powerful city in the world. Raised to expect a distinguished public career, Aemilianus never doubted that it was his destiny to be a great leader. In time he would serve with distinction in all three of the Republic's principal imperial spheres—and then serve as one of the principal authors of Rome's ultimate imperial triumph.[17]

Aemilianus's first taste of action came in Greece when his natural father, Lucius Aemilius Paullus, brought his seventeen-year-old son along on campaign to observe how Rome conducted a war. In June 168, Paullus's legions crushed the Macedonians, deposing its young, ambitious king, Perseus, who had tried to overthrow the hegemony of Rome. He watched as his father seized the Macedonian royal treasury, enslaved upward of three hundred thousand people, and literally erased the Kingdom of Macedon from the map. What had once been the Kingdom of Alexander the Great was now divided into four small republics.[18]

After this harsh settlement, however, the Senate returned to their habit of ruling with a light hand. They demanded the inhabitants of the four new Macedonian republics continue to pay taxes, but at half the rate they had been paying to the kings of Macedon. If you managed to survive the war and not get sold into slavery, life under the Romans was pretty good.[19]

In the midst of his conquest, Aemilius Paullus also took a thousand prominent Greeks hostage to secure the good behavior of their kin. Among them was a brilliant politician and scholar named Polybius. A civic leader from the city of Megalopolis, Polybius had counseled neutrality toward the Romans in its wars with Macedon, which was enough to mark him as a dangerous element. But though Polybius was now slated for banishment it would prove a fortuitous calamity. When the Roman senior command passed through Megalopolis, the teenage Aemilianus borrowed books from Polybius, and their subsequent discussions created a friendly bond. Paullus arranged for Polybius to spend his exile in Rome and tutor his son in rhetoric, history, and philosophy.[20]

Under Polybius's tutelage Aemilianus embraced a new Greco-Roman spirit that was sweeping the age. The flood of educated Greek slaves into Italy led an entire generation of young nobles to become fully steeped in Greek literature, philosophy, and art. Some more conservative Romans railed against the importation of Greek ideas and believed they eroded the austere virtues of the early Romans. But while young leaders like Aemilianus reveled in Greek culture, they never questioned Rome's right to rule the world. And despite conservative moral agonizing, there was nothing soft about Scipio Aemilianus, who believed that obedience was taught with a whip hand. He would be in a prime position to be that whip hand when those who chafed under Roman rule began to rise up and the Senate decided to finally teach the Mediterranean obedience.[21]

WHILE POLYBIUS SPENT his exile in Rome, he came to admire the Roman Republic—or at the very least came to believe that Roman power was irresistible and that his fellow Greeks better get used to it. An energetic observer of the world, Polybius took endless notes and maintained extensive correspondence that allowed him to make a thoroughgoing investigation of these obscure Italian barbarians who were now masters of the universe. Eventually Polybius would write a history of Rome to explain how and why the Romans had risen so far so fast. Polybius argued that beyond their obvious military prowess, the Romans lived under a political constitution that had achieved the perfect balance between the three classical forms of government: monarchy—rule by the one; aristocracy—rule by the few; and democracy—rule by the many.[22]

According to Aristotelian political theory, each form of government had its merits but inevitably devolved into its most oppressive incarnation until it was overthrown. Thus a monarchy would become a tyranny, only to be overthrown by an enlightened aristocracy, which slid to repressive oligarchy until popular democracy overwhelmed the oligarchs, opening the door for anarchy, and so back to the stabilizing hand of monarchy again. Polybius believed the Romans had beaten this cycle and could thus keep growing when other cities collapsed under the shifting sands of their own inadequate political systems.[23]

The monarchical element of the Roman constitution was the executive consuls. Thanks to the Roman aversion to kings, the Republic did not have a single executive and instead elected a pair of consuls who would share supreme military, political, and religious authority. To limit the risk of a tyrannical power grab, each executive partner had the ability to veto the decisions of his colleague. But even more importantly, the term of office was just a single year. At the end of their year in office, the consuls would return to the ranks of the citizen body and a new pair of leaders would replace them.[24]

The practical Romans, however, did create an emergency office called the Dictatorship. In times of crisis, the consuls could pass power to a single man who would hold absolute power in order to deliver Rome from danger. And this did not just mean foreign threats: the first dictator was appointed due to plebeian unrest in Rome rather than threat from a hostile neighbor. But, critically, the Dictatorship expired after six months. As the Romans held an implacable hatred of kings, the Senate authorized any citizen, at any time, to kill another citizen caught seeking regal power. For nearly five hundred years Roman dictators never failed to lay down their power.[25]

The aristocratic element was, of course, the Senate. Originally one hundred old men organized by Romulus to act as a council of state, the Senate numbered about three hundred old men in Polybius's age. Drawing its members from the richest and most powerful families in Rome, the Senate had evolved into the central political institution of the Republic. With the Senate composed of former magistrates, it served as the principal adviser for the annually elected leaders. Rarely did consuls pursue a policy without the Senate's deliberative input.[26]

Finally, the democratic element was found in the Assemblies, which were open to all Roman citizens. By the time of Polybius there were three principal Assemblies: the Centuriate Assembly, which elected senior magistrates; the Tribal Assembly, which elected junior magistrates, passed laws, and rendered legal judgment; and the Plebeian Assembly, which had many of the same powers as the Tribal Assembly but which elected the tribunes and were open only to men of plebeian birth. The democratic element of the Roman constitution is often underrated, but the Assemblies were incredibly powerful. Only an Assembly could enact a law or pass capital sentence on a citizen. And while a citizen could always appeal a verdict *to* the Assemblies, there was no appeal *from* the Assemblies. (Because the Greek and Roman literary sources are not always clear which of the three Assemblies they are talking about, hereafter they are referred to collectively as "the Assembly.")[27]

In Polybius's construction, the three elements of the Roman constitution existed in a balance that prevented any one element from dominating. But though Polybius was a gifted theorist, by the time he was writing his history in the mid-100s the balance he admired had already been disrupted. The Senate had emerged from the Punic Wars stronger than it had been since the First Secession of the Plebs in the 400s. During the Punic Wars the annual changeover of senior military commanders became a hindrance to war planning and the Senate collectively began to take the lead in developing and executing policy. The senators also became adept at ensuring subservient clients were elected tribunes. By the end of the Punic Wars the consuls, the tribunes, and Assemblies no longer acted as a check on the Senate, but as an extension of it. Even as Polybius wrote his paean to Roman constitutional balance, the senatorial aristocracy was sliding into repressive oligarchy.[28]

O NE OF THE ways the Senate wielded power was by keeping tight control on who would be elected to the highest magistracies. By the mid-200s the Conflict of the Orders had destroyed most distinctions between patrician and pleb. But as one elite aristocracy falls, another is always right there to take its place, and a new distinction emerged: any family—patrician or pleb—that could claim a consular ancestor was now referred to as *nobile*. Men born without consular ancestors were derisively called *novus homo*, or New Man. This new patrician/pleb nobility worked hard to ensure that their families continued to monopolize the consulship, and New Men were almost never allowed to attain a consulship. Lucius Mummius was among those who felt the effects of this slide toward oligarchy. He was an ambitious young man. He was also novus homo.[29]

Almost nothing is known about Mummius's early life—even his year of birth is a mystery and can only be calculated to have been somewhere between 200 and 190. Assuming he followed a standard trajectory, Mummius would have joined the legions after finishing his education sometime between the ages of eighteen and twenty-two. Ten years' service in the legions was a prerequisite for public office, and Mummius would have served as a cavalry officer at various provincial garrisons. After his ten years' service, Mummius qualified to begin his ascent up the *cursus honorum*, the "path of honors" that comprised the hierarchy of elected magistracies.

The first step in the cursus honorum was *quaestor*. Each year the Assembly elected ten quaestors who were tasked with the Republic's finances, accounting, and record keeping. Usually acting as an assistant to a senior magistrate, the quaestors spent their year in office learning the ropes of Roman administration. Election to quaestorship also qualified a man to be enrolled in the Senate—though as junior officers in their early thirties they were typically seen and not heard during great senatorial debates. Mummius might have spent his year as quaestor assigned to the state treasury in Rome or placed on a provincial assignment to Sicily, Sardinia, or Spain.[30]

Above the quaestors were *aediles*. Each year the Assembly elected four aediles who were tasked with overseeing public works and games. A year as aedile was a great way for a rising politician to cultivate name recognition and popularity by throwing lavish games or overseeing a high-profile project like a new road or aqueduct. Ambitious young men often took on enormous debt to fund these projects—on the understanding that their future political success would afford them opportunities to pay back their creditors.[31]

When former quaestors and aediles approached their fortieth birthdays they were allowed to run for *praetor* and cross the threshold from junior to senior magistracies. Since the two annual consuls could not be everywhere, each year the Assembly elected four praetors who held sovereign power when the consuls were not present. Praetors helped shoulder the responsibilities of provincial administration, military operations, and judicial proceedings. Undoubtedly with the help of noble patrons who saw promise in the young officer, Mummius was able to secure election as praetor for 153 BC. Given his novus homo status, however, this was as far as Mummius could reasonably expect to rise. The consulship, after all, was not a place for a New Man.[32]

But a crisis in Spain helped Mummius break the streak that had seen no novus homo elected consul for a generation. The Senate assigned Mummius the task of restoring order in Further Spain, which was reeling from a revolt by the native Lusitanians. Marching into the interior, Mummius located the main body of Lusitanians and drove them back, but his army lost cohesion while chasing the rebels, allowing the Lusitanians to turn the tables. Mummius was forced to retreat all the way back to the coast. Undaunted, Mummius regrouped and then proceeded to best the Lusitanians repeatedly. By the end of the year, he was sitting on top of a pile of slaves and plunder. For his victories, the Senate and the People of Rome awarded Mummius a triumph—a rare enough honor to begin with, almost never granted to a novus homo.[33]

The triumph was not just an honor; it was the ultimate in Roman political pageantry. A returning general would enter Rome along with his victorious troops and the spoils of war and follow a ritualized path to the Temple of Jupiter on the Capitoline Hill. Along the way the citizens of Rome would behold the gold, silver, jewels, exotic artifacts, trophies, and slaves accumulated by the legions during the campaign. When the parade was over the triumphant general often hosted banquets and games—the more memorable and exotic, the better. Every Roman leader jockeyed to be awarded a triumph, but not everyone got one. It is a testament to Mummius's ability and political connections that this novus homo paraded through Rome in triumph. If Mummius decided to run for consul, his name was now known far and wide.[34]

I F THE NOVUS homo Mummius needed methodical and steady steps to climb the cursus honorum, the patrician nobile Scipio Aemilianus simply breezed along without a care in the world. Aemilianus was elected quaestor around 155, but prior to his consulship that was the only official magistracy he held. In 151, he volunteered to accompany the consul to Spain, where further revolts necessitated continued military engagement. While in Spain Aemilianus developed a reputation for courage and physical prowess. Once he received an award for being first over an enemy wall; another time he rescued three cohorts of trapped legionaries, and then later he defeated a boastful Spanish warrior in single combat. This was the resume of a dashing young hero, and the Romans delighted in his exploits.[35]

As Aemilianus's popularity grew, his destiny came into focus as the sleeping giant of Carthage woke from its fifty-year slumber. In 152, the aging Cato the Elder traveled to Carthage to arbitrate a dispute and was appalled at how splendid and wealthy Carthage had become since the end of the Punic Wars. Detecting newfound self-confidence, Cato returned to Rome and advocated immediate war to prevent the Carthaginians from ever again threatening Rome. In every speech he subsequently delivered in the Senate—no matter the topic—Cato famously concluded by saying, "furthermore Carthage must be destroyed." The Senate finally succumbed to Cato's nagging, and in 150 they found the pretext to attack. But the defensive fortifications of Carthage were impressive, and instead of destroying the city quickly the Romans found themselves mired in a two-year-long siege.[36]

Promised a quick and easy war, the citizens of Rome grew impatient at the Senate's inability to finish the job. In 148 they went looking for a new leader. As the consular elections approached, a movement to draft the popular Scipio Aemilianus broke out in Rome. But there was a problem: Aemilianus was both too young for the job *and* had never served a magistracy higher than quaestor. According to both the letter and spirit of the law, Aemilianus was ineligible for the consulship. But the power of the Assembly was vast and by simple majority vote they suspended the qualifications, elected Aemilianus consul, and then dispatched him to Carthage. After arriving in the spring of 147, Aemilianus set to work putting the city to a methodical siege. He walled off the harbor to prevent Carthaginian boats from slipping the Roman blockade and built extensive siege works to finally bring the city to its knees.[37]

THE YEAR AFTER Aemilianus's irregular consular election saw another irregular election as Lucius Mummius prepared to do the impossible. Helped by noble patrons and buoyed by the memory of his triumph, Mummius ran for the consulship of 146. It had been a full generation since the nobility let even a single ounce of new blood into their body, but Mummius was deemed worthy of the honor. When he won the consulship he was the first novus homo consul in almost forty years.[38]

The Senate dispatched newly minted consul Mummius to Greece, where Roman hegemony was once again being challenged. Since their victory over Macedon in 168, the Senate continued to play an influential but detached role in Greek affairs, acting as impartial arbitrators of political and economic disputes between various cities and kingdoms. But though the cities of the Greek east often sought Roman arbitration and guidance, that did not mean it always respected the Senate's decrees. In 148, envoys from the Achaean League—an alliance of cities in central Greece—petitioned Rome to prevent disgruntled members of the league from leaving the alliance. But when the Senate decreed that any city choosing to withdraw could do so, the leaders of the Achaean League launched a war to stop the Senate's will from being enforced. Of this inevitably doomed bid, the geographer Pausanias said, "Audacity combined with weakness should be called madness."[39]

As if that was not enough, just as war in Greece was brewing a pretender to the Macedonian throne launched a campaign to restore the Kingdom of Macedon. When word of this latest threat from Macedon reached Rome, the Senate dispatched the praetor Quintus Caecilius Metellus, who made quick work of the Macedonian army—forever earning Metellus the cognomen "Macedonicus." After this latest Macedonian uprising Rome decided they had had enough of Macedonian uprisings. Instead of returning sovereignty to the native inhabitants, the Senate annexed the whole region and created a new province of the Roman Republic called Macedonia.[40]

But while the Macedonians were crushed, down in Greece the Achaeans still held out. When Lucius Mummius arrived in the spring of 146, he found the last intransigent Achaeans holed up in Corinth. Mummius took over the siege and prepared for a massive final assault. Knowing they would not be able to withstand an attack, most of the Corinthians escaped out the back. Mummius allowed the inhabitants to flee, and when the city was mostly empty, he ordered his legions to break down the gates. Likely acting on senatorial instructions, Mummius ordered his men to collect every valuable object they could find, kill or enslave any residents they came across, and then systematically demolish the city.[41]

When word came back of Corinth's destruction, the Senate dispatched a commission to Greece to settle affairs in the east for all time. After fifty years of trying to maintain the pretense of Greek liberty, the Romans finally gave up. Greece was merged with Macedon into the single Roman province of Macedonia. Greek liberty was dead. The Romans now ruled.[42]

BACK IN NORTH Africa, the Romans prepared for final victory over their greatest enemy. After a year of careful preparation, Aemilianus launched the final assault on Carthage in the spring of 146. The legions breached the walls and rushed into the city, but it took a week of bitter house-to-house fighting to subdue the last Carthaginian holdouts. When the city was finally conquered, Aemilianus likely acted on the same set of instructions that had been given to Mummius. He stripped the city of its wealth, enslaved any fighters left alive, and forcibly moved the remaining inhabitants inland. He then ordered Carthage put to flame. Soon enough a senatorial commission would arrive to annex Carthaginian territory into the domains of Rome and create a new province called Africa.[43]

But as he stood watching Carthage burn, Scipio Aemilianus reflected on the fate of this once great power. Overcome with emotion, he cried. His friend and mentor Polybius approached and asked why Aemilianus was crying—what better outcome could any man hope for? Aemilianus replied, "A glorious moment, Polybius; but I have a dread foreboding that some day the same doom will be pronounced on my own country." According to Roman tradition Aemilianus then quoted a line from Homer: "A day will come when sacred Troy shall perish, And Priam and his people shall be slain." Aemilianus knew that no power endures indefinitely, that all empires must fall, and that there is nothing mortals can do about it.[44]

CHAPTER 1

THE BEASTS OF ITALY

Thieves of private property pass their lives
in chains; thieves of public property in riches
and luxury.

C<small>ATO THE</small> E<small>LDER</small>[1]

T<small>IBERIUS</small> S<small>EMPRONIUS</small> G<small>RACCHUS WAS WATCHING AS</small> C<small>AR</small>-
thage burned. In 146 BC the teenager was on his first campaign
and serving under the famous commander Scipio Aemilianus—a
typical posting for the scion of an illustrious family. And the Gracchi were
an illustrious family. First ennobled by Tiberius's great-grandfather, the
family had risen in stature with each generation, culminating with Tiberius's
father, whom Livy called "by far the ablest and most energetic young
man of his time." Over the course of his storied career, Gracchus the Elder
served two consulships and was awarded two triumphs. Though his father
died when Tiberius was just ten years old, the boy knew his father's
exploits well. He knew he had much to live up to.[2]

Tiberius's mother, Cornelia, was herself one of the most respected matrons
in Roman history. She was the daughter of Scipio Africanus and
wielded enormous influence inside the extended Scipione family. After
her husband, Gracchus the Elder, died in 154, Cornelia elected not to remarry—even
turning down a marriage proposal from the king of Egypt—
and instead dedicated herself to Tiberius and her other son, Gaius. She

cultivated their education and hired renowned Greek tutors to expose the boys to the most advanced theories of the age. In an apocryphal but telling story, a wealthy noblewoman once showed off a set of beautiful jewels to Cornelia, who herself pointed to Tiberius and his younger brother Gaius and said, "Those are *my* jewels."[3]

As he grew to maturity, young Tiberius was admired for his intelligence and dignity. He was possessed of "brilliant intellect, of upright intentions, and . . . the highest virtues of which a man is capable when favored by nature and by training." A generous spirit and eloquent speaker, Tiberius was on track to meet the high standards set by his father and become the leading man of his time.[4]

To keep the family fortunes under one house, Cornelia arranged for her daughter Sempronia to marry her adopted nephew Aemilianus—even though she did not like Aemilianus personally. Cornelia found him pretentious and did not think him worthy of the honor of being head of the family. In fact, much of Cornelia's focus on her children was an effort to keep Aemilianus from outshining her jewels. She pushed her sons' ambitions by reminding them that the Romans still called her the mother-in-law of Aemilianus, but not yet mother of the Gracchi.[5]

Despite all this family drama Aemilianus was obligated to bring his teenage brother-in-law Tiberius to the siege of Carthage. In Africa, Tiberius was exposed to the basics of military life. By all accounts he performed well as a soldier, earned the respect of the men, and even won a coveted award for being the first man over an enemy wall. When Carthage fell in 146, Tiberius Gracchus was there to watch the city burn.[6]

After Tiberius returned from North Africa, Cornelia maneuvered him into a marriage with the daughter of Appius Claudius Pulcher. Tiberius's new father-in-law came from one of the oldest patrician families in the Republic and had recently been named *princeps senatus*—a prestigious position that meant he was listed at the top of the senatorial roll and was allowed to speak first in any debate. But the marriage was not without complications: Claudius was a bitter opponent of Scipio Aemilianus, and Tiberius was now caught in the middle of their rivalry. But that said, by his early twenties Tiberius was positioned to achieve a preeminence that might even surpass his father. He was well educated, well connected, and already recognized as a man with "great force of character, eloquence, and dignity." But unlike most Romans, Tiberius would not win fame on the battlefield fighting a foreign enemy. Instead he would win fame in the Forum combating the domestic threat of skyrocketing economic inequality.[7]

AFTER THE SECOND Punic War ended in 202 BC, the economy of Italy endured a massive upheaval. The legions that conquered Spain, Greece, and North Africa returned home with riches on an unprecedented scale. A proconsul returned from a campaign in the east bearing 137,420 pounds of raw silver, 600,000 silver pieces, and 140,000 gold pieces. Tiberius's own father returned from a campaign in Spain with 40,000 pounds of raw silver. This was an insane load of treasure that would have been unimaginable to the frugal and austere Romans of the early Republic. But by the middle of the second century BC, Rome was rolling in the Mediterranean's dough.[8]

The newly enriched Romans spent their money on a variety of luxuries: fine carpets, ornate silverware, embellished furniture, and jewelry made of gold, silver, and ivory. The effect of this influx of wealth began to concern some alert senators. As early as 195, Cato the Elder warned his colleagues, "We have crossed into Greece and Asia, places filled with all the allurements of vice, and we are handling the treasures of kings . . . I fear that these things will capture us rather than we them." Every few years, the Senate would attempt to rein in ostentatious displays of wealth, but the resulting limitations inevitably went unheeded and unenforced: "by a fatal coincidence, the Roman people, at the same moment, both acquired a taste for vice and obtained a license for gratifying it."[9]

But this story of fabulous riches leading to moral decay only affected the small group of noble families who controlled the spoils of war. For the majority of Roman citizens, the conquest of the Mediterranean meant privation, not prosperity. In the early days of the Republic, service in the legions did not interfere with a citizen's ability to maintain his property—wars were always fought close to home and in rhythm with the agricultural seasons. But when the Punic Wars spread the legions across the Mediterranean, citizens were conscripted to fight in campaigns that dragged on for years a thousand miles from home. Thanks to these endless wars, lower-class families were "burdened with military service and poverty," and their property would fall into a state of terminal neglect. Upon returning home, a discharged soldier was likely to find the time, effort, and resources required to restore his land to its former productivity beyond his means.[10]

Wealthy noble families exacerbated the sharpening divide between rich and poor. As they looked to invest their newly acquired riches, they found thousands of dilapidated plots just waiting to be scooped up. Sometimes destitute families sold willingly, happy to get something for property they could no longer afford to work for themselves. But holdouts were often bullied into quitting their land. As these newly acquired small plots combined into larger estates, the Roman agricultural landscape began to transform from small independent farms to large commercial operations dominated by a few families.[11]

The plight of the dispossessed citizens might not have been so dire had they been allowed to transition into the labor force of the commercial estates. But the continuous run of successful foreign wars brought slaves flooding into Italy by the hundreds of thousands. The same wealthy nobles who bought up all the land also bought slaves to work their growing estates. The demand for free labor plummeted just as poor Roman families were being pushed off their land. As the historian Diodorus observed: "Thus a few men became extremely rich while the rest of the population of Italy grew weak under the oppressive weight of poverty, taxes and military service."[12]

Tiberius first confronted the new economic realities early in life. According to a pamphlet written later by his brother, "Tiberius was passing through Tuscany, and observed the dearth of inhabitants in the country, and that those who tilled its soil or tended its flocks there were barbarian slaves." According to Gaius this was the moment Tiberius first seriously confronted the need for economic and social reform. This apocryphal story is no doubt a fine piece of exaggerated propaganda, but it captures the essential dislocation of the poor families from their traditional way of life.[13]

Some of these dislocated citizens migrated to the cities in search of wage labor, only to find that slaves monopolized the work in the cities, too. So most remained in their rural homelands, forming a new class of landless peasants who would continue to work their land as mere tenants and sharecroppers rather than owners. Their new landlords loved the arrangement—tenant farmers could be used to produce low-margin cereals, which would allow landlords to save their slaves for more lucrative crops like olives and grapes. Politically minded landlords had an added incentive to promote tenancy: these peasants remained political clients whose votes could be counted on in the Assembly. This new breed of poor tenant-farmers would be tied to their landlords forever unless someone came along and offered them a way out.[14]

EXACERBATING THIS ECONOMIC and social dislocation was the Spanish quagmire the Romans had gotten themselves stuck in. When Carthage and Corinth fell in 146, Roman power seemed invincible, but Roman commanders in Spain had indulged in greedy atrocities that continued to provoke stiff resistance from the Spanish natives. So each year the Senate was obliged to raise new recruits and ship them off to the Iberian Peninsula, to serve on campaigns of undefined length against an enemy who specialized in demoralizing skirmishes. As a reward for their service these conscripts would come home to find their farms ruined.[15]

While the unpopularity of the Spanish wars grew, potential conscripts began to defy the consuls. With no other recourse, they once again turned to the tribunes for protection. The tribunes were the ancient guardians of the plebs, but over the past century they had been co-opted by the Senate. With citizens once again suffering under the arbitrary whims of the nobility, the tribunes returned to their sacred mandate of protecting the people from abuse. In both 151 and 138, aggressive conscription by the consuls climaxed with tribunes placing the consuls under arrest until they backed off. The tribunes had every right to throw the consuls in jail, but it was still a shocking challenge to noble authority.[16]

The Senate attempted to mollify potential conscripts by making life in the army a little less harsh. They capped service at six years and gave soldiers the right to appeal punishments handed down by their officers. But ultimately, this did little to improve the morale of the legionaries in Spain. In 140, veterans who had served six years were mustered out and replaced by raw recruits. These new soldiers were "exposed to severe cold without shelter, and unaccustomed to the water and climate of the country, fell sick with dysentery and many died." Not exactly something you can put on a recruitment poster.[17]

As the tribunes watched their constituents driven off the land or hauled off to fight in the quagmire in Spain, they took their first steps toward curbing the power of the nobles. For the entire history of the Republic, citizens had declared their vote out loud, making it easy for powerful patrons to ensure clients voted the way they had been ordered to. In 139, a tribune defiantly passed a law requiring secret ballots for elections. Two years later the secret ballot was extended to judicial assemblies. It would take time for the effects of these reforms to be felt, but the introduction of the secret ballot would prove a hammer blow to the foundations of the senatorial oligarchy.[18]

Surveying the state of Italy in the 130s, some among the nobility could see that there was a greater problem. Conscripts still had to meet a minimum property requirement to be enrolled, but with the rich pushing the poor off the land fewer citizens could meet the minimum requirement to be drafted. The Romans had faced crises like this in the past and responded by lowering the property requirements to bring more men under arms. But by the mid-second century, many citizens could not even meet minimal standards of service. The consuls were forced to rely on an ever-shrinking pool of men to fight wars and garrison the provinces.[19]

WITH ALL THESE social and economic problems swirling, Tiberius Gracchus was elected quaestor for 137. This was supposed to be the routine first step on his ascent up the cursus honorum, but instead it nearly ended Tiberius's public career before that career even began. Attached to the command of consul Gaius Hostilius Mancinus, Tiberius landed in Spain in the spring of 137 to continue the war against the Numantines, a Celtiberian tribe who had managed to resist all Roman attempts at pacification. Upon arrival Tiberius found himself caught up in one of the most embarrassing defeats the legions ever suffered. The consul Mancinus was far more a scholar than a soldier and the experienced Numantine guerrillas ran circles around his clumsy maneuvers. After a series of poorly executed skirmishes, Mancinus attempted a strategic retreat under cover of darkness, but discovered as the sun rose that his army was surrounded.[20]

Having fallen prey to Roman treachery in the past, the Numantine leaders demanded young Tiberius Gracchus be sent forward to negotiate. While serving in Spain a generation earlier, Tiberius's father had brokered an equitable peace treaty with the Numantines, and they remembered the name Gracchi and trusted the son to play as fair as his father. On his first campaign and with as many as thirty thousand lives on the line, Tiberius negotiated a treaty that allowed the legions safe passage out of the region in exchange for a pledge of future peace.[21]

Though there was little else Tiberius could have done under the circumstances, when Rome heard about the surrender, senators tripped over themselves bewailing the humiliating terms. The Senate recalled Mancinus and his senior staff to Rome to explain the cowardly capitulation. Though the embarrassed Mancinus attempted to justify his conduct, the Senate brutally smacked him down. They stripped Mancinus of his consulship and ordered him deposited at the gates of Numantia in chains to signal Rome's rejection of the treaty. The Numantines responded by sending Mancinus back to Rome with a message that "a national breach of faith should not be atoned for by the blood of one man."[22]

Tiberius and his fellow junior officers escaped official censure for their role in the scandal, but that did not spare them a severe tongue lashing. Tiberius cannot have expected to return home to a hero's welcome, but the intensity of the invective the Senate laid on him seemed disproportionate to his "crime." All he had done was save tens of thousands of men from certain death—did the Senate really expect him to choose voluntary mass suicide? But in contrast to the self-righteous fury of the old men in the Senate, when Tiberius emerged from the Senate house, he was greeted by cheers from the families of the men he had saved.[23]

W HILE TIBERIUS LICKED his political wounds, the road to re-
demption was already being paved by a group of senators intent
on rebuilding the population of small citizen-farmers. These reformist
senators were crafting a novel piece of legislation called the *Lex Agraria*
that would hopefully reverse the decades-long trend of growing economic
inequality. They believed they had hit upon an ingenious method of redistributing land from rich to poor without running afoul of the iron-clad
private property rights that defined Roman law. They would focus exclusively on *ager publicus* illegally occupied by wealthy squatters.

As you might have guessed from squinting at the Latin, ager publicus
was publicly owned land. As the Romans conquered Italy, they typically
confiscated a third of a defeated enemy's territory and turned it into state-
owned ager publicus. In the early days of the Republic, this public land
was converted into a Roman colony, but by Tiberius's day it was usually
leased to individual renters who would work the land in exchange for a
portion of the produce. To prevent rich families from monopolizing the
state lands, the Assembly passed a law that no family was allowed to lease
more than five hundred *iugera* (about three hundred acres) of public land.
But this prohibition was mostly ignored. The magistrates tasked with
enforcing the limits were themselves wealthy landowners occupying excessive public land, so everyone colluded to get away with it together.[24]

The legal rationale of the *Lex Agraria* was simple: the five-hundred-
iugera prohibition would be strictly enforced. Anyone caught occupying
ager publicus over the legal limit would be forced to relinquish the excess
back to the state. The excess could then be divided up into small manage-
able plots and redistributed to landless citizens. Since the whole point of
the reform was to rebuild the class of small holders, the bill stipulated that
the newly created plots could not be broken up and sold. The authors of
the *Lex Agraria* did not want to hand a plot of land to a poor man just so
he could turn around and sell it back to a rich man.[25]

Somewhat counterintuitively, the senators crafting this piece of radical
reform legislation were not backbench agitators, but rather some of the
most powerful men in Rome. The group was led by Tiberius's father-in-
law, Appius Claudius Pulcher, who was princeps senatus. Joining him were
a prominent pair of brothers: the wealthy jurist and scholar Publius Li-

cinius Crassus Mucianus and Publius Mucius Scaevola, one of the most respected legal theorists of his generation. There were other prominent senators and rising young nobles surrounding Claudius's group of reformers; among them was Tiberius Gracchus.[26]

For historians, one of the most controversial aspects of the *Lex Agraria* is whether the authors intended only Roman citizens to qualify for allotments or whether the noncitizen Italian Allies also qualified. The Italians provided much of the manpower for the legions and Tiberius himself was personally anxious about their plight, "lamenting that a people so valiant in war, and related in blood to the Romans, were declining little by little into poverty and paucity of numbers without any hope of remedy." But whatever the original intent, there is no evidence the Italians were ultimately included in the redistribution program. It seems an obscure point, but the fight over the *Lex Agraria* was an early test of Roman willingness to treat the Italians as equals. It was a test they failed.[27]

Historians also still argue about the motivations of the authors of the bill. Maybe they were acting on high-minded principle and simply wanted to restore the citizen-farmer and rebuild the manpower reserves of the legions. But it could also be that the law was cynically designed to add thousands of new clients to the political networks of its authors. Traditionally, the man tasked with distributing land absorbed the families that benefited onto his client rolls. And it is here that we might also detect the source of the intransigent opposition to the bill. Because what the *Lex Agraria* proposed to do was take all the miserable tenants attached by default to their landlords and transfer their political allegiance to the Claudian faction—an intolerable shift in the balance of senatorial power.[28]

A piece of legislation this controversial and far-reaching was not drafted on a whim. Claudius, Scaevola, and Mucianus would have spent years carefully picking through Roman law, laying out how the survey process would work, and who would arbitrate contested claims. But once the law was written they simply had to wait for the right time and the right person to introduce the bill. And for that, Claudius had his eye on his talented young son-in-law Tiberius, who was now trying to recover from the shame of the Numantine Affair.

Wʜɪʟᴇ ᴛʜᴇ ᴀᴜᴛʜᴏʀѕ of the *Lex Agraria* waited for the right time to introduce their bill, the unpopular war in Spain continued. After the Senate rejected Tiberius's treaty, two more years of inconclusive fighting followed—more men dead, more farms ruined, more families dislocated—all for no discernable gain or purpose. The people of Rome were getting fed up, so just as they had done during the war against Carthage, they turned to Scipio Aemilianus to end the war once and for all. But they faced a similar problem to one they had faced back then: Aemilianus was technically prohibited from running. During the Carthaginian war fifteen years earlier, the problem was that he was too young. Now the problem was that a law had been passed barring a man from serving more than one consulship in his career. But just as the Assembly had voted an exemption that allowed Aemilianus to stand for the consulship of 147, they exempted Aemilianus from the prohibition on multiple consulships. He was duly elected for the consulship of 134.[29]

With his ability to secure special treatment from the Assembly, the career of Aemilianus became a prototype for ambitious politicians in the years to come. Aemilianus showed how easy it was to manipulate the mob to serve personal ambition—inducing them to suspend inconvenient rules. But that was not the only dangerous example Aemilianus set. During the campaign for the consulship of 134, he promised to raise new recruits from his own extensive client network. The Scipione were a major center of political gravity in Rome, and many friends and allies readily agreed to accompany Aemilianus to Spain—among them Tiberius's younger brother Gaius. Raising a personal legion of four thousand men, Aemilianus was able to depart for Spain without the need for forced conscription. This was, for the moment, a welcome answer to an emergency situation, but it also set the precedent of a powerful noble raising a personal army from his own client network—an army whose loyalty to the powerful noble might outweigh their loyalty to the Senate and People of Rome.[30]

From the perspective of Claudius, though, all Aemilianus's departure for Spain meant was that a formidable political opponent would now be absent from Rome for at least a year. With his biggest rival out of the way,

Claudius wasted no time dispatching his son-in-law Tiberius Gracchus to ram through the *Lex Agraria* before anyone could stop it.

WITHIN MONTHS OF Aemilianus's departure for Spain, Tiberius Gracchus stood for the tribunate. The office was slightly beneath his standing, and had the Numantine Affair not darkened his prospects, it is likely Tiberius would have moved right on to an aedileship to set up his inevitable runs for praetor and consul. But given that he had to over-come the shame of the debacle in Spain, he could use his year as tribune to boldly vault back to the forefront of Roman politics.

Before Tiberius took office, the Claudian reformers floated the con-tents of the *Lex Agraria* to their senatorial colleagues, but met with in-credulous resistance. After occupying the ager publicus for many years, these wealthy landowners had come to regard the public land as their personal property. They had invested in it, improved it, used it as col-lateral for loans, given it away as dowries, and bequeathed it to their heirs. The authors of the bill wrote a number of concessions to lessen opposition: offering compensation for the ager publicus seized, giving clear title to the five hundred iugera that remained, making allowances for larger families to hold more land. But even with these concessions, a large faction in the Senate planned to resist the bill no matter what. To have their land confiscated and handed over to the shiftless rabble was simply out of the question.[31]

With the majority of the Senate hostile, the Claudians elected to break with mos maiorum and have Tiberius present the bill directly to the As-sembly without giving the Senate a chance to register their opinion. There was no law stating that a bill *must* be presented to the Senate before it was introduced in the Assembly—it was simply the way things had always been done. Tiberius's provocative gambit set everyone on edge. Shortly after taking office in December 134 Tiberius appeared before the Assem-bly and announced his intention to pass a law redistributing ager publicus from the rich to the poor.[32]

According to Roman law, after a bill was introduced three market days had to pass before it could be voted on. With market days occurring about once a week, the interval between the introduction and the vote could be anywhere from eighteen to twenty-four calendar days. This delay allowed time for voters to make their way to Rome for the vote. Since Tiberius was tapping into real resentment, dispossesed citizens flooded into Rome over the next three weeks "like rivers flowing into the all-receptive ocean." Even nonvoting Italians came in to support the bill. Though they could not vote they could still register their physical and psychological support for land redistribution. During these weeks, Tiberius regularly addressed the citizens in the Forum to harness and solidify their energy. He planned to have a large and eager majority in the Assembly when it came time to vote.[33]

After three market days had passed, Tiberius convened the Assembly on the Capitoline Hill to consider the *Lex Agraria*. The space would have been packed with voters, giving the area in front of the Temple of Jupiter "the appearance of stormy waves on the sea." Before the official presentation, Tiberius defended the *Lex Agraria* with the speech of his life. The Gracchi had been trained by the best orators in the Mediterranean, and Tiberius perfected an irresistibly calm and dignified presence on stage. He did not pace the rostra or beat his chest. He stood perfectly still and allowed the inherent force of his argument to hold the audience's rapt attention. According to Plutarch, Tiberius composed himself in the center of the rostra and delivered an impassioned defense of the common citizens of Rome.[34]

"The wild beasts that roam over Italy have every one of them a cave or lair to lurk in," he said, while "the men who fight and die for Italy enjoy the common air and light . . . but nothing else; houseless and homeless they wander about with their wives and children." Invoking the imagery of an Italian population dislocated by war and poverty, he said, "It is with lying lips that their commanders exhort the soldiers in their battles to protect sepulchers and shrines from the enemy . . . but they fight and die to support others in wealth and luxury." These ruinous wars had led to an unacceptable irony for the average Roman: "though they are styled masters of the world, they have not a single clod of earth that is their own."[35]

After bringing the Assembly to tears, Tiberius requested the clerk read the bill in preparation for the vote that he would surely win. But as it turned out senatorial opponents of the *Lex Agraria* had themselves been busy over the past three weeks. Knowing they would lose the vote, they had recruited Marcus Octavius, one of Tiberius's fellow tribunes, to prevent the vote from even taking place. One of the most powerful weapons a tribune wielded was the *veto*—which meant "I forbid." A tribune could veto anything, at any time, for any reason, and not even another tribune could overturn it. So when the clerk rose to formally read the *Lex Agraria*, Marcus Octavius stepped forward and vetoed the reading of the bill. Everything stopped. The vote could not take place until the clerk read the bill, so as long as Octavius maintained his veto, the bill could not be read and the vote could not take place. With the proceedings ground to a halt, Tiberius adjourned the Assembly for the day.[36]

A FTER FAILING TO avoid senatorial opposition with a generous bill, Tiberius and his Claudian backers decided the best play was to rally his popular base by making villains of the rich. Tiberius stripped out the friendly concessions before the next vote so that the *Lex Agraria* would be "more agreeable to the multitude and more severe against the wrongdoers." With luck, pressure from the populace would force Octavius to give up his veto and allow the bill to come to a vote—a vote they would surely win.[37]

In between sessions of the Assembly, Tiberius and Octavius came every day to the Forum to debate the merits of the *Lex Agraria*. The Forum is not a large area and like the stages at a music festival, there were few rostras available for speechmaking and their audiences often overlapped. In such close quarters, Tiberius and Octavius often engaged each other directly in debate. As Tiberius grew more and more exasperated, he promised to purchase all the ager publicus Octavius owned at a fair price if Octavius would drop his opposition the bill—hinting that Octavius's opposition was rooted in crass self-interest rather than high-minded public spirit. But Octavius refused to give up.[38]

With traditional debate and persuasion failing to break the deadlock, Tiberius turned to radical action. Tiberius promised he would veto every piece of public business until Octavius relented. Then he marched up the

Temple of Saturn and locked the state treasury with his personal seal
so that "none of the usual business was carried on in an orderly way: the
magistrates could not perform their accustomed duties, courts came to
a stop, no contract was entered into, and other sorts of confusion and
disorder were rife everywhere." Tiberius then ratcheted up the dramatic
atmosphere further. Alluding to reports that his enemies planned to assassinate him, he now carried a concealed short sword in his cloak and
surrounded himself at all times with thousands of dedicated followers.[39]

But when the Assembly once again convened to consider the *Lex
Agraria*, Octavius remained intractable. He vetoed the reading of the
bill again and the session descended into a fiery storm of mutual denun-
ciations. Two senators then stepped forward and asked the deadlocked
tribunes to put the matter before the Senate. Tiberius still had some
hope the Senate might help broker a deal. There was no question that if
the *Lex Agraria* came to a vote, it would pass by an overwhelming mar-
gin. When past tribunes had levied vetoes against popular bills, they
withdrew it after expressing their symbolic disapproval—but no one
had ever permanently defied the people's will. By the traditional force
of mos maiorum, Octavius should allow the vote on the *Lex Agraria* to
proceed. Never before had a tribune so obstinately blocked the clear will
of the people. Surely the Senate would induce Octavius to withdraw his
opposition.[40]

But rather than mediating a fair compromise, the assembled senators
took the opportunity to heap abuse on Tiberius—just as they had after
the Numantine Affair. There is no record of who said what, but Appian
reports that Tiberius was "upbraided by the rich." Not only did they fail
to pressure Octavius into accepting a compromise, they actively joined in
the attacks on Tiberius. Senators opposed to the *Lex Agraria* no doubt
railed against the contents of the bill, Tiberius's political tactics, and probably his personal character. The meeting ended with no resolution to the
dilemma and Tiberius himself angrier than ever.[41]

Unable to make headway by traditional measures, Tiberius introduced an unprecedented bill at the next scheduled Assembly. Arguing
that a tribune who defied the will of the people was no tribune at all,
Tiberius moved that the Assembly depose Octavius from office. There

was no law that said a tribune could not be deposed from office, but the proposal broke with all mos maiorum. No tribune had ever induced the Assembly to depose a colleague. It was unheard of. But Tiberius had once again packed the Assembly with his supporters, who now ominously surrounded the rostra and dared anyone to stand in their leader's way.[42]

Not wishing to spark a riot, Octavius settled on principled martyrdom, rather than suicidal intransigence, and did not veto the deposition bill. The Assembly was free to depose him if they wished and Tiberius called on the voters to prepare to vote. For the purposes of voting, the Romans were divided into thirty-five tribes that would each receive one collective vote. Individual members of a tribe would file through voting stalls and deposit their ballot in an urn. When they were finished the ballots would be tallied with the majority opinion determining the single collective vote of the whole tribe. Then the process would repeat for the next tribe until a majority of tribes agreed.[43]

When the first tribe completed their balloting, the herald announced the result: one vote for depose. Since Tiberius understood that he was suborning an unprecedented attack on a fellow tribune, he halted the proceedings after this first vote and begged Octavius to withdraw his veto. But Octavius refused. The next sixteen tribes deposited their ballots and every single one voted in favor of deposition. On the brink of victory, Tiberius again halted the proceedings and gave Octavius one last chance to stand down. Octavius again refused. The eighteenth tribe then cast their ballots. When they were done, the herald announced that a majority had been reached: Octavius was deposed from office. Stripped of his tribunate, Octavius no longer enjoyed the protections of his office and found himself menaced by the looming mob. He was only able to escape thanks to a group of friends who pushed their way through the crowd and escorted Octavius out of the Assembly.[44]

The deposition of Octavius was a decisive turning point in the battle over the Lex Agraria. Until Tiberius took this fateful step, he still enjoyed a great deal of support from his fellow tribunes and senatorial backers. But this reckless assault on a fellow tribune made Tiberius toxic to the naturally conservative elite. His father-in-law Claudius stuck with him but many others who supported the reform in theory were happy to lay the bill aside in the face of relentless opposition, let things cool off, and then try again a year or two later. But Tiberius could not afford to lose. His future career depended on passing the *Lex Agraria*, so he was willing to go to any lengths to push it through. And for the moment it had worked. Tiberius Gracchus won the battle. With Octavius out of the way, the Assembly overwhelmingly passed the *Lex Agraria*. The controversial land bill was now law.[45]

T HE *LEX AGRARIA* called for a panel of three commissioners to survey the ager publicus, determine ownership, and parcel out land. To make sure the job was done properly (and to monopolize political credit for the distribution of land) Tiberius induced the Assembly to elect Tiberius himself, his father-in-law Claudius, and his twenty-one-year-old brother Gaius to serve as the first three land commissioners. So far so good. But Tiberius soon learned that passing the law and enforcing its provisions were two very different things.[46]

Unable to prevent the bill from becoming law, conservatives in the Senate hit back with their own bag of tricks. This opposition was now led by the *pontifex maximus* Publius Scipio Nasica, who hailed from a more conservative branch of the Scipione clan. Nasica personally possessed far more than five hundred iugera of ager publicus, so he engineered an insulting blow to the new land commission. It was the Senate's responsibility to appropriate funds to pay for the men and material necessary to complete the surveying work, which required a small army of secretaries, clerks, surveyors, architects, carts, and mules. At Nasica's urging, the Senate voted a pittance to cover merely the daily expenses of the commissioners themselves. This calculated stinginess left Tiberius the captain of a boat with no oars. It was infuriating but there was nothing he could do about it.[47]

Shortly after being dealt this blow, one of Tiberius's closest supporters suddenly died and foul play was suspected. The increasingly paranoid Tiberius already kept his family surrounded by an informal group of friends and clients who acted as permanent bodyguards—and this protection now seemed more necessary than ever. Whether he was just playing to the crowd or genuinely afraid for his life, Tiberius donned mourning garb and brought his children to the Assembly where he "begged the people to care for them and their mother, saying that he despaired of his own life."[48]

But then fate intervened to alter the course of Roman history—and as will so often be the case, domestic Roman politics were shaped by events far beyond the shores of Italy. In this case the far off event was the death of King Attalus III of Pergamum. Pergamum was a Greek kingdom, occupying what is today the Aegean coast of Turkey, and had been an ally of Rome for close to a century. Since King Attalus III had no sons and believed his death would lead to a bitter power struggle among his potential heirs, he willed his entire kingdom and royal treasury to the people of Rome.[49]

Rome learned about Attalus's death shortly after the passage of the *Lex Agraria*, and Tiberius was himself among the first to be told of the terms of the will. Tiberius's father had once served on a senatorial embassy that confirmed the alliance between Rome and Pergamum—and when the envoy bearing King Attalus's will arrived in Rome, he stayed in the Gracchi home. One step ahead of his enemies, Tiberius convened the Assembly and announced that because Attalus's will said "Let the Roman people be heir to my estate," that both the disposal of the royal treasury and subsequent administration of the new province would be handled by the Assembly. Then Tiberius announced that a portion of King Attalus's royal treasury would be used to fund the work of the land commission and even provide startup capital for the new owners.[50]

This bold gambit sent conservatives in the Senate through the roof. By every right of custom the Senate enjoyed full discretion over both state finances and foreign policy. Polybius, a close student of the Republican constitution, said the Senate "has the control of the treasury, all revenue and expenditure being regulated by it," and "it also occupies itself with the dispatch of all embassies sent to countries outside of Italy for the purpose . . . of settling differences." The people, he said, "have nothing to do with it." By laying claim to Pergamum, Tiberius was attempting to wrestle both away at the same time. The Senate met in a furious session to denounce Tiberius as a reckless demagogue aiming to make himself a tyrannical despot.[51]

Soon after, either to retain the legal immunity his office provided or to protect the integrity of the land commission (or both), Tiberius made another shocking announcement: he was going to run for reelection. No law forbade a tribune from serving consecutive terms, but the overwhelming force of mos maiorum made his bid unprecedented. To his political enemies, this was all iron-clad proof that Tiberius planned to make himself a tyrant. If he controlled the state finances, distribution of property, foreign policy, and claimed the right to permanent reelection, Tiberius Sempronius Gracchus would be the king of Rome in all but name.[52]

UNFORTUNATELY FOR TIBERIUS, his political strength was at an all-time low as the summer elections approached in 133. During the battles over the Lex Agraria he had been able to count on a solid block of rural voters to stand with him. Perhaps it was because harvest was then in full swing that Tiberius had difficulty remobilizing his supporters for another contentious vote. Just as likely, however, is that conservatives now decided that Tiberius must be denied reelection at all cost. If they let it be known that they no longer opposed the Lex Agraria and land redistribution would go forward whether Tiberius was tribune or not, the urgency of the coming election would be undercut and many voters would stay home.[53]

Without his usual base of supporters, Tiberius turned to the urban population for the votes he needed. Land reform had never been of much interest to the urban plebs, so Tiberius broadened his platform to include further limits on military service, the right to appeal the verdicts of judges, and barring senators from serving on juries. This last drew one of the great political battle lines of the late Republic, though for the moment it was an empty suggestion not yet acted upon.[54]

Ever dramatic, Tiberius donned black mourning clothes in the lead-up to the election and again went round with his children securing pledges from his supporters to protect them if something were to happen. The night before the final election, Tiberius slept surrounded by armed bodyguards.[55]

Early the next morning, Tiberius's supporters packed the area near the Temple of Jupiter on the Capitoline Hill to ensure they controlled the voting space. Accompanied by bodyguards, Tiberius himself arrived and was greeted by cheers and applause from the crowd. When opponents of Tiberius arrived, they found themselves unable to push through the pro-Gracchan mob. Prevented from accessing the voting stalls, when the anti-Gracchan voters heard the call for the tribes to begin voting, scuffles erupted on the edge of the crowd as opponents tried to push their way in. The fighting halted the voting.[56]

Meanwhile, the Senate convened for a session in the Temple of Fides, located just around the corner on the Capitoline. Rumors swirled that Tiberius had deposed all the other tribunes and was preparing to assume regal powers. The consul presiding over the Senate that morning was none other than Mucius Scaevola—one of the authors of the *Lex Agraria*. Nasica and the hard-liners in the Senate demanded Scaevola do something, but the consul replied that "he would resort to no violence and would put no citizen to death without a trial; if, however, the people, under persuasion or compulsion from Tiberius, should vote anything that was unlawful, he would not regard this vote as binding."[57]

This was not good enough for the incensed Nasica, who rose in response and said, "Let those who would save our country follow me." Nasica then donned the formal attire of the pontifex maximus and put himself at the head of a mob of like-minded senators and clients. Together they marched to the Temple of Jupiter. As weapons were not permitted to be carried inside the Pomerium—the sacred city limits—Nasica and his followers armed themselves mostly with table legs and other bludgeons. Though the coming attack was not premeditated, it was clear they were willing to use force to beat back the mob trying to make Tiberius Gracchus king of Rome.[58]

Meanwhile, up on the rostra, Tiberius was warned about the approaching mob. Tiberius's men turned and readied for battle, but hesitated when they saw the mob included senators and was led by the pontifex maximus himself. Though the Gracchans started to give way, Nasica's men aggressively pushed and beat the crowd anyway. Once the shoving and hitting began, Tiberius's supporters naturally fought back, leading to a line of clashes throughout the Assembly. The casualties in the resulting mêlée were entirely one-sided—Tiberius's people were unarmed and made easy targets for Nasica's gang. Trapped in the confined space in front of the Temple of Jupiter, many people were trampled underfoot or fell to their deaths off the steep cliffs of the Capitoline. When the dust cleared three hundred people lay dead.[59]

The principal target of the attack was, of course, Tiberius himself, and it didn't take long for the reactionary senators to locate their prey. Near the entrance of the Temple of Jupiter, Tiberius tripped over the body of a man who had already fallen and before he could get up, he was set upon by a fellow tribune and a senator. Though he was a tribune and allegedly sacrosanct, these two men proceeded to beat Tiberius Gracchus to death with the legs of a bench. As the historian Appian records: "So perished on the Capitol, and while still tribune, Gracchus, the son of that Gracchus who was twice consul, and of Cornelia, daughter of that Scipio who robbed Carthage of her supremacy. He lost his life in consequence of a most excellent design too violently pursued; and this abominable crime, the first that was perpetrated in the public assembly, was seldom without parallels thereafter from time to time."[60]

IT WAS ONE of the bloodiest days in Roman political history, though Plutarch overstates things when he says, "This is said to have been the first sedition at Rome, since the abolition of royal power, to end in bloodshed and the death of citizens." But at least in living memory Roman politics had always been waged without resorting to violence. Now hundreds of citizens lay dead on the Capitoline Hill. Whatever one felt about Tiberius Gracchus and his *Lex Agraria*, it must have been a shocking sight.[61]

The principal cause of the crisis of 133 was a dangerous game of mutual brinksmanship. Tiberius had bypassed the Senate, so Octavius vetoed the reading of the bill, so Tiberius shut down all public business. When Octavius remained intractable, Tiberius deposed him from office, so the Senate denied the land commission money to operate, so Tiberius seized the bequeath from Pergamum, and then ran for reelection. All of this culminated with Nasica leading an armed mob to kill three hundred people. In just a few short months, a simple land redistribution bill had escalated to violent massacre.

The Senate made no apologies for the attack. Tiberius and his dead supporters were denied traditional funeral arrangements and dumped en masse into the Tiber. This was, in itself, a shocking affront to tradition. The Gracchi were still a powerful noble family; denying their son a proper burial was fraught with religious and social implications. But the story was now that Tiberius had been trying to make himself king—the most taboo of political offices. And the Senate determined that they could not afford a funereal becoming a venue for renewing violent revolution.[62]

With all the taboos of mos maiorum now breaking down left and right, "this was the beginning in Rome of civil bloodshed, and of the license of the sword." The definitive triumph of naked force was a lesson no one could unlearn. As the ancient Greek historian Velleius Paterculus later observed: "Precedents do not stop where they begin, but, however narrow the path upon which they enter, they create for themselves a highway whereon they may wander with the utmost latitude . . . no one thinks a course is base for himself which has proven profitable to others."[63]

CHAPTER 2

THE STEPCHILDREN OF ROME

For when those in power act cruelly and wickedly, the character of their subjects is inflamed to reckless action . . . if they are denied the kindness which they deserve, they revolt against the men who act like cruel despots.

DIODORUS[1]

THE YEAR 132 BC DAWNED WITH THE SENATE READY TO bury the revolution of Tiberius Gracchus. They created a special commission whose purpose was to punish those who had supported Tiberius's illegal bid for monarchy. This commission would be led by the new consuls—Publius Rupilius and Publius Popilius Laenas— who were given the authority to pass capital sentences. But there were questions about the legality of this extraordinary tribunal. According to the ancient Law of the Twelve Tables, "Laws concerning capital punishment of a citizen shall not be passed . . . except by the Assembly." Neither the Senate nor the consuls had the right to bring capital charges against citizens on their own authority—but here they were, doing it anyway.[2]

The populace was outraged at the brazen flouting of the law and their outrage grew when only lower-class plebs or resident foreigners were targeted for prosecution. The aristocratic senators who had participated in the affair—for example, the authors of the *Lex Agraria*—were never called to account despite their central role in the crisis. For the next few weeks the common people of Rome lived under the ominous shadow of the tribunal. Men were hauled before the consuls for the most tenuous connection to the Gracchan movement. Some were executed, many more driven into exile.[3]

If it was obnoxious to many that no senators were called to account for themselves, it was downright sacrilegious that Scipio Nasica still walked free. Nasica had done nothing less than orchestrate the murder of a sacrosanct tribune. That he had yet faced no consequences was literally a crime against the gods. So Marcus Fulvius Flaccus, a young reformist senator and ally of the Gracchans, announced his intention to bring Nasica to justice. Whatever they thought of Nasica's conduct, the Senate could not stand by while an angry mob prosecuted the pontifex maximus. Luckily a convenient solution presented itself. With Tiberius dead, the Senate had taken back control of the Kingdom of Pergamum, and they named Nasica to an embassy that would travel to Pergamum, assess the situation, and begin the process of annexation. The pontifex was incensed that he was being shuffled out the back door, but complied with the will of his colleagues. Nasica departed for the east, where he would live just long enough to witness a giant slave revolt before dying bitterly, "without any desire to return to his ungrateful country."[4]

Having defused this crisis the Senate also refused to ignite a new one. They knew there were limits to how far they could go with their repressive antics, so they did not attempt to repeal the Lex Agraria or to shut down the land commission. Either because they finally admitted the efficacy of reform or because they believed that stopping the process now would spark a riot, the Senate allowed the commission to continue its work. They assigned Mucianus—one of the senatorial authors of the Lex Agraria— to take Tiberius's place on the commission alongside Claudius and young Gaius Gracchus. The redistribution of ager publicus continued.[5]

WHILE ALL OF this was unfolding in Rome, Scipio Aemilianus was half a world away wrapping up the conquest of Numantia. He had arrived eighteen months earlier and found the Spanish legions demoralized, inert, and lacking discipline. Aemilianus cleaned them up and ran them around on daily exercise to get them back into fighting shape. After a full year of preparation, Aemilianus then called in the full weight of Rome's available manpower. In the spring of 133 more than 60,000 Italian, African, and Spanish soldiers surrounded the pitiful city of Numantia, which was now manned by just 8,000 holdouts. In the face of this overwhelming force the Numantines admitted defeat: "Despairing, therefore, of escape and in a revulsion of rage and fury they made an end of themselves, their families and their native city with the sword, with poison and with general conflagration." When the few remaining traumatized survivors exited the gates, Aemilianus ordered them thrown in chains and Numantia razed to the ground.[6]

Aemilianus expected this victory to be the talk of Rome, but shortly after the fall of Numantia word came of a major political crisis in Rome. After passing a controversial land bill, Tiberius Gracchus and three hundred of his followers had been killed and dumped in the Tiber. Aemilianus did not respond diplomatically to the news. With the official story being that Tiberius had conspired to make himself a king, Aemilianus responded with another dose of Homeric wisdom: "So perish all those who attempt such crimes." But when Aemilianus's Homeric quip landed back home, the streets murmured with displeasure. Had Aemilianus just sanctioned the murder of a tribune—his own brother-in-law, no less? The same people who had carried Aemilianus to two extraordinary consulships now saw him as just another out-of-touch noble.[7]

Aemilianus was oblivious to the shift in mood back in Rome, however, and continued to believe that thanks to his latest conquest his star burned brighter than ever. When he returned home in the summer of 132, he was shocked by the reception he received. Rather than adoring throngs he found people in Rome glowering and standoffish. A distressed Aemilianus hardly recognized the people that had unanimously elected him consul just two years earlier.[8]

Things might have gone differently for Aemilianus had he been able to lavishly spread the wealth from his conquest in Numantia, but unfortunately there was no wealth to spread. Compared to his triumph after the sack of Carthage, Aemilianus's Numantine triumph was a pathetic affair. Few riches. Few slaves. Nothing exotic or beautiful or wondrous to behold. For all the lives that had been ruined in the Spanish wars, it must have been infuriating to discover that all Rome had to show for it was a few trinkets and some gaunt Spaniards.[9]

Shortly after Aemilianus's meager triumph, a rising Gracchan partisan named Gaius Papirius Carbo was elected tribune for 131. A passionate young reformer, Carbo introduced a bill that would extend the secret ballot to all legislative assemblies. If passed, it would complete the transformation of Roman voting from public voice to secret ballot—as all electoral, judicial, and legislative Assemblies would now be secret. Carbo also introduced a bill to retroactively confirm the legitimacy of Tiberius's reelection bid to undercut the conservative argument that Tiberius's murder was justified because he broke the law.[10]

Believing that things were moving too far in a popular direction, Aemilianus spoke in the Forum against Carbo's bill. He said the traditional prohibition on recurring office holding was in keeping with republican virtue—which must have struck the crowd as hypocritical since Aemilianus had secured an exemption from those very same prohibitions. During one of Aemilianus's public appearances, Carbo himself stepped forward to demand what Aemilianus *really* thought about the murder of Tiberius. Aemilianus said, "If he intended to seize the state he was killed justly." When the audience turned hostile Aemilianus returned the compliment. As he looked out at the angry mob Aemilianus did not see true Romans, but instead a gaggle of foreign interlopers: immigrants, freedmen, and slaves who did not know what Roman virtue and dignity meant. "How can I," he bellowed, "who have so many times heard the battle shout of the enemy without feeling fear, be disturbed by the shouts of men like you, to whom Italy is only a stepmother?" Not surprisingly, this only led to further heckling and Aemilianus's bitter withdrawal from the Forum. The measure confirming the right of reelection did not pass, but the fight had done irreparable damage to Aemilianus's reputation.[11]

I N SOME WAYS, Aemilianus was right about the crowd he faced in the Forum that day. In the early days of Rome, there was no difference between the *plebs urbana*—the residents of the city—and the *populus Romanus*—the citizens of Rome. The residents of the city were citizens of Rome, and the citizens of Rome were the residents of the city. But by the end of the second century, Rome was by far the largest city in the Mediterranean. Where other cities of the day boasted tens of thousands of citizens, Rome boasted *hundreds* of thousands. As the largest and most powerful city in the Mediterranean, Rome became a center of migratory gravity. Noncitizen Italians frequently moved to the growing metropolis, and were followed by Greek philosophers, and Spanish artisans, and North African merchants, and Syrian ambassadors, and Gallic mercenaries. By the 130s, Rome had transformed into a polyglot mix of every language and ethnicity in the known world.[12]

As it was with the rural peasants, the mass influx of slaves also played a dramatic role in the transformation of the urban population. Wealthy Romans purchased skilled artisans from across the Mediterranean and put them to work in the city manufacturing goods for sale. But unlike their less-skilled brethren, skilled slaves often only stayed slaves for a limited amount of time. Owners allowed a man to buy his way out of slavery and go into private business under the auspices of his former owner. These freedmen clients allowed senators to engage in the kind of commercial enterprises they were supposedly forbidden from participating in. Senators used their freedmen as legal fronts to operate apartment complexes and retail shopping stalls and engage in overseas trade. Freedmen also expedited the transformation of senatorial estates into commercial ventures, while allowing the senator's hands to remain clean of the grubby business of business.[13]

Unlike the mostly rural residents of Italy, the plebs urbana lived entirely on wage labor. Work was principally in retail and trade as Rome became the great clearinghouse of imperial trade. The docks, warehouses, and shops teemed with life every single day. Slaves worked alongside wage laborers on large public works projects—aqueducts and roads—with new projects always started as old projects were completed. Since the city of Rome was a strictly cash economy and all food, lodgings, and fuel required coins, there was never desperate poverty. If you did not have money to live you either departed for the countryside or died in a back alley. Poverty was fatal.[14]

Politically, the plebs urbana hadn't had a collective political identity since the now ancient Conflict of the Orders. Though the democratic Assemblies operated through the thirty-five tribes, all citizens domiciled in Rome were lumped together into just four of those tribes. So though they often outnumbered all other voters at an Assembly, they still only wielded four collective votes. But though their voting influence was limited, their very presence in the city made them a latent force in Roman politics. As the crisis over the *Lex Agraria* had shown, physically controlling the Assembly space was now a critical part of winning political battles. The permanent presence of the plebs urbana meant that however muted their electoral voices might be, their *actual* voices could be heard loud and clear, as Scipio Aemilianus discovered when they heckled him for his intemperate remarks against Tiberius Gracchus.[15]

As the plebs urbana again found their political voice, they discovered they could demand aspiring politicians cater to their particular needs. Land redistribution did not particularly appeal to them—they were traders, artisans, and merchants, not farmers. But what did appeal to them was the promise of a stable supply of cheap grain. Since the plebs urbana could not feed themselves, they relied on the surrounding countryside to produce the grain that kept them alive. As every budding Roman politician would learn, what the plebs urbana really wanted was food security. They were all acutely aware that the supply was susceptible to sudden shortages caused by the weather, transportation mishaps, and crop failures. Or, for example, a massive slave revolt in Sicily.[16]

I N THE TIME of the Gracchi, the grain that fed Rome mostly came from Sicily. Ceded by the Carthaginians in 241, Sicily was the first overseas province acquired by Rome. The incredibly fertile island was an endless bounty waiting to be harvested. Roman owners flooded in, bringing with them slaves "driven in droves like so many herds of cattle." The working conditions on the Sicilian estates were atrocious as slaves were "vilely beaten and scourged beyond all reason." They were also so ill-provided-for that they took up banditry to survive, preying on native Sicilians who, like their cousins in Italy, were being squeezed by growing slave estates. Complaints rained in, but there were only a handful of junior Roman magistrates to administer the whole island—as long as the profits made everyone rich, there was little reason to reform the cruel system.[17]

Without hope, the Sicilian slaves began plotting rebellion. The man who emerged as the principal leader was a Syrian named Eunus. Eunus arrived in Sicily as a talkative and charismatic con artist. Claiming to be a prophet and fire-breather, he charmed his masters with tales that one day he would be their king. In 135, a group of slaves approached him secretly. They wanted to kill their masters and asked the prophet Eunus for advice. Eunus said the gods favored their plot, and soon four hundred armed men put themselves under Eunus's command. That night they attacked the city of Enna. Contrary to his jovial promises, Eunus was not benevolent in victory. He rounded up the inhabitants of Enna, separated out skilled blacksmiths, and executed the rest. When word of the massacre spread it sparked a general uprising. Within weeks, ten thousand slaves had joined the rebellion. Eunus then fulfilled his own prophecy. Placing a stolen diadem on his head, he proclaimed himself King Antiochus of Sicily.[18]

In the wake of Eunus's revolt, a second revolt erupted on the other side of the island just a few weeks later. A Cilician slave named Cleon heard about Eunus's rebellion and launched his own insurrection, attracting five thousand men to his banner. Cleon's army then overran the southern port of Agrigentum and sacked it. There was some hope among the beleaguered Sicilians that the two slave armies would come into conflict and destroy each other—and were horrified when Cleon instead bent his knee to "King Antiochus of Sicily." Combined, the slave armies were now unbeatable.[19]

Inside the Senate, the assumption was that this revolt would soon peter out, but every new batch of reinforcements sent to Sicily never came back. The Senate dispatched a praetor to bring the province back under control, and when he failed they had to send another the following year. But by now the slaves numbered some two hundred thousand and no Roman force appeared capable of defeating them. And it wasn't just the slaves. Many of the poor Sicilian peasants had taken to raiding wealthy estates out of a mix of greed, desperation, and revenge. Anarchy reigned.[20]

So as the Senate dealt with the quagmire in Spain, and the sudden Gracchan Revolution, they also dealt with this ongoing Sicilian slave revolt. The Senate was frustrated by the whole affair, and were aware that out in the streets of Rome the disruption to the food supply was making the plebs urbana angry. With the rebellion still ongoing in the summer of 132—fully three years since the initial revolt—the Senate dispatched consul Publius Rupilius to Sicily. Having wrapped up his work on the anti-Gracchan tribunal, Rupilius was now off to crush yet another seditious insurrection.[21]

If Rupilius succeeded where other Roman commanders had failed, it was thanks to the devastation of Sicily. The insurrectionary slaves had naturally cast aside their plows, so the farms and pastures of the island went uncultivated. By the time Rupilius arrived in 132, the great bread-basket of Rome was barren. With conditions so grim, it was not hard for Rupilius to find desperate souls inside each slave-held city to open the gates in exchange for food and leniency. When the Romans arrived at Enna, Cleon led a slave army out into the field, but Cleon himself was killed in the subsequent battle and his army defeated. Rupilius then found a willing traitor to open the gates of Enna and King Antiochus fled out the back door. The King was found hiding in a cave a few days later with "his cook, his barber, the man who rubbed him in the bath and the jester at his banquets." Rupilius tossed King Antiochus in a cell where he was consumed by lice and died. After three years, what later became known as the First Servile War was over.[22]

The Senate was thrilled by the end of the slave rebellion, and coupled with the victory in Numantia and the eradication of the Gracchan men-ace, the noble leadership of Rome was no doubt ready to enjoy a measure of peace and quiet. But within months of the victory in Sicily, reports came in from the east that Rome had *another* massive provincial revolt on its hands. The embassy sent to annex the Kingdom of Pergamum dis-covered that many did not want their independent kingdom to be turned into a mere province of Rome's growing empire.

FOR THE ROMANS a *provincae* originally meant the general sphere within which a magistrate would wield authority in Rome's name. It could be a geographic area, or a military assignment, or a legal jurisdiction. But as Rome accepted its permanent imperial responsibilities, the annual provincae of the various magistrates began to take on stable geographic boundaries. By 146, the Senate annually assigned magistrates to the provinces of Sicily, Sardinia, Nearer and Further Spain, Macedonia, and Africa. Though it was not a term used by the Romans, these provincial magistrates can reasonably be called provincial governors. In the early days of Rome's empire, a governor's work was primarily focused on military security. Political affairs were limited to securing alliances with local cities and tribes, and economic matters restricted to collecting taxes and paying for the military occupation.[23]

The administration in a province consisted of a small group of functionaries. A newly arrived praetor or consul would bring with him a household staff and an informal group of advisers called *legati* drawn from among the magistrate's friends and family. The governor was also assigned a quaestor—a young man entering public service for the first time who would be entrusted with the provincial treasury. For some young quaestors this was a nerve-wracking experience, for others an opportunity to prove their virtue, and still others an opportunity for graft and bribery.

Because the Roman administrative presence was so slight, provincial governors mostly relied on local leaders and existing legal and social institutions. The aristocracy of a given city were courted and co-opted, their sons sent back to Rome as hostages, where they would be well treated and given a full Roman education. As a matter of practical governance, local laws, social customs, and institutions were retained—the final fount of authority now simply Rome rather than a local royal court.[24]

Though the regular administration was small, and the official burdens of being a subject of the Republic light, that did not mean being a provincial was easy to bear. Each governor arrived at the pinnacle of his career and had often taken on loads of debt to make it this far. Governing the provinces was understood to be a time to remake a man's fortunes. But an incoming governor only had so much time, and with the great wars of conquest now past, they often resorted to extorting money from various tribes and cities in exchange for *not* going to war. Governors wanted to make as much money as they could before they got out. Unfortunately for the provincials, the next governor would arrive in exactly the same circumstances and the cycle would repeat.[25]

This type of abuse by the governors was cited as a frequent cause of revolts, so in 149—just as they were annexing the central Mediterranean—the Romans established their first ever permanent court, the *quaestio de repetundis:* the Extortion Court. The purview of the court was investigating and punishing Roman magistrates who used their power to wring unjust revenue from the provincials. But, of course, jurors for the Extortion Court were drawn exclusively from the senatorial ranks—you can guess how often they found one of their wayward colleagues guilty.[26]

The new province of Asia was destined to become one of the most lucrative provinces in the empire, and thus a hotbed of extortion and abuse. But before the Romans could exploit their new province they had to organize it—which was about to prove very difficult. When Scipio Nasica and his fellow senatorial ambassadors arrived in 132, they found that not everyone in Pergamum believed that they were the property of the Roman people.

A FTER KING ATTALUS III died, a pretender to the throne named Aristonicus rejected the handover of the kingdom to Rome and claimed the crown for himself. He went around drumming up support, but most of the rich coastal cities had good relations with Rome and there was little interest in joining a revolt. Driven into the interior, Aristonicus had better luck recruiting by promising freedom to slaves in exchange for service. Raising an army of impoverished peasants and field slaves, Aristonicus promised that after they defeated Rome they would all be equal citizens in a free utopia he dubbed Heliopolis—the City of Sun.[27]

So just as Spain and Sicily were put to bed, the Senate had to turn and deal with Asia. The command went to the new consul, and recently appointed land commissioner, Mucianus. Mucianus lobbied hard for the command, which held the promise of massive eastern riches, but upon arrival in Asia, nothing went right. Mucianus led his legions into the mountainous interior of Anatolia but found himself repeatedly bested by Aristonicus. In a final humiliating blow, Mucianus himself was captured by the enemy. Furious at being made a prisoner, the consul provoked his captors and "blinded with a stick the barbarian who was guarding him." The guard, "smarting from the pain and burning with rage, stabbed him through the side with a sword."[28]

Mucianus's failure necessitated sending another consular army in 130. This army successfully besieged Aristonicus's capital and forced Heliopolis to surrender. Most of the inhabitants were either killed or reenslaved; Aristonicus was put in chains and subsequently displayed in a triumphal parade back in Rome. When the parade ended, an executioner strangled Aristonicus to death in a prison cell. The short-lived dream of a slaveless utopia died with him.[29]

With all of these battles and sieges proceeding over months and years, it was not until 129 that the Romans finally started organizing the old Kingdom of Pergamum into the new province of Asia. The Senate dispatched consul Manius Aquillius with a ten-man senatorial commission to oversee arrangements. But Aquillius turned out to be a man of questionable character. A few scattered cities still resisted Roman occupation, and not wishing to waste his time with mop-up operations, Aquillius turned to "the wicked expedient of poisoning the springs" to bring the last holdouts to their knees. Hardly the tool of honorable conquest.[30]

But with Rome now firmly in charge, Aquillius and the new senatorial embassy settled the province of Asia. The process still dragged on, however, as the ambassadors had to demarcate the boundaries between royal property and free cities in accordance with Attalus's will. The former would become state-managed ager publicus, the latter exempt from taxation. While these demarcations were being established, Aquillius took the opportunity to make a little profit on the side. He accepted bribes from neighboring kings to hand over lucrative territory as a "reward" for their help containing Aristonicus. In particular, Aquillius gifted the kingdom of Phrygia to King Mithridates V of Pontus—a shady transaction that would still be disputed a generation later.[31]

But with Asia finally brought into the Roman fold, the Republic was about to see yet another enormous transfer of wealth to Italy. Asia became by far the most lucrative imperial holding and delivered riches into both private and public hands, exacerbating the rising inequality that had already been undermining the stability of the Republic.

H ISTORY BOOKS ARE filled with the names of Roman military and political leaders because those were the men Roman historians wrote about—giving the impression that every Roman was a triumph-hunting political intriguer. But plenty of wealthy Roman citizens had no interest in the lunatic jockeying for consulships and triumphs that consumed the great noble houses. And because no member of the Senate was allowed to engage in commerce, there was plenty of room for the nonpolitical rich to take on the business of the growing empire and make huge fortunes without the pathos of high politics.[32]

The families who constituted the nonpolitical rich of Rome were called the Equestrian class. Originally these were men with enough wealth to equip and maintain a warhorse so they filled the ranks of Rome's early cavalry—hence the name "Equestrians." But by the age of the Gracchi, the Equestrian name referred generally to the class of families worth more than four hundred thousand sesterce. To say these families formed the "middle class" of Rome is technically accurate—their fortunes fell somewhere in between the senatorial oligarchs and the mass of subsistence peasants—but Equestrian fortunes were still considerable, and they were a part of the economic elite.[33]

At the intersection of private and state business was a special group of Equestrians called the *publicani*. The Republic had a variety of public obligations to fulfill, from equipping armies, to maintaining temples, to building roads and aqueducts. With senators prohibited from conducting business, someone had to handle the logistical details. The first recorded publicani contract was simple: procure feed for the Sacred Geese, a special flock of birds the superstitious Romans believed to be favored by the gods. But by the time of the Punic Wars the publicani handled a significant chunk of state business. With nearly fifty thousand men in the legions there was a constant demand for shoes, tunics, horses, blankets, and weapons. One order called for 6,000 togas, 30,000 tunics, and 200

Numidian horses to be delivered to Macedon—*someone* had to arrange it. Men would buy shares in joint-stock companies and then bid on the right to fulfill a contract. As the breadth and depth of the Republican Empire grew—the profits to be made from state contracts were enormous—some publicani fortunes came to surpass those of minor senators.[34]

The most lucrative contracts were for operating the state-owned mines. The first batch of state mines came under Roman control during the Punic Wars after Rome expelled Carthage from Spain. The Romans discovered the Carthaginians had opened rich silver mines and so claimed these mines as state-owned ager publicus. Every five years contracts would be auctioned off to operate the mines, and though it is difficult to calculate actual figures, the revenue involved dwarfed anything the Romans had ever handled. Conditions in these mines were awful. Diodorus describes that slaves "wear out their bodies both day and night in the diggings under the earth . . . dying in large numbers because of the exceptional hardships they endure . . . For no respite or pause is granted them in their labors, but compelled beneath blows of the overseers to endure the severity of their plight, they throw away their lives in this wretched manner." The work was fatal, but the profits astronomical.[35]

The second-most lucrative contracts were for tax collection. The Roman provincial administrators did not directly collect provincial taxes. Instead publicani investors would form companies to buy five-year contracts, offering a lump sum of cash in exchange for the right to go collect what was owed Rome—the amount of money a company made over the amount paid was their profit. It was a system begging to be abused because the publicani had every incentive to extort as much as they could—even if it was more than what was legally owed. With limited oversight out in the provinces, the publicani tax farmers soon gained a notorious reputation that wherever they went there was neither law nor freedom. But despite this reputation for vigorous avarice, the publicani was still the one group that could actually handle the logistical load of empire. The Republic had no standing bureaucracy, so someone had to do it.[36]

The Senate was not thrilled at the rise of these publicani corporations. Senators were themselves prohibited from participating in commercial enterprises, so they naturally considered base commerce beneath the dignity of a reputable man and distrusted the publicani as greedy parasites. After the conquest of Macedonia in 168, the Senate intentionally withheld its extensive mines, forests, and infrastructure from the publicani. It was a deliberate attempt to block the further ascendency of the publicani, but it didn't last long. Five years later the province was opened and the money started rolling in. From that point on, wherever Rome went, so too came the publicani. And publicani conduct in the rich province of Asia would become a special source of future conflict.[37]

WHILE ASIA WAS proving itself to be a major source of conflict abroad, the seeds of an even more disastrous conflict were being sewn back home as the work of the agrarian commission exposed major fault lines in the social and political landscape of Italy.

Italy in the second century was not a unified state, but rather a stratified confederation of cities, each with different social and political rights depending on when and how they fell under the Roman umbrella. At the top of the citizenship hierarchy were, of course, full Roman citizens. There was no wealth requirement to be a citizen—the wealthiest senator and the poorest beggar both shared equally in the rights of citizenship, rights that collectively established their *libertas*, or civil liberty. The most important of these liberties was the right to vote in the Assembly and protection from abuse by senior magistrates.[38]

Below the full Roman citizens in the hierarchy were the communities or individuals who held so-called Latin Rights. After unilaterally annexing Latium in 338, the Senate did not offer full citizenship for their new Latin citizens but instead granted them a set of rights that allowed them to operate on a semi-equal footing with true Romans. Latins could marry, enter into contracts, and engage in land claims with a full Roman citizen. They even had the right to vote in the Assembly, though the Senate was not going to give too much of a voice: the Latins were collectively lumped into just one of the thirty-five voting tribes.[39]

Eventually the concept of Latin Rights outgrew its original ethnic origin. When Rome planted new colonies around Italy, the Roman colonists were downgraded to holding mere Latin Rights in exchange for the free plot of land and place in the colony they were about to receive. Individual Italians could also win Latin Rights by special grant by the Senate or senior Roman magistrate—often as a reward for battlefield heroics or rendering some special service to Rome. Holding Latin Rights soon became a civil distinction rather than an ethnic one.[40]

Finally, at the bottom of the hierarchy were the *foederati* or *socii*—known collectively as the "Allies." As Rome had spread across Italy they forced defeated cities and tribes to sign mutual defense pacts with Rome that required both sides to come to the other's aid. But those defeated cities were never formally annexed, hence they remained merely "Allies" of Rome. The majority of inhabitants in Italy were Allies with only limited civil and political rights. But as a trade-off they also had few responsibilities. Rome demanded no regular taxes and left local administration to local magistrates. All Rome asked was that the Allies provide troops to fill the ranks of the legions. The hierarchical, confederal relationship that defined Roman Italy worked tolerably well for two centuries. It was now coming undone.[41]

B Y 129, ONLY young Gaius Gracchus remained of the original land commissioners. Tiberius had died on the Capitoline Hill and his successor Mucianus had been killed in Asia. Mucianus's seat was filled by Marcus Fulvius Flaccus, the friend of the Gracchi who had helped drive the hated Nasica out of Rome. Now in his mid-thirties, Flaccus was gearing up for a run at the consulship when he joined the commission. Then in 129, the old princeps senatus Claudius died and his seat went to Gaius Papirius Carbo, the tribune who had introduced the secret ballot law in 131 and clashed with Aemilianus over the legacy of Tiberius's death. Where once the Gracchan faction had been run by eminent elder statesmen, it was now in the hands of young firebrands.[42]

The problem facing the new-look agrarian commission was that any ager publicus that was easy to identify and parcel out had already been identified and parceled out. All that remained was disputed property. For every disputed boundary the commission had to undertake a thorough investigation to assess rival claims. This was a process made nearly impossible if owners could not produce deeds, and if sellers could not produce receipts. Hostile ambiguity often reigned and the work of the commission slowed considerably.[43]

No boundaries created more hostility than those between Rome's ager publicus and land owned by her Italian Allies. It was nearly impossible to disentangle ager publicus held by the Senate and People of Rome from ager publicus held by an Allied city. No less than their Roman counterparts, wealthy Italians had absorbed public land onto their estates while poor shepherds relied on public land to graze their flocks. The arrival of these Roman land commissioners looking to confiscate property threatened everyone's livelihoods, but without the ability to stand for themselves in a Roman judicial proceeding, the Italians needed a Roman patron to protect their interests. They found a champion in Scipio Aemilianus, now taking the stage for the final public act of his long and storied career.[44]

Aemilianus's reasons for entering the fray on behalf of the Italians were varied and not wholly magnanimous. First, it would boost his own prestige enormously. His aristocratic disdain for the fate of Tiberius had estranged him from the populace of Rome, so he now positioned himself to broaden his base of political support. Second, by pushing back against the land commission, Aemilianus hoped to reconcile with his colleagues in the Senate. He had spent his life thumbing his nose at their traditions, but Aemilianus would earn back much goodwill if he killed the despised land commission. Finally, there may have been a collective desire on the part of the Senate to at least appear to take the complaints of the Italians seriously. Full integration of Italy was not what the Senate desired, but by positioning themselves as sympathetic to the Italians, they might buy enough support to permanently avoid calls for more drastic reform.[45]

In 129, Aemilianus delivered a speech in the Senate arguing that the commissioners were violating treaties, and that because borders with Allied land was a matter of foreign policy and not domestic affairs, disputes between the commission and the Italians should be arbitrated by a consul. The Senate agreed and passed a decree supporting Aemilianus's recommendation. This decree did not have the literal force of law, but now that the land commission was run by three relatively junior politicians, the weight of the Senate's opinion prevailed. But by now nearly all available land bordered Italian property, so the senatorial decree brought the work of the land commission to a grinding halt. The commission was not formally abolished, but its ability to act was fatally curtailed.[46]

Aemilianus then moved the debate into the Forum where he held forth in front of the crowds, laying the groundwork for either significantly amending, or outright repealing, the Lex Agraria. But he was, once again, greeted by the plebs urbana, who were angry he was taking the side of the Italians. Cries went out that Aemilianus was "determined to abolish the law of Gracchus utterly and for that end was about to inaugurate armed strife and bloodshed." Soon, the already hostile mob turned very hostile and men started shouting, "Kill the tyrant!" But Aemilianus stood his ground and said, "Very naturally those who feel hostile towards our country wish to make away with me first; for it is not possible for Rome to fall while Scipio stands, nor for Scipio to live when Rome has fallen." But though he all but dared the mob to attack, they did not, and Aemilianus's friends escorted him home after the meeting had adjourned.[47]

After his friends saw him safely home, Aemilianus told them that he planned to spend the evening working on a major speech that he would deliver the following day. But the next morning Aemilianus failed to emerge from his house. Concerned friends soon found his lifeless body in his bed. Only fifty-six years old and still in the prime of his political life, Scipio Aemilianus was dead.[48]

Given the atmosphere that surrounded his sudden death it would have been impossible not to suspect foul play, and over the years the list of suspects has included the entire Gracchi family: Gaius, his sister Sempronia, and their mother Cornelia Africana. All three had good reason to now consider their erstwhile kin an enemy. But also suspected were the two other land commissioners Flaccus and Carbo—both of whom had clashed with Aemilianus in the past. But for whatever reason, the Senate did not care to pry too deeply into the affair: "Great man though [Aemilianus] was, no inquest was held concerning the manner of his death." It may well be that Aemilianus's death was natural and that the timing of his demise mere coincidence. We will never know.[49]

T HE STORIED AND controversial career of Publius Scipio Aemilianus created a template for future generations of Romans to emulate. He embodied a new spirit of what it meant to be Roman. He embraced Greek philosophy and was comfortable in luxurious surroundings. This new breed of Roman nobles detested old scolds like Cato the Elder, and they saw no reason to reject good wine and elegant conversation. As the years progressed, the worldview of the Scipione circle would take over the upper classes, who were soon sending their sons to be educated in Athens as a matter of course. Aemilianus even introduced the habit of shaving one's face daily, which became standard custom of the Roman aristocracy for the next three hundred years.[50]

On the political front, Aemilianus figured out how to use the Assembly to bypass inconvenient hurdles. He had held two consulships in his career, both secured after special dispensation from an Assembly. As consul, he fought two great wars, both assigned by a special vote of the Assembly rather than by traditional drawing of lots. It was a powerful example that would be used by all future dynasts of the Late Republic. The Assembly was incredibly powerful—the people's unified voice could override everything. A man who controlled the Assembly could do anything he wanted.

Aemilianus also set a dangerous example when he used his extensive client network to raise a personal legion. In an age wracked by fights over conscription, Aemilianus had no trouble raising men to go conquer Numantia—he was able to call in favors and obligations from across the Mediterranean that raised fully sixty thousand troops. Aemilianus was living proof of what a charismatic and well-connected general could do. Marius, Sulla, and Caesar all followed Aemilianus's basic principles of operations: raise a personal army and then use the Assembly to legislate your opponents into oblivion.

But though his career pointed to the future Aemilianus himself departed this world as an anachronism. The future would not be defined by noble princes who ruled the world by day and debated Greek philosophy at night. Instead it would be driven by a harder set of men. Publicani merchants steering the empire toward their own profits. Poor farmers squeezed off their land. Urban artisans dealing with recurring grain shortages. Italian Allies frustrated with their lack of civil rights. Slaves by the thousands constantly on the verge of revolt. The next generation would be defined by men who would attempt to harness these forces to control the Republic. But as Aemilianus himself noted, "Those who make themselves up for political competition or the race for glory, as actors do for the stage, must necessarily regret their action, since they must either serve those whom they think they should rule or offend those whom they wish to please."[51]

CHAPTER 3

DAGGERS IN THE FORUM

> Citizens were not called "good" or "bad" according to their public conduct because in that respect they were all equally corrupt; but those who were wealthiest and most able to inflict harm were considered "good" because they defended the existing state of affairs.
>
> SALLUST[1]

GAIUS GRACCHUS HAD A DREAM. IN THIS DREAM, HE WAS visited by the ghost of his dead brother Tiberius who said, "However much you may try to defer your fate, nevertheless you must die the same death that I did." Another version of the dream has Tiberius asking, "Why do you hesitate, Gaius? There is no escape; one life is fated for us both, and one death as champions of the people." Gaius liked to tell the story of his dream because it gave the impression that he was not just another politician indulging personal ambition: instead he was being called to public service by a higher power. But though he feigned humility it is clear that from a young age, Gaius Gracchus aimed to become the greatest Gracchus of them all.[2]

Though they were raised in the same house, by the same mother, and with the same tutors, the personalities of Tiberius and Gaius could not have been more different. Plutarch makes much of their divergent temperaments. Where Tiberius was "gentle and sedate," Gaius was "high-strung

and vehement." Tiberius lived "simple and plain" while Gaius was "ostentatious and fastidious." When speaking in public, Tiberius relied on quiet
empathy while Gaius exuded exaggerated charisma.[3]

Gaius saw his older brother for the last time in the spring of 134 BC.
Twenty-year-old Gaius departed for his first campaign in Spain believing that the family was on the cusp of greatness. His older brother was
preparing to introduce the *Lex Agraria* and vault the next generation of
Gracchi to the forefront of Roman politics. But while in Spain Gaius
learned that it had all gone terribly awry. Tiberius had carried the *Lex
Agraria* but he had paid for the victory with his life.[4]

Gaius returned to Rome in 132. It had been less than a year since Tiberius's death, and Gaius now found himself not just the patriarch of the
household, but also expected to be the leader of a political movement his
brother had started. Gaius took his first step onto the public stage a few
months later when he was called to defend a family friend in court. The
power of Gaius's oratory was the stuff of instant legend. Gaius pioneered
a new form of theatrical oratory: he was the first Roman to pace the rostra energetically and pull his toga off his shoulder as he spoke. Even Cicero—an unrelenting critic of the Gracchi—reckoned that Gaius was the
finest orator of his generation: "How great was his genius! How great
his energy! How impetuous his eloquence! So that all men grieved that
all those good qualities and accomplishments were not joined to a better
disposition and to better intentions." Gaius also had a hand in changing
speechmaking "from an aristocratic to a democratic form; for speakers
ought to address themselves to the people, and not to the Senate." We do
not have any record of this first great speech. The only thing we *do* know
is that Gaius's performance "made the other orators appear to be no better
than children." He was just twenty-two years old.[5]

The following year, Gaius continued to put his oratory to use in defense
of his family's legacy. He publicly supported Carbo's bill to retroactively
legitimize Tiberius's attempt at reelection. Though the bill failed, Gaius's
performances put the political elite on notice that Tiberius would not be
the only Gracchus to be reckoned with. Indeed, the leading nobiles began
to fret about the power of Gaius, and there was a general consensus that
he must not be allowed to become a tribune.[6]

The nobles were right to fret because the visit from his dead brother was not the only dream Gaius had. Over the past century the Republic had undergone a massive transformation without any comprehensive attempt to refit the ship of state to survive the new waters within which it sailed. Where Tiberius had proposed a single piece of radical agrarian legislation to blunt the effects of rising economic inequality, Gaius dreamed of an entire slate of reforms to ameliorate the most destabilizing aspects of Rome's imperial expansion. Gaius Gracchus had a dream, and this dream would lead him to share one life with his brother and die a champion of the people.

WHILE GAIUS PUT together the early pieces of his reform package, one thing had already become clear: the future of Rome lay in Italy. As his brother had likely recognized in the early draft of the *Lex Agraria*, restoring the health of the Republic meant restoring the health of all Italians—not just Roman citizens. It was time to stop treating the Italian Allies as foreigners rather than what they really were: integral members of the Roman community. The loose, Roman-led confederation that had knitted the peninsula together over the last two hundred years was exhausted. With the Mediterranean now revolving around Italy it was time for the peninsula to unify.[7]

In the years after Tiberius's death, fellow land commissioner Marcus Fulvius Flaccus had become something of an older brother to Gaius. While Gaius was just starting his public career, Flaccus was on the cusp of a consulship. When it came time to run, he introduced a provocative idea that he most likely discussed with Gaius in advance: to make every Italian a full Roman citizen. While this proposal had enormous long-term implications, it was premised on the more immediate and practical concern of resolving disputes with the land commission. Flaccus believed that "the Italian Allies should be admitted to Roman citizenship so that, out of gratitude . . . they might no longer quarrel about the land." And though their gratitude was key, even more important was that by accepting citizenship the legal roadblock that had stalled the agrarian commission would be resolved. Flaccus and Gaius both believed the Italians would make that deal.[8]

Offering the Italians full citizenship was, of course, a radical proposition that sent shivers up the spines of the conservative nobility in Rome. They could not stand the thought of their subjects becoming their equals. But Flaccus also ran into difficulty with the common plebs urbana who jealously guarded the privileges of citizenship. To guard against the proposal, the Senate induced a tribune to expel all noncitizens from Rome in preparation for the consular election. If Flaccus wanted to win on a platform of citizenship for the Italians, he was going to have to sell it to the Roman citizens. Periodic expulsions of foreigners became a recurring feature of the later Republic, and Cicero deplored the practice, saying, "It may not be right . . . for one who is not a citizen to exercise the rights and privileges of citizenship," but actually expelling non-Romans was "contrary to the laws of humanity."[9]

But Flaccus won the consulship anyway and in January 125 he unveiled his plan for Italian citizenship. But though he was now consul Flaccus still had the problem of convincing the Assembly to vote it into law, especially since now only Romans were present in the city. It is difficult to say what would have happened had the bill actually come to a vote, but fortunately for the Senate, an opportunity arose to deflect Flaccus's attention. Envoys from the allied Greek city of Massilia (modern Marseilles, in France) arrived in Rome to complain about marauding Gallic tribes. The Senate assigned Flaccus to go repel the attackers. Either because he sensed that his bill wasn't going to pass, or because he prioritized military glory over social reform, Flaccus left for Gaul and did not return to Rome before his consulship expired. The bill for Italian citizenship expired with his consulship. This would be the first step in a long and tortuous battle for full Italian citizenship that would not end until thirty years later—and then only after hundreds of thousands lay dead and the Republic itself was nearly extinguished by civil war.[10]

WHEN THE ITALIAN citizenship bill died, at least one Italian city did not take the news well. In late 125 the city of Fregellae went into revolt. A former Roman colony that had been planted in 328 during the heat of the Samnite Wars, Fregellae had subsequently stayed loyal to Rome during the long struggle against Hannibal. The city was, in fact, noted for its exemplary service against the Carthaginians. Citizens of Fregellae destroyed a key bridge to stymie Hannibal's advance in 211 and then resisted pressure to capitulate even after Hannibal laid waste to their farms in retaliation. For their steadfast loyalty, the Senate included them among those cities by whose "aid and succor the dominion of Rome was upheld."[11]

The details of the Fregellae revolt are practically nonexistent, but it was not considered threatening enough to demand consular attention. Instead, the Senate dispatched praetor Lucius Opimius to end the rebellion in early 124. As Roman leaders go, Opimius was forged from a particularly brutal mold. Opimius proceeded to sack and demolish Fregellae so that "of the city whose brilliance but yesterday irradiated Italy, scarce the debris of the foundations now remains." The brutality of the sack was possibly a direct warning to other Italian cities who might in the future think of following Fregellae's lead. Future Romans would link the destruction of Fregellae to the string of demolished cities that stood as bare witnesses to Rome's expanding imperial self-confidence: "By the Roman people Numantia was destroyed, Carthage razed, Corinth demolished, Fregellae overthrown." But when Opimius returned to Rome the Senate denied his request for a triumph. They felt that while the object may have been to cow the Italians, rubbing their noses in it was a bit over the top.[12]

Opimius's brutal suppression of Fregellae turned out to be only the first example of the cold-blooded tactics he was willing to employ in defense of the existing order. Opimius would be elected consul in 121 and take center stage in the final showdown of the Gracchan revolution—a revolution that reignited just as Opimius returned home from the sack of Fregellae.[13]

Gaius Gracchus was not in Rome as this drama played out. He was elected quaestor in 126 and posted to the island of Sardinia, where he continued to make a name for himself. The winter of 126–125 was particularly hard and the legionaries suffered badly from a lack of proper supplies and clothing. The Roman governor forcibly requisitioned material from the towns of Sardinia to feed and clothe his men, but when the Sardinians sent an embassy to Rome to complain, the Senate canceled the requisitions and ordered the governor to supply his men some other way. This "some other way" turned out to be Gaius Gracchus making a circuit of the island during which he used the full power of his persuasive oratory to convince the Sardinians to supply the Romans of their own free will. The Sardinians were convinced and contributed voluntarily.[14]

When the Senate heard of Gaius's successful campaign, they did not congratulate him so much as fret over what would happen when his persuasive brand of charismatic oratory returned to the Forum. So they conspired to keep him in Sardinia for as long as possible. It was perfectly normal for a consul to transition into a proconsul when his annual term of office expired, and it was also normal for his staff to stay on with him. So the Senate extended the Sardinian command for another year, and Gaius remained in Sardinia. But then the following year the Senate extended everyone again, which was highly irregular. Not since the Punic Wars had such multiple extensions been necessary—and with Sardinia peaceful and subdued, it was a curious decision.[15]

Gaius suspected that the extensions had less to do with the necessity of keeping the consul in Sardinia than with keeping Gaius Gracchus out of Rome. So to counter these highly irregular orders, Gaius broke out a highly irregular response. Ignoring the mos maiorum that a staff officer was obligated to stay with his commander for the duration of their provincial assignment, Gaius simply packed up his belongings and headed back to Rome in the spring of 124. The Senate was outraged at his unexpected appearance in the city. Seeing happy throngs of cheering citizens greet him at the docks only darkened their mood.[16]

But though their plan to trap Gaius in Sardinia had failed, that did not mean conservatives were going to let him waltz into the tribunate unopposed. Immediately upon his return Gaius was hauled before the censors to answer for the abandonment of his commander. It was while defending himself from this charge that Gaius delivered one of his most famous speeches. With his honor besmirched, he defended his conduct in Sardinia, saying that while others used their provincial postings to oppress the locals and make themselves rich, "when I left for Rome, I brought back empty from the province the purses which I took there full of money. Others have brought home overflowing with money the jars which they took to their province filled with wine." This was a pointed rejoinder to the men accusing *him* of civic immorality, many of whom had indeed spent their service abroad drinking wine and filling the empty bottles with treasure.[17]

There were limits, though, to the powers of the censors to punish Gaius for his alleged transgressions. It is possible however that the moral approbation was meant to merely lay the groundwork for a more serious charge—one that *would* be heard in a criminal court. Conjuring up a vague Italian conspiracy theory, Gaius's enemies accused him of helping foment the rebellion of Fregellae. Gaius's pro-Italian bias would have been well known by now, and conservative senators tried to link that bias to actual treason against the Senate and People of Rome. The charges were of course ridiculous, as Gaius had been in Sardinia for the whole length of the uprising, but they still created a scandalous cloud that forced Gaius to respond. Records are scant, but we know that Gaius successfully dodged the accusations and began campaigning for his destined tribunate.[18]

THE TRIBUNATE ELECTION for 123 was particularly fierce as the bulk of the nobles organized their clients to oppose Gaius's election. But the broad popularity of the Gracchi name and the power of Gaius's oratory were irresistible. Citizens poured into Rome from the surrounding countryside, and in the days leading up to the election there was not housing enough for all of them. Even the wide-open Campus Martius was soon overcrowded to the point where men occupied the rooftops.[19]

While Gaius campaigned, a bill came before the Assembly to finally ratify the settlement of Asia that had been engineered by Aquillius. Ten years had now passed since the death of King Attalus, and the settlement of Asia was only just now ready for ratification. It had run into an unexpected delay when reports of Aquillius's shameful conduct filtered back to Rome. Among other things, Aquillius stood accused of taking bribes from King Mithridates V of Pontus to settle the border to Mithridates's advantage. Since the charges were 100 percent true, all signs pointed to an open-and-shut conviction. But instead the jury acquitted Aquillius. This was partly thanks to the incomparable oratory of Marcus Antonius, a rising young star who defended Aquillius in court. But it was also thanks to the money Aquillius spread among the jurors—essentially using bribe money to bribe his way out of accusations of bribery.[20]

After the scandal died down, the final bill to ratify Aquillius's settlement of Asia came before the Assembly and Gaius came out strongly in opposition. Whether there was anything particularly objectionable in the administrative regime established by Aquillius is lost to history and likely beside the point. Gaius not only wanted to use the issue of Asia to lambast the corruption of the Senate, but he had his own plans for how to settle Asia and wanted to ensure he had a clean slate to work with.[21]

But while the issue of Asia made for good antisenatorial fodder, there was no issue Gaius exploited more than the tragic story of his brother. "Before your eyes," he would say, "these men beat Tiberius to death with clubs, and his dead body was dragged from the Capitol through the midst of the city to be thrown into the Tiber . . . those of his friends who were caught were put to death without trial." And though much of this was intentionally manipulative there is no reason to think it was pure cynicism. Tiberius *had* been murdered by powerful men who had escaped punishment. No Roman would ignore the chance to settle matters of family honor, especially in such a public way.[22]

When election day came Gaius was elected easily, and upon taking office in December 124 the force of his reputation and power of his ambition made him indisputably the "first of all the tribunes."[23]

T HE BREADTH AND depth of Gaius's reform package was unprecedented. After what must have been years of careful preparation, Gaius Gracchus entered the tribunate of 123 with a multifaceted platform designed to appeal to different interest groups. If enacted in full, that platform would curb the power of the Senate and restore the balance of the Polybian constitution. It was later said that when Gaius was done, "he left nothing undisturbed, nothing untouched, nothing unmolested, nothing, in short, as it had been."[24]

But before he could get to ambitious sociopolitical reform, Gaius had some family business to settle. The first bill he introduced was aimed squarely at Octavius, the tribune whose obstinacy had contributed so much to Tiberius's death. Gaius introduced a bill making it illegal for a man deposed from office by the Assembly to serve as a magistrate ever again. If enacted, this would end Octavius's public career. But famously, Cornelia interceded and Gaius withdrew the bill, which some historians have suggested may have been a stage-managed affair to establish Gracchan benevolence while slyly confirming the principle that the Assembly *could* depose a magistrate if it wanted to—which was still not yet an established point of law.[25]

Gaius next aimed for the men who had persecuted his brother's followers. Gaius claimed that the extraordinary tribunal of 132 had violated the Assembly's supremacy in capital cases. To make sure it never happened again Gaius introduced a bill saying that the Senate could only convene a tribunal after receiving permission from the Assembly. The Senate would never again be able to repeat the repressive tribunal of 132. But the new law went further than simply ensuring such tribunals would be illegal in the future—Gaius's law was also *retroactive*. There was no prohibition against ex post facto legislation of this kind, and a person could find themselves guilty of breaking a law that did not exist at the time of the alleged crime—for example, Rupilius and Laenas, the two consuls who had led the tribunal in 132. By the time Gaius was passing this ex post facto law Rupilius was already dead, but his colleague Laenas was alive and well. When the law passed, tearful friends accompanied Laenas to the gates of Rome and he departed for exile.[26]

With family business settled, Gaius moved swiftly to implement his reforms. First up was restarting the work of the land commission. The commission still technically existed and Gaius, Flaccus, and Carbo were all still commissioners, but their work had been stalled for years by the Senate decree that consuls had jurisdiction over disputes with the Italians. Flaccus had tried to circumvent the problem by making the Italians full Roman citizens, and when that failed, the commission remained in dry dock. Gaius cut through the legal red tape by passing a bill establishing that the land commissioners had final jurisdiction over all disputed boundaries. The rural poor had always been the bedrock of Gracchan support, and they thrilled at the idea that more ager publicus could now be identified and parceled out.[27]

But Gaius now wanted to do much more than settle landless plebs on small private plots—he wanted to create whole new communities. Gaius envisioned a whole network of new colonies in Italy, stretching from Etruria in the north, all the way down to Tarentum in the south. All the colonies would be situated on good harbors and improve trade in and out of the Italian interior. To fill these colonies Gaius would not just need landless peasants, but also rich Equestrians who would become the principal merchants of the new colonies; profits both in trade and state contracts to build the roads and streets and harbors made his colonization project attractive to everyone. He even dreamed of overseas expansion, targeting the great harbor of vanquished Carthage as the perfect location for a permanent Roman colony.[28]

Gaius also launched a broad project to improve and extend the roads of Italy. Introducing for the first time uniform methods and specifications, Gaius's roads became known for their utility and elegance. They were made from good stone laid on tightly packed sand. They were of uniform height and width and equipped with excellent drainage systems. Gaius also ordered the work crews to mark each mile with a stone pillar so travelers could calculate distances easier. In the long run, Gaius's roads helped improve lines of communication, supply, and trade. And for short-term political purposes, the roads promised profits for publicani contractors and steady work for rural laborers.[29]

Since this roadwork would occur way off in the rural hinterlands it offered little for the plebs urbana of Rome. So to secure their support, Gaius promised them what they always wanted: a stable supply of cheap grain. Just as Gaius was coming to office, a plague of locusts decimated crops in North Africa, causing food shortages back in Rome. Gaius introduced legislation directing the state to purchase and stockpile grain and then sell it to citizens for a fixed price. Cicero later denounced the project as an obvious handout to secure political support and said that better men at the time "resisted it because they thought that its effect would be to lead the common people away from industry to idleness." But this was not the free-grain dole that would later become a hallmark of imperial municipal policy. It was simply offering grain at a fixed price to create some semblance of stability. The plebs urbana loved the bill so much they made further expansion of subsidized grain their central political demand for the next hundred years.[30]

Gaius then introduced measures to redress thirty years of complaints about the ruinous cost of service in the legions. The state had provided arms, equipment, and clothes for the legions through publicani contractors but always deducted expenses from a soldier's pay—a ruinous burden for the already impoverished legionaries. Gaius passed a law that the state would stop deducting the expenses. As with the evolution of the grain dole, it would take a century to move from the ad hoc armies of the middle Republic to the permanent legions of Augustus, but Gaius's law to move expenses from the citizens' pockets to the state treasury was a big step.[31]

Finally, Gaius put the capstone on his project with two major pieces of legislation in support of the Equestrians generally but, more specifically, the publicani. The first addressed an issue Gaius had already campaigned against: Aquillius's settlement in Asia. All the old royal domains had now been converted into Roman ager publicus and were available for taxation, the profits from which would be astronomical. But a controversial clause in the settlement stipulated that tax-farming contracts for Asia would be sold by the Roman governor in Asia, giving the governor control over the flow of enormous wealth. Gaius passed a law stipulating that Asian tax-farming contracts would be sold by the censors back in Rome. It was billed as a measure to curb senatorial power, but it also ensured the largest and most powerful of the publicani companies would be able to monopolize the business. This earned Gaius backing from some of the richest and most influential men in Rome who were already impressed with Gaius's public works projects. These men were not yet part of the political power structure but were fast being integrated into the system.[32]

Gaius helped further politicize the publicani with his second major piece of legislation: reform of the Extortion Court. The jury pool of the Extortion Court had always been drawn from the Senate, and the senatorial jurors had long turned a blind eye to each other's misdeeds. These were, after all, the jurors that had just found Aquillius innocent despite clear evidence of his guilt. Gaius passed a law that barred senators from serving on the jury; instead jurors would be drawn from the ranks of the Equestrians. But not just any Equestrians. To be available for jury duty a man had to be permanently domiciled in Rome. Since the official residence for the majority of Equestrian families was their country estates, the only men "permanently domiciled in Rome" were those who supported themselves strictly through business—especially the publicani. The publicani now had a powerful mechanism to defend their own interests.[33]

When Gaius was done with all this legislation he not only introduced reforms that anticipated by a hundred years the stable imperial structure of Augustus, but it also put Gaius at the center of a powerful antisenatorial coalition. The plebs urbana, the rural poor, the Equestrians generally, and the publicani particularly were all now arrayed behind Gaius—his success would be their success; his ruin, their ruin. The coalition forged by Gaius would become familiar in years to come as men like Marius, Saturninus, Drusus, Sulpicius, and Cinna would all use the same basic mix to pursue their own antisenatorial agendas.

A S ELECTIONS FOR the next year's tribunate approached, Gaius appeared ready to pass the baton to his old friend and ally Flaccus, who put himself forward as a candidate. Flaccus running for tribune was all on its own another chink in the unspoken armor of mos maiorum—a former consul had never before stood for the lesser office of tribune. With the backing of Gaius, Flaccus won election easily but then—as a result either of careful planning, unexpected luck, or some combination of the two—Gaius himself won reelection to the tribunate. The very thing that had once been so controversial it had literally gotten his brother killed.[34]

As shocking as it was, Gaius's reelection remains historical mystery. We know that Gaius was still not technically a candidate when the elections occurred, but when the results came, a few of the ten tribune slots remained vacant—an unusual but not unheard of outcome. In such cases, it was the tribunes' prerogative to assign men to fill the vacant seats and Gaius Gracchus was among those appointed. The question is, how much of this drama was preengineered? Was the first vote manipulated to ensure open seats remained? Or was it the spontaneous work of the goddess Fortuna, and Gaius was as surprised as anyone to find himself reelected? We do not know. We only know that Gaius was now tribune for a second consecutive year.[35]

G AIUS ENTERED HIS second term at the peak of his powers. He was "closely attended by a throng of contractors, artificers, ambassadors, magistrates, soldiers, and literary men, with all of whom he was on easy terms ... Thus he was a more skillful popular leader in his private inter-course with men and in his business transactions than in his speeches from the rostra."[36]

But there was a core of conservative senators opposed to him. This group had gotten steamrolled during Gaius's first term but had regrouped for his second term. As had happened to Tiberius, Gaius's enemies tapped a rival tribune named Marcus Livius Drusus to do their dirty work. Drusus was himself a rising star in Roman politics. Like Gaius he was eloquent, wealthy, and had been raised to expect a public career. But where Gaius sought advancement through popular reforms, Drusus planned to advance by blocking them. He entered office on a mission to undermine Gaius at every turn—if he was successful he would gain pow-erful allies in the Senate. Drusus opened by offering a new colonization project of his own. Though Gaius's plan had until that point been the most ambitious colonization project in history, Drusus now promised *twelve* new colonies—each with generous land grants and startup capital for three thousand colonists. Fully thirty-six thousand families stood to benefit, and the news sent shockwaves through the population. Drusus also very carefully made sure everyone knew that only Roman citizens qualified for the new colonies. Italians would not be allowed.[37]

Drusus's clever dividing of Roman from Italian came just as Gaius was preparing to introduce the measure Flaccus had failed to carry during his consulship: citizenship for the Italians. As a matter of principle and political interest, Gaius supported a broader franchise and had been a frequent spokesman on behalf of the Italians. Gaius proposed those with Latin Rights be elevated to full Roman citizenship, while Allies would be granted Latin Rights. Gaius's bill fell short of blanket equality proposed in 125 by Flaccus, but this was a massive bomb to lob into the middle of the Forum—especially as it came on the heels of Drusus's Romans-only colonization project.[38]

Just as had happened during Flaccus's consulship, the Senate dealt with Gaius's call for Italian citizenship by once again expelling non-Roman Italians from entering the city in the run-up to the vote. The decree stated, "Nobody who does not possess the right of suffrage shall stay in the city or approach within [five miles] of it while voting is going on concerning these laws." Facing a population thoroughly hostile to the bill, Gaius let it die rather than risk his other plans. Another attempt at reform having failed, the issue of Italian citizenship would remain a persistent problem for the Romans. Especially because the Italians were already detecting a pattern: citizenship would be dangled only to be snatched away at the last minute. It was not a game that amused them.[39]

A FTER LOSING THE vote on Italian citizenship, Gaius sailed for North Africa in the spring of 122. The first of his colonies being built was the most controversial of all. Located on the site of old Carthage, the colony would control a strategically advantageous port, but the superstitious Romans were wary of occupying haunted ground. Leaving Flaccus behind to mind Rome, Gaius personally traveled to Carthage to oversee the founding of the colony. It's hard to say exactly why Gaius departed Rome at this moment—perhaps it was because he felt that his presence during the building of the colony was important both practically and symbolically. But his support among the people would not hold in his absence.[40]

Gaius spent seventy days in Africa, and during those seventy days nothing went right. The survey team laying out the plots of land and design of the colony were plagued with problems. A post planted to mark the center of town was hit with a gust of wind and snapped. The entrails for a required sacrifice were similarly scattered by winds. Then wolves set upon the boundary markers and carried them away. And to the superstitious Romans, these problems were not just setbacks, they were proof that the gods did not approve of Gaius's plans. The Senate would soon be able to use the reports of ominous portents to mount their final attack on Gaius and his followers.[41]

Meanwhile, back in Rome those followers were dwindling by the day. Flaccus was not nearly as deft as Gaius when it came to politicking and Drusus was running circles around him. With the fabled twelve colonies already making the Gracchan program look stingy, Drusus announced that the land Gaius, Flaccus, and Carbo had distributed as land commissioners—which stipulated rent must be paid to the state—would now be rent-free. Drusus was successfully outflanking the Gracchans from the popular side, and Gaius was now painted as an ungenerous skinflint.[42]

Gaius returned after his two-month absence to find his political standing had plummeted. The people who once supported him now cheered Drusus. The stories that had come out of Carthage hinted that Gaius was now courting the wrath of the gods themselves. But Gaius refused to back down. When he returned, he vacated his house on the Palatine Hill and took up residence in a smaller house near the Forum—he would live among the people to try to prove that it was he—not Drusus—who had their interests at heart.[43]

To ensure the survival of his legislation Gaius decided against all precedent to run for a *third* consecutive term. On election day, Gaius emerged with the necessary number of votes to secure reelection, but the observers who monitored the election tripped over themselves challenging Gaius's ballots, alleging that most were fraudulent and that the ballot box had been stuffed. It did not take long for the magistrates in charge of the election to agree, toss out most of Gaius's votes, and declare him defeated. Gaius protested, but there was nothing he could do. The election results were verified and that was that. When the new year arrived, Gaius was out of office, stripped of the immunity from prosecution and the sacrosanct protection from physical harm. Left powerless and unprotected, he was about to be forced to watch his legislation die.[44]

Nearly as bad as losing the election in 121 was watching Lucius Opimius win the consulship. An avowed enemy of the Gracchi, newly elected consul Opimius made it his personal mission to destroy

Gaius Gracchus as he had once destroyed Fregellae. Opimius's plan was not just to repeal the Gracchan legislation, but to also provoke Gaius into doing something illegal that would justify prosecution and banishment. For his part, Gaius tried to avoid taking the bait, but when Opimius let it be known that he was going to abandon the colony at Carthage, Gaius finally organized some of his old supporters to stage a demonstration. How much genuine support Gaius actually had left is unknown, and there is a passing hint in Plutarch that his mother Cornelia paid non-Romans to sneak back into the city and support her son in his hour of need.[45]

On the morning that the fate of the colony was slated for debate, two rival factions filtered into the Forum. While Gaius paced in an adjacent portico, Flaccus delivered an energetic speech attacking the tyranny of Opimius and the Senate. With the Gracchan faction riled up, one of Opimius's servants started making his way through the crowd bearing the entrails for a sacrifice. Some reports state that the servant merely approached Gaius and begged him to not do anything that would destroy the Republic. Plutarch, however, says the servant pushed his way through the crowd, demanding that the Gracchan rascals make way and cursing their impetuousness. Both versions of the story end the same, though: a band of Gracchan supporters surrounded the servant. One of the Gracchans then pulled out a writing stylus that had been sharpened into a shiv and stabbed Opimius's servant to death.[46]

When word of the murder filtered through the crowd, the Forum erupted. In the ensuing commotion, Gaius berated his followers for giving the Senate the excuse they needed to crack down and then rushed forward to try to explain that the murder of Opimius's servant was not what it appeared. But no one wanted to hear it. In the chaos no one *could* hear it. But a final confrontation was avoided when a heavy rain started to fall, and it drove both sides out of the Forum. As Gaius considered which way to run, he cried, "Whither shall I, unhappy wretch, betake myself? Whither shall I turn? To the Capitol? But that is drenched with the blood of my brother! Or to my home, that I may see my distressed and afflicted mother in all the agony of lamentation?"[47]

The next day the consul convened the Senate to discuss a response to the events of the previous day. Just as debate was beginning a din broke out in the Forum. The funeral procession bearing Opimius's murdered servant coincidentally arrived at the Forum as the Senate met. Emerging from the Senate to view the procession, the senators denounced the reckless political violence of the Gracchans and grieved for its victims. But pro-Gracchan citizens present in the Forum heckled the moralizing senators, asking why they were so worked up over a dead servant when ten years earlier they had dumped the bodies of Tiberius Gracchus and three hundred of his followers into the Tiber without a second thought.[48]

Insulted by the crowd, the Senate gave Opimius the authority he needed to restore order. They instructed Opimius to do "whatever he thought necessary to preserve the State." The intent of this vague decree was clearly to authorize Opimius to act as a dictator would—without resurrecting the cumbersome and archaic authority of the Dictatorship itself. Though they did not know it at the time, the Senate's improvised decree set a precedent for the future. In times of civil unrest the Senate would invoke the same formula, which became known as the *senatus consultum ultimum*—the Senate's Final Decree. Opimius promptly ordered every senator to provide two armed men from their households and muster them in the Forum the next morning.[49]

Gaius Gracchus spent his final night as his brother had—surrounded by bodyguards and partisans, knowing that a great confrontation loomed in the morning. Gaius had spent years telling people about his dream: "However much you may try to defer your fate," the ghost of his brother told him, "you must die the same death that I did." What had once been a stirring bit of propaganda now seemed morbidly specific. Flaccus seemed unconcerned—even eager—about the looming clash. He and his friends stayed up late drinking and boasting of the fight they would give the no-good bastards in the morning. Gaius was sober. And somber.[50]

In the morning, Flaccus had to be roused from a hungover stupor, but when he woke he distributed weapons to the men from his own private collection. As they left the house Gaius had to disentangle himself from his wife, who begged him to stay: "Not to the rostra, O Gaius, do I now send you forth, as formerly, to serve as tribune and law-giver, nor yet to a glorious war, where, should you die . . . you would at all events leave me in honored sorrow." Instead, he was exposing himself to men who likely aimed to murder him. "The worst has at last prevailed; by violence and the sword men's controversies are now decided . . . Why, pray, should men longer put faith in laws or gods, after the murder of Tiberius?" But Gaius pushed his way past her—honor would not be satisfied by staying home.[51]

The Gracchan faction occupied the Aventine Hill, which lay across a shallow valley from the Palatine Hill and along a plebeian enclave going back to the founding of the city. Flaccus was clearly spoiling for a fight, but Gaius prevailed upon them all to give reason one last chance. They dispatched Flaccus's young son Quintus to the Forum to find out what— if anything—would defuse the crisis.[52]

In the Forum, Opimius waited with his forces arrayed. Reinforced by some auxiliary slingers and archers recently returned from a campaign in the Balearic Islands, Opimius had at his command about three thousand men. When Flaccus's son arrived Opimius told the young man that at a minimum the Gracchans had to lay down their arms, come to the Forum, and beg forgiveness. He also said that if the answer was anything less than total capitulation, the boy best not come back at all. Gaius, for one, appeared ready to back down, but Flaccus and his more radical supporters talked him out of it. Ignoring Opimius's threat, they sent Flaccus's son back to reject the terms. Good to his word, Opimius arrested the young man, tossed him in jail, and then led his small army toward the Aventine. Before leaving he offered a bounty of gold for the heads of Flaccus and Gaius—the amount of gold determined by the weight of the head.[53]

When Opimius's small legion ascended the Aventine, the archers lobbed arrows and the assembled Gracchans were forced to disperse. In the chaos they lost cohesion, and the strength they might have had in numbers never materialized. Just minutes into the fight, it was already every man for himself. Gaius led a party to the nearby Temple of Diana, while Flaccus went into hiding either in a vacant bath or the workshop of one of his clients. Opimius's men knew Flaccus was somewhere in the area but no one would identify which house he was in. When they threatened to burn the whole block down, someone came forward and ratted Flaccus out. So it was that Marcus Fulvius Flaccus, senator, consul, tribune, and citizen of Rome, was apprehended and summarily executed on a random street on the Aventine Hill.[54]

Gaius meanwhile could see that it was all falling apart. Rumors flew that Opimius was now offering immunity to anyone who laid down their arms. The same cocky crew that had spent the night drinking and boasting now tossed down their weapons and begged for mercy. Gaius's few remaining supporters urged him to run for it. So Gaius ran for it. With a small handful of his most loyal friends, Gaius ran from the Aventine down to a bridge across the Tiber. But a company of Opimius's men were in hot pursuit. As Gaius fled across the Tiber, his loyal friends posted themselves at the head of the bridge to fight off their pursuers and give Gaius time to get away. They were cut down to a man.[55]

Gaius and a single slave made it as far as the Sacred Grove, an ancient patch of trees on the outskirts of Rome. It was there that Gaius decided that he would run no more and that his time was at hand. Handing a dagger to his slave, Gaius exposed his neck and ordered the slave to plunge the dagger into his throat. The slave obliged. Another Gracchus now lay dead in a pool of blood.[56]

After his body was found, Gaius's head was duly cut off and secured by a savvy former supporter. The erstwhile Gracchan carried the head home and "bored a hole in the neck, and drawing out the brain, poured in molten lead in its place." Then he carefully "stuck the head of Gaius on a spear and brought it to Opimius, and when it was placed in a balance it weighed seventeen pounds and two thirds." Opimius paid him in full.[57]

A S WITH TIBERIUS, the day of sharp violence was followed by a more methodical purge. As many as 250 people died that same brutal morning as Gaius and Flaccus. But thousands more were identified and executed in the days to come as Opimius rid Rome of Gracchan partisans. Even the son of Flaccus—arrested for being the messenger of his father—was only given the courtesy of choosing his method of death. The Gracchan faction was broken.[58]

Carbo, the last remaining Gracchan land commissioner, only survived the purge by switching sides. He likely secured a consulship for 120 by promising to defend Opimius's conduct in front of the Assembly. But since no one likes a traitor, Carbo was himself arraigned on vague charges of treason the minute he left office in 119. The prosecution was led by a rising young noble named Lucius Licinius Crassus. Just twenty years old, Crassus dazzled the crowd with incisive wit and eloquence that shredded Carbo's attempt to escape his past: "Although, Carbo, you defended Opimius, this audience will not on that account esteem you a good citizen; for it is clear that you dissembled and had other views." For a decade Carbo had been a radical Gracchan—the last-minute defense of Opimius didn't fool anyone. Loathed by all and his reputation destroyed, Carbo "rescued himself from the severity of the judges by a voluntary death" (as Cicero so eloquently put it). Gaius Papirius Carbo was the last victim of the Gracchan purge.[59]

But though the Gracchi were now dead, many of their reforms lived on. The Extortion Court remained staffed by Equestrian jurors. The grain dole remained in place, and though for the moment it was merely a small price-controlled ration, it entered permanently into the fabric of Roman administration. The road building and public works continued, and though the colonies were never completed, any early colonist who had secured land was allowed to keep it. Drusus's magical twelve colonies were never heard from again now that Gaius's headless body had been dumped in the Tiber.

As for the land commission, it remained existent but inert. Within a few years the Assembly amended the *Lex Agraria* to allow possessors of the Gracchan allotments to sell their land. It did not take long for wealthy magnates to buy up the majority of the lots. By 111, a further law transferred all currently held ager publicus to outright private property. The *Lex Agraria* had been a creative attempt to solve the problem of widening inequality in Italy and reverse the gradual disappearance of the small Roman farmer—a problem that ultimately would not be solved until after the fall of the Republic.[60]

After their deaths, the Gracchi brothers themselves were transformed into legendary martyrs of the people. The Romans erected statues of them where each had been slain. Citizens dropped offerings and sacrifices at these quasi-religious shrines. Their mother Cornelia was moved by the devotion and said, "the sacred places where her sons had been slain . . . were tombs worthy of the dead which occupied them." Cornelia herself retired to a villa at the port city of Misenum and lived for another twenty years. She maintained a running salon of Greek intellectuals and philosophers and welcomed visitors from all corners of the Mediterranean including the kings from the Hellenic east. Of her sons, she always spoke "without grief or tears, and narrated their achievements and their fate . . . as if she were speaking of men of the early days of Rome." Some found her calm demeanor off-putting, but as Plutarch says, "While fortune often prevails over virtue when it endeavors to ward off evils, she cannot rob virtue of the power to endure those evils with calm assurance." When Cornelia died, the Romans built a statue of her in the Forum.[61]

As the years passed the Gracchi name came to mean more than just the brothers: it stood for an array of programs and tactics that collectively represented a new *populare* movement in Roman politics. The standard populare programs included a grain dole for the urban poor, land for the rural poor, control of the courts with the Equestrians, secret ballots in the Assembly, subsidies for military service, and punishment of corrupt nobles. Tactically, the populare harnessed the democratic power of the Assembly rather than the aristocratic weight of the Senate. While populare leaders came and went, the citizens of Rome remained the same and would support those who offered them what they wanted.

Opposing the populares were the *optimates*. Meaning literally "the best" or "the good," the term invoked a variety of characteristics. But since Cicero is our main source, those characteristics tended to align with his own worldview. For Cicero, an optimate was a well-educated senator with an active interest in oratory, politics, and war, and skewing away from the severe Roman virtues in the mold of old Cato the Elder. An optimate senator was comfortable with exotic food and Greek ideas. These grandly sophisticated statesmen were the natural guardians of the Republic, standing as sentinels against enemies both foreign and domestic.

For the great historian Sallust—himself an active partisan in the politics of the Late Republic—the divide between populare and optimate meant that "the institution of parties and factions" had come to Rome. He felt both sides were to blame for the treacherous polarization because "the nobles began to abuse their position and the people their liberty . . . thus the community was split into two parties, and between these the state was torn to pieces." But despite Sallust's observation, the Romans did not have political parties in the modern sense. There was no "Populare Party" and "Optimate Party." Tactics, strategies, and alliances were fluid to all factions. But though Cicero deplored the tribunes and the Assembly, his beloved optimate were just as adept at using the Assembly to get their way as the populare. In fact, most of the greatest popular orators of the coming generation spoke on behalf of the optimate rather than populare.[62]

But though there were no formal parties, it is true that there were now two broadly opposing worldviews floating in the political ether waiting to be tapped as needed. As the crisis over the *Lex Agraria* revealed, it was no longer a specific issue that mattered so much as the urgent necessity to triumph over rivals. Reflecting on the recurrent civil wars of the Late Republic, Sallust said, "It is this spirit which has commonly ruined great nations, when one party desires to triumph over another by any and every means and to avenge itself on the vanquished with excessive cruelty." Accepting defeat was no longer an option.[63]

In fact, memories of that excessive cruelty doled out to the Gracchans lived on the minds of those who had been witness to the methods of the noble optimates. Though it was the Gracchi who Cicero later accused of "throwing daggers in the Forum," it was the optimates who had murdered thousands in the name of public order. Most insulting was the Senate's order to Opimius to rebuild and refurbish the Temple of Concord, which had been damaged during the fighting in 121. The temple was dedicated to the unity of the Roman people, but for many in Rome, calling a bloody purge the foundation of unity was an insult. After the restoration was complete an anonymous vandal inscribed at the base of the temple: "A work of mad discord produces a temple of concord."[64]

CHAPTER 4

A CITY FOR SALE

> We are silent when we see that all the money of
> all the nations has come into the hands of a few
> men; which we seem to tolerate and to permit
> with the more equanimity, because none of these
> robbers conceals what he is doing.
>
> CICERO[1]

Gaius Marius was born in 157 BC in Arpinum, an Italian city that had only recently been enfranchised by the Senate. Though later denigrated as "a man of rustic birth, rough and uncouth, and austere in his life," Marius was in fact the son of a respected Equestrian family, raised in comfort and privilege. But though he was the well-educated son of a prosperous family, Roman politics in the second century seemed designed to make a mockery of his ambitions. Marius was a novus homo Italian without sufficient ancestry or connections to dream of anything more than a respectable career in local government. But Marius wanted more than that. So upon completing his education he took the only path to political prominence available to a relative outsider: service in the legions. Marius had "no sooner reached the age for military life than he had given himself the training of active service, not of Grecian eloquence."[2]

A family connection to the Scipione allowed twenty-three-year-old Marius to join the personal legion Scipio Aemilianus raised for the final expedition to Numantia in 134. Contrary to long-standing myth, Marius did not begin his career as a common legionary: his Equestrian status qualified him to be an officer. During his service in Spain, Marius's superiors commended his bravery, diligence, and honesty. Marius proved time and again that he was a man to be counted on. According to an oft-told story from the end of the siege of Numantia, Aemilianus's friends asked him one night where the Roman people would find a man to replace him. Aemilianus tapped young Marius on the shoulder and said, "Here, perhaps."[3]

After Numantia fell, Marius likely joined the scramble for a piece of commercial spoils, which in Spain meant mining. If he did acquire a share of the mining rights, it would explain how he had enough money to fund an expensive political career in Rome. But even as he benefited from these business connections, Marius was acutely aware of the resistant social pressures to a public career. He had "neither wealth nor eloquence, with which the magnates of the time used to influence the people," but "the very intensity of his assurance, his indefatigable labors, and his plain and simple way of living, won him a certain popularity among his fellow citizens."[4]

DESPITE HIS SOCIAL background, Marius did have one thing going for him. He was a hereditary client of the Caecilii Metelli, a noble family just emerging as the dominant faction in Rome. A plebeian family ennobled for five generations, the Metelli rose to prominence thanks to one great man: Quintus Caecilius Metellus Macedonicus. A contemporary of Scipio Aemilianus, Macedonicus earned his triumphant cognomen by crushing the last remnants of Macedon in 147.* This victory heralded a long and impressive career that took Macedonicus across the empire from Spain to Greece. But as he rose, Macedonicus avoided throwing his family's lot in with either the Scipione circle or the Claudians, instead remaining aloof to both.[5]

---

* See prologue.

The real strength of the Metelli, though, lay in manpower. Macedonicus and his brother Lucius had, between them, six sons and three daughters. This brood of Metelli went forth into high Roman politics in the 120s and took it over for a generation. Wherever a war was being fought, a Metelli was sure to be there. From 123 to 106 the Metelli cousins held six consulships. Their name dominates the rolls of triumphal honor that recorded successful campaigns in Macedonia, Thrace, Sicily, Gaul, Spain, and North Africa. This herd of cousins filled all ranks of the cursus honorum through the 120s and 110s. By the time the eldest attained their consulships, the youngest filled the ranks of quaestors, aediles, and praetors. This domination of the magistracies gave the family direct control over the levers of power.[6]

But the Metelli were not just successful because there were so many of them; they also cultivated talent. In fact, the real mastermind behind the Metellan faction was not one of the cousins at all, but rather a shrewd young operator named Marcus Aemilius Scaurus. Scaurus hailed from a noble family, but recent generations had seen their political and economic fortunes collapse. Scaurus's father didn't even bother with a public career and instead spent his life as a coal merchant to rebuild the material fortunes of the family. Coming from such humble origins, Scaurus was later slandered as the novus homo son of a publicani, but he was neither. Scaurus was not a great orator like Gaius Gracchus, but he had a knack for persuasion in intimate conversations, relying more upon "his judgment in affairs of consequence, than upon his ability in speaking." He talked his way into the Metelli just as the family was rising in status and he married one of Macedonicus's daughters. From the moment Scaurus entered the family, he began to take the reins. Cicero would later say of Scaurus that "nothing happens without his word." Sallust recalls that Scaurus "was greedy for power, fame, and riches, but clever in concealing his faults."[7]

While Scaurus was a consummate backroom operator, the Metellans also needed men to command attention in the Assembly. Among the most promising was the vibrant young orator Lucius Licinius Crassus. The quintessential optimate, Crassus came from an illustrious family and had a keen intellect and a born talent for oratory. He had burst on the scene in 119 as the prosecutor of the turncoat land commissioner Carbo. He was now considered the greatest orator in Rome, a mantle he inherited from the dead Gaius Gracchus. But Crassus was more of a scholar than the Gracchi—a student of the law, philosophy, and literature. The only thing missing from his sterling resume was an interest in battlefield glory. While a man like Gaius Marius was stamped by service in the legions, Crassus was stamped by the Forum. He later said, "I entered the Forum quite a youth, and was never absent from it longer than during my quaestorship." No one better knew the Forum, or was better known in the Forum, than Lucius Crassus the Orator.[8]

The Metellans also recruited Crassus's great friend and political ally Marcus Antonius. Four years older than Crassus, Antonius acknowledged Crassus's superior ability: he said that while men listened to him and dreamed of equaling his own skill, when Crassus spoke, "no one is so conceited as to have the presumption to think that he shall ever speak like him." Though loyal to his friends, Antonius was also a subtle player who understood the power of circumspection. He once said that he never wrote his speeches down so that if later "he had said anything which was not desirable, he might be able to deny that he had said it." He carried this basic inscrutability throughout his entire life, and where Crassus was the master of the great public occasion, Antonius shined in judicial proceedings. With the skill of the best Greek sophists, Antonius could argue any side of a debate and win. He was a formidable force in the courts and often deployed in defense of Metellan interests.[9]

Aside from these rising young nobles, the Metelli also cultivated allies within the Equestrian class, the merchants and bankers who provided funding for the wars of foreign conquest that maintained domestic supremacy. With Metellans taking part in nearly every censorship between 131 and 102, they controlled the state publicani contracts for an entire generation. There is no evidence that the Metelli were abnormally corrupt, but in that era it was taken for granted that one would help his friends and stymie his enemies. These connections made the Metelli the most powerful single faction in Roman politics.

Gaius Marius was himself a rising Equestrian client of the Metelli. After ten years of service, Marius stood for election as a military tribune, a legionary staff officer elected by the soldiers themselves. He most likely spent his year as military tribune in the Balearic Islands helping one of the eldest Metelli cousins achieve the generation's first triumph. He parlayed this service into a successful run for his first true magistracy, winning a quaestorship in 122. In office, Marius probably served in the legions that were by then advancing into southern Gaul. There he would see for the first time the hills and streams where twenty years later he would win one of the most spectacular victories in Roman history.[10]

W HEN ROME EXPANDED beyond the borders of Italy it moved in three directions: west to Spain, south to Africa, and east to the Aegean. But their northern border remained unchanged, partly because the Alps loomed as an enormous natural boundary. But after the great conquests of the mid-second century, Rome needed to maintain supply and communication lines with its far-flung territories in Spain and Macedonia. As a result, the legions crossed the Alps and became embroiled in a series of conflicts with the tribal powers beyond the new frontiers.[11]

Until the 120s, however, the swath of coastline between the Alps and Pyrenees was not under Roman jurisdiction. They instead left the protection of the region to the city of Massilia. A Greco-Phoenician colony founded in the 600s, Massilia had been a friend and trading partner of Rome going back to the early days of the Republic. In 125, Massilia was attacked by the Salluvii—a Gallic tribe that dominated the plains between the Alps and the Rhône river—and they requested aid from Rome. Happy to help a friend (and even happier to get the consul Flaccus out of town before he pushed through his bill for Italian citizenship), the Senate dispatched legions north. After several years of inconclusive fighting the Romans finally occupied a settlement about twenty miles inland from Massilia and organized it as a permanent military colony called Aquae Sextiae (modern Aix-en-Provence). After its founding in 122, Aquae Sextiae became the principal base of Roman operations in Gaul.[12]

Repulsed by the Romans, the king of the Salluvii took the remnants of his people and sought refuge with the Allobroges, another powerful tribe that controlled territory in the upper reaches of the Rhône. With the Allobroges lurking, the Senate dispatched the consul for 122 to guard the frontier. Late in the year, the legions won a huge battle against the

Allobroges near modern-day Avignon, and followed that up a few months later with an even bigger victory—a victory that quaestor Gaius Marius likely participated in. The climax of these early Gallic wars came in the late summer of 121. The Romans met a coalition of Gauls eighty miles north of Aquae Sextiae on the banks of the Isère River. We have no details of the battle but with total Gallic losses estimated at 120,000, it must have been a huge affair. Only a lack of specifics in the record keeps the Battle of the Isère River from being one of the most famous battles in Roman history. The victory established Roman political and military hegemony over southern Gaul.[13]

With the Romans ascendant in Gaul, a faction of senators and Equestrian merchants pushed to found a permanent civilian colony in the region to facilitate supply lines in case of future emergencies. The Senate twisted itself into contortions resisting the proposal, but just as they were achieving terminal paralysis, the dazzling young orator Lucius Crassus delivered another impressive performance in the Assembly. He strongly advocated for the founding of the colony and carried the Assembly—and most of his senatorial colleagues—along with him. When the new city of Narbo (modern Narbonne) was finally founded in 118, the whole region of southern Gaul became known as Gallia Narbonensis. With permanent settlements in the area, the Romans then constructed the famous Via Domitia, the permanent road linking Italy to Spain that is still visible along the southern coast of France.[14]

A FTER PARTICIPATING IN wars in Spain in the 130s and Gaul in the 120s, Gaius Marius transitioned from military to civilian life and stood for the tribunate of 119. He secured election thanks to the patronage of the Metelli. But rather than use his year as tribune to win new friends and allies, Marius spent his time alienating nearly everyone.[15]

Despite the introduction of the secret ballot, there were still plenty of ways for a patron to make sure his clients voted the way they were supposed to. One common practice was to confront a voter *after* he had filled out his ballot, but *before* he deposited it in the ballot box. Over the objections of his Metelli patrons, Marius introduced a bill to redesign the voting stalls to prevent such confrontations. One of the consuls—who happened to be a Metelli—induced the Senate to condemn Marius's bill and order Marius to present himself. Unintimidated, Marius threatened to toss the consul in prison if he stood in the way of the Assembly. The consul backed down, but the Metelli were furious their dog was biting the hand that fed him.[16]

Having angered his principal senatorial patrons, Marius then refused to cater to the plebs urbana, who had supported his voting reform efforts. Another tribune introduced a bill expanding a citizen's allotment of Gracchan price-controlled grain. The bill was extremely popular in Rome, but Marius vetoed it on the grounds that it was a needless handout that ruined the moral fiber of the Republic. The plebs urbana had asked for cheap grain, not moral hectoring, and thus Marius managed to leave the tribunate as disliked in the Forum as he was on the Palatine Hill.[17]

But despite his shaky political instincts, Marius let his ambition propel him forward and he stood for an aedileship in either 118 or 117. Marius may have viewed a year as aedile as a good way to build back public goodwill, but elections for the aedileship were much more competitive than the lower offices. Rather than ten annual tribunates or ten annual quaestorships, there were just four aedileships available. Being a well-connected noble with money was not a guarantee to winning—there was certainly no guarantee for a novus homo Italian who had just angered both the optimates and populares.[18]

Marius entered his name first for the senior aedile seat, but as the voting proceeded his announced vote totals were alarmingly small. Seeing that he faced certain defeat, Marius withdrew his name and put it in for junior aedileship. It was an unconventional gamble, but not against the law. Not that it mattered. Marius promptly lost that election, too. Marius's humiliating double defeat left his budding political career near death. But on the other side of the Mediterranean, events unfolded that would propel him to the inner circle of Roman power.[19]

THE KINGDOM OF Numidia lay on the north coast of Africa, corresponding roughly to modern-day Algeria. The kingdom was built on animal husbandry and maritime trade, but was famous for its expert horsemanship. The Numidians produced some of the finest cavalry in the Mediterranean. For generations, that cavalry had been at the disposal of the neighboring Carthaginians, but in the midst of the Second Punic War, the great Numidian king Masinissa defected to the Romans, and joined Scipio Africanus for the final battle against Hannibal in 202. Masinissa then ruled North Africa on Rome's behalf for the next fifty years and did not die until 148, just as Rome was returning to destroy Carthage once and for all. As proconsul of Rome, and personal friend of the Numidian royal family, Scipio Aemilianus settled the late king's estate between his three sons but by either luck or foul play one of the sons, Micipsa, emerged as the sole king of Numidia.[20]

King Micipsa was among those Aemilianus called in 133 to provide auxiliary units for the final conquest of Numantia. Not only was Micipsa happy to oblige, he had the perfect man to lead the expedition— his illegitimate nephew Jugurtha. Though the product of an extramarital liaison, Jugurtha remained in the royal family's orbit and was popular at court. Jugurtha was blessed with "physical strength, a handsome person, but above all with a vigorous intellect." For a few years, Micipsa saw Jugurtha as a potential heir, but when the king had sons of his own, Jugurtha became a problem. Sending the dashing prince to war might get him killed, which would be a convenient solution to the problem. But it was a gamble with a clear risk—what if Jugurtha came back more popular than ever?[21]

Once at Numantia, Jugurtha impressed everyone. "The young Numidian failed neither in judgment nor in any enterprise. He had, besides, a generous nature and a ready wit, qualities by which he had bound many Romans to him in intimate friendship." As he interacted with Romans, Jugurtha learned how Roman war and politics *really* worked. He learned their military tactics. He learned their political fault lines. Most especially he learned their vices. Aemilianus noticed the lessons Jugurtha was learning and took the young Numidian prince aside to caution him against relying too much on bribes and gifts to get his way. "It is dangerous," Aemilianus said, "to buy from a few what belonged to the many." This was not a lesson Jugurtha would learn.[22]

When the siege of Numantia concluded, Jugurtha returned home not only alive, but bearing a glowing letter from Scipio Aemilianus, who wrote, "The valor of your Jugurtha in the Numantine war was most conspicuous, as I am sure you will be glad to learn. To us he is dear because of his services, and we shall use our best efforts to make him beloved also by the Senate and People of Rome." Micipsa now had a real dilemma on his hands—he could not get rid of Jugurtha now that Jugurtha had the Roman stamp of approval. The only thing to do now was embrace him. The king formally adopted Jugurtha as his son, making him one of now three legitimate heirs to the throne.[23]

In 117, old Micipsa died and Numidia fell into the hands of three men: Jugurtha and his younger "brothers" Adherbal and Hiempsal. The three agreed to partition the kingdom and treasury equally, but Jugurtha was not interested in sharing. His agents bribed their way into Hiempsal's house, found the king cowering in a closet, and chopped his head off. Alerted to the assassination, Adherbal raised an army but Jugurtha's years of leadership in the Numidian military gave him the allegiance of all the best men. Adherbal could only raise fresh conscripts who were neither loyal nor well trained. In their one engagement, Jugurtha's army swept Adherbal's force aside. Unsafe anywhere in Numidia, King Adherbal fled to the only place of refuge he could think of: Rome.[24]

The Senate was vexed by the unrest in Numidia and agreed to let Adherbal and envoys from Jugurtha explain themselves. Each side predictably blamed the other. Adherbal called his brother "the wickedest of all men on the face of the earth," who had murdered his brother and provoked a war. Jugurtha's envoys claimed Adherbal and Hiempsal were the real problem, that Jugurtha had only acted in self-defense. The envoy said Adherbal was only "complaining because he had been prevented from inflicting injury." The Senate debated the matter and agreed to send a ten-man commission to Numidia to investigate further and render an informed judgment.[25]

The head of the commission was none other than Lucius Opimius, who was now an elder statesman after a career spent crushing Fregellae and the Gracchi. Jugurtha greeted Opimius's commission with all due honor and respect, and swore that he would abide by their judgment. After interviewing participants and surveying maps, the commission decided to oust neither king and instead return to the principle of joint rule. They divided Numidia in half—the fertile interior went to Jugurtha and the coastal plains to Adherbal. Then the senators packed up and left and hoped to hear no more from squabbling Numidian kings.[26]

In the course of the debates over Numidia, some senators were more supportive of Jugurtha than others, and it was well known Jugurtha's agents had come to Rome with "a great amount of gold and silver, directing them first to load his old friends with presents, and then to win new ones—in short, to make haste to accomplish by largess whatever they could." The defense of Jugurtha offered by these new friends was a touch embarrassing as the Numidian bribery was "notorious and brazen." It got to the point where Scaurus castigated his colleagues for their conduct. Scaurus was afraid "such gross corruption would arouse popular resentment."[27]

But this tale of shameless bribery does not tell the whole story. Many men in the Senate would not have needed money to support Jugurtha. Many had served alongside him at Numantia and believed him to be brave, educated, and a worthy ally of Rome. It is not unreasonable to think that those old friends needed very few presents to believe their one-time comrade-in-arm's side of the story. They did not know Adherbal. But they knew Jugurtha and liked him very much. As for the rest, money and gifts from a foreign delegation would have been accepted as the respectful price of admission to the atrium of any senator's villa. That said, some men are always prepared to let their wallets rule their politics; Jugurtha exploited as many of these men as he could.

WHILE THESE EVENTS unfolded, Gaius Marius was climbing back on the horse. Undeterred by his failure to secure an aedileship, Marius aimed higher and ran for praetor in the elections of 116. Though the Metelli opposed their erstwhile client's attempt to attain a praetorship, the novus homo Marius won the last spot.[28]

Stories swirled immediately that Marian partisans had snuck slaves into the voting lines to put their friend over the top. Shortly after the election, Marius was charged with electoral fraud. The trial lasted for days

and witnesses for both sides testified, including Cassius Sabaco, one of
Marius's friends who had allegedly slipped noncitizens into the voting
line. Also called was one of Marius's other noble patrons, Gaius Herennius. But Herennius refused to appear, citing the long-established legal
principle that a patron did not have to testify against a client. Marius himself released Herennius from that obligation, saying that the moment he
became a praetor he stopped being any man's client. The trial seemed to
be going against Marius, but when the jury returned, there was a surprise
verdict: they were tied. In Roman courts, a tie went to the defendant.
Marius was now a praetor.[29]

Despite Marius's victory, 115 was still a banner year for the Metellans. The shrewd Scaurus was elected consul alongside one of the Metelli cousins, while another Metelli secured a censorship. Proof of the
power Scaurus wielded behind the scenes, the Metellan censor named
Scaurus princeps senatus. Not only was this honor usually reserved for
an older senator, it had never been given to a sitting consul. Still only
in his mid-forties, Scaurus would remain princeps senatus for the next
twenty-five years, influencing the course of Roman history from atop the
senatorial rolls and speaking first in every debate. After putting Scaurus
first on the rolls, the censors then purged the Senate of thirty-two men,
most of whom we can assume were not friends of the family. Marius's
good friend Cassius Sabaco became a casualty and was expelled for his
part in the previous year's electoral fraud scandal.[30]

After an uneventful year minding his business in Rome, Marius was
sent to Further Spain. Little is known of his time in Spain, but we do
know he advanced Roman authority into areas that had become a hotbed
of brigands. By 114, Marius had cleared the brigands out of the region,
and publicani contractors moved in to open up new mining operations.
Like most Roman administrators, Marius saw his time abroad as the time
to build a fortune. We assume that he staked a lucrative claim to the un-
exploited mines, because when he returned to Rome in 113 he was a very
rich man.[31]

Back in Rome, the now forty-five-year-old Marius parlayed his wealth
and promising political prospects into a mutually advantageous alliance when he married sixteen-year-old Julia Caesaria. The Julii were an

ancient patrician house with roots older than the Republic itself. But their influence had waned over the centuries, and though their name was noble, their purses were empty. Bringing Marius into the family injected both energy and cash into their house. Marius was still a novus homo, but the Julii connection lent him the respectability he would need to attempt to make the leap from praetor to consul—a gap even the most well-connected men often found impossible to clear.[32]

As Marius's hunt for the elusive consulship began, the Kingdom of Numidia exploded into chaos. Jugurtha and Adherbal maintained a tense coexistence for three years, but in 113, Jugurtha made a second bid to become sole ruler of Numidia. He sent raiding parties into his brother's territory to try to provoke a response so he could portray himself as the victim. But Adherbal did not take the bait. Instead, he sent envoys back to Rome to complain about Jugurtha's provocation. Tired of the bickering in Numidia and with far bigger concerns on their plate, the Senate wrote to Adherbal, essentially telling him to handle the problem himself.[33]

When Jugurtha realized the Senate was not coming to Adherbal's aid, he mustered an army and marched into Adherbal's half of Numidia. Adherbal raised an army to defend himself, but once again Jugurtha's superior troops blew right through them. Adherbal fled to his capital of Cirta and closed the gates. The young king was probably pessimistic about his chances, but a group of Italian merchants who lived in Cirta convinced Adherbal to hold out—they told him *they* supported his claim and so would the Senate. So Adherbal sent a final letter to Rome begging for help while preparing to withstand a siege.[34]

The Senate's second response wasn't much better. They dispatched three junior senators who arrived in Numidia with instructions to order Adherbal and Jugurtha to resolve their quarrel peacefully. Jugurtha told these young senators his side of the story, spinning a tale that he had uncovered a nefarious plot by Adherbal and was only defending himself. But when the envoys requested they be allowed to enter Cirta and hear Adherbal's side, Jugurtha refused. Flummoxed, the envoys returned to Rome to make their report. The Senate was not stupid, and given Jugurtha's high-handed disdain for the envoys it was clear that he was most likely the aggressor in all this. But Jugurtha still had powerful friends in the Senate who killed any talk of sending legions to restore order.[35]

Instead, the Senate dispatched yet another commission, this one led by the princeps senatus Scaurus. Scaurus had been a consistent critic of Jugurtha and upon arrival in Africa sent orders for the wayward king to present himself at once. Jugurtha knew Roman politics well and knew Scaurus was a man to be feared. After one last failed attempt to take Cirta, Jugurtha gave up and presented himself to the Romans. But while enduring Scaurus's admonishments, Jugurtha noticed he did not hear any firm threat to introduce the legions. It dawned on him that Scaurus was there to avoid a military entanglement, not provoke one. As it turned out there was not much to fear from the Romans—they wanted no part of a war in Numidia.[36]

With Scaurus in Africa negotiating a settlement, the Italian merchants in Cirta, who had been urging Adherbal to resist, now advised him to submit. They told him to surrender to Jugurtha and that both kings should swear to abide by whatever settlement the Senate decreed. Adherbal could demonstrate his own goodwill by demanding nothing more than his own life be spared. Adherbal agreed—which turned out to be a fatal error. After Adherbal walked out of the gates of Cirta, Jugurtha wasted no time dispensing with his troublesome younger brother. The unfortunate Adherbal was apprehended and tortured to death.[37]

Had Jugurtha stopped with the execution of Adherbal, the whole affair might have ended right there. The Senate likely would have recognized him as the sole king of Numidia and life would have gone on. But as soon as his forces entered Cirta, Jugurtha's men took bloody vengeance on everyone in the city. The order went out that any "who were found with arms in their hands" were to be killed, but the order was interpreted loosely and led to a general massacre that consumed hundreds of people, including most of the Italian merchants. This was the moment that it all went wrong for Jugurtha. Even a Senate that did not want to get involved in Numidia could not ignore the slaughter of their countrymen.[38]

Back in Rome, the clear consensus was that Jugurtha had gone too far. But even more than that, public opinion now recognized that the Senate had been mismanaging Numidian affairs for years. The rumors of bribery and corruption had long been swirling in the Forum. When news hit of Jugurtha's latest outrage—the sadistic massacre of Italians—the tribunes demanded the Senate take action. Real action. Military action.[39]

The Senate relented. That year's consul, Lucius Calpurnius Bestia, was assigned to the province of Africa and ordered to raise legions. While he assembled his army, Bestia also selected an influential group of legati to serve as his senior advisers. Among those was Scaurus, who made sure he was placed on Bestia's staff. Having failed once to keep the legions out of Numidia, Scaurus still sought a peaceful resolution to the crisis. The discussions between Bestia and Scaurus would have revolved around how much of a show of force was necessary to bring Jugurtha to heel.[40]

Jugurtha was surprised to find Rome now mobilizing for action. He believed that his money had been spread lavishly enough—and that the Romans disdained military intervention in Numidia enough—that he would never have to face them in battle. He could think of only one thing to do. Jugurtha dispatched one of his sons and two close friends to make the trip to Rome with even *more* money to try to bribe the Senate back into docility. But the political winds had shifted. The Senate barred the Numidians from Rome and passed a decree ordering them to vacate Italy within ten days.[41]

In the summer of 111, Bestia's legions sailed for the province of Africa and from there advanced across the Numidian border. Hearing the legions had entered his territory, Jugurtha sent agents to the Bestia. Jugurtha's envoys told the consul that conquering Numidia would be a long and expensive affair and that it would be much better for everyone if an agreement could be reached. Then Jugurtha presented himself personally to Bestia and Scaurus and the three sat down for a private conference. During this conference it was agreed that in exchange for an indemnity payment of "thirty elephants, many cattle and horses, and a small amount of silver," Rome would recognize Jugurtha as the sole king of Numidia and everyone would go home.[42]

The perfunctory campaign and easy terms raised hell back in Rome, but Scaurus hoped the charade would end the crisis. With Jugurtha now sole king of Numidia, he would cease to be a threat and the Senate could focus on Rome's far more porous and dangerous northern border.

B UT THE CHARADE was not enough. The plebs urbana expected Bestia to return with Jugurtha's complete capitulation; instead messengers brought the shocking news that Bestia was withdrawing after securing a paltry indemnity. One young leader in particular grabbed onto the scandals surrounding Jugurtha as his ticket to power: Gaius Memmius. Memmius had been one of the vocal proponents of sending Bestia to Numidia in the first place, and after being elected tribune for 111, he denounced the Senate's foot dragging and claimed that they were complicit in Jugurtha's crimes. The facts were plain: Roman honor had once again been "nullified by avarice."[43]

When word of the settlement reached Rome, Memmius launched a full broadside on the vicious cupidity of the Senate: "Men stained with crime, with gory hands, of monstrous greed, guilty, yet at the same time full of pride, who have made honor, reputation, loyalty, in short everything honorable and dishonorable, a source of gain." But he also scolded the people for allowing it to go on: "You were silently indignant that the treasury was pillaged, that kings and free peoples paid tribute to a few nobles, that those nobles possessed supreme glory and vast wealth." He then addressed all of Rome: "the Senate's dignity has been prostituted to a ruthless enemy, your sovereignty has been betrayed, your country offered for sale at home and abroad." [44]

But Memmius took pains to not let things get out of hand. Specifically invoking the martyred Gracchi, he said: "After the murder of Tiberius Gracchus . . . prosecutions were instituted against the Roman commons. Again, after Gaius Gracchus and Marcus Fulvius were slain, many men of your order suffered death in the dungeon. In both cases bloodshed was ended, not by law, but by the caprice of the victors." Illegal violence was the tactic of reactionary nobles. Taking the high road, Memmius

said: "Let those who have betrayed their country to the enemy be punished, not by arms or by violence, which it is less becoming for you to
inflict than for them to suffer, but by the courts." And Memmius had a
very specific thing in mind: he wanted Jugurtha himself to testify against
the corrupt Senate.[45]

Memmius induced the Assembly to order a praetor to go to Numidia,
fetch Jugurtha, and bring him back to Rome to identify the senators he
had bribed. The king was to remain under the full protection of the tribunes' authority and could expect full immunity for his testimony. Whatever the true scope of their individual guilt, the Senate cannot have liked
the sound of this. Jugurtha did not like the sound of it, either, but he
didn't really have much choice in the matter. If he did not come, it would
prove he was a traitor to Rome. So when the praetor arrived to fetch him,
Jugurtha got on the boat and they departed Numidia.[46]

After years of scandal, Jugurtha's arrival in Rome was a sensation. Ever
the savvy operator, Jugurtha made sure to dress in humble clothes without any of the finery he usually wore. If he hoped to make it out of this
in one piece, he couldn't come parading into Rome like King Moneybags.
But even in humble dress, he couldn't resist throwing around some cash.
With his testimony scheduled for the Assembly, he set out to find an
agreeable tribune and retain his services. Jugurtha found such a man in
Gaius Bebius, who, after pocketing Jugurtha's cash, promised to act on
the king's behalf.[47]

When the Assembly met, the crowd was agitated and hostile. Once
Jugurtha himself came out, Memmius launched into a full recounting
of how deeply Jugurtha had corrupted the Senate. But he reminded everyone that Jugurtha himself was here to testify, not be punished. The
crowd waited expectantly for the big moment when Jugurtha would reveal all. But the king did not move and did not speak. Instead, Gaius
Bebius stepped forward and told the king to remain silent. Bebius said
that he was vetoing the proceedings. The crowd was stunned and then
erupted in anger. But much like Octavius's vetoing of Tiberius Gracchus's
land bill, nothing would persuade or intimidate Bebius into changing
his mind. That was it. Jugurtha would not testify. The Assembly shook
with rage as Jugurtha was escorted off the rostra, but when he was gone

the crowds dissipated peacefully. They did not, however, forget the prize they had been denied.[48]

During his sojourn in Rome, Jugurtha resolved to tie up some loose ends. His prior conduct had triggered a diaspora of anyone with Numidian royal blood, all of whom rightfully considered themselves targets for assassination. A few of these refugees wound up in Rome, and one of them positioned himself as a replacement king if the Romans squashed Jugurtha—a grandson of the late Numidian king Micipsa named Massiva. Jugurtha caught wind of this plot and determined to do to Massiva what he had already done to Hiempsal and Adherbal.[49]

Jugurtha delegated the task to Bomilcar, one of his most loyal supporters. Bomilcar trolled the seedy underbelly of Rome until he made contact with a small group of men who were "adept in such business." These men stalked Massiva until they learned his regular schedule, set a trap, and jumped him. But the hit was not carried out with anything resembling ninja stealth. Massiva was killed but it was such a reckless, loud fight that the murder was discovered and the assassins apprehended. Dragged before the consul, the killers made a full confession and implicated Bomilcar as the mastermind.[50]

Skirting the protection that had been offered Jugurtha, the consul prepared to bring Bomilcar to trial for the crime—and hopefully implicate Jugurtha along the way. The Numidian king tried to laugh off the charges and handed over fifty of his retainers to guarantee Bomilcar's appearance in court. But unable to halt the proceedings with his usual array of bribes, Jugurtha decided to cut his losses. Abandoning the fifty hostages to their fate, Jugurtha arranged for Bomilcar's escape from Rome. When the Senate discovered the defendant had escaped, they ordered Jugurtha himself to vacate Rome immediately. As he departed, Jugurtha looked back at Rome and issued his famous judgment: "A city for sale and doomed to speedy destruction if it finds a purchaser."[51]

CHAPTER 5

THE SPOILS OF VICTORY

For the first time resistance was offered to
the insolence of the nobles, the beginning of
a struggle which threw everything, human and
divine, into confusion, and rose to such a pitch
of frenzy that civil discord ended in war and the
devastation of Italy.

SALLUST[1]

SOMETIME AFTER 120 BC, A GREAT NORTHERN TRIBE CALLED
the Cimbri left their homeland near modern Denmark and migrated south. Over the following months and years they progressed
toward the Danube, and then followed the course of the river west toward
the Alps. Since no one is thrilled when a horde of three hundred thousand strangers comes wandering over the horizon, wherever the Cimbri
went, they were met by hostile natives. But since the Cimbri were not a
conquering horde, they were willing to move on when faced with hostility
from the existing inhabitants. All they were looking for was a peaceful
place to settle where they could build a new life.[2]

Like so many "barbarian" tribes who inhabited the world beyond the
Mediterranean, identifying who the Cimbri were, and where they came
from, is difficult for historians. The Romans were never too particular
about getting the details right and had a tendency to make sweeping gen-
eralizations, lumping completely different peoples into single catch-all

categories. The Cimbri are alternatively described as being Gauls, Scythians, Celts, and Germans—and even when they are successfully identified in 114 as the "Cimbri," the sources are unclear whether it was really one homogenous people or whether it was a roving confederation that also included groups like the Teutones and Ambrones. The Romans also tended to describe every barbarian tribe as enormous, hairy, painted, dirty, and loud—more beasts than men. Mustering every ounce of hackney stereotyping, the historian Diodorus says the Cimbri "had the appearance of giants, endowed with enormous strength." But since this is how the Romans described *every* Germanic tribe, it is difficult to know what the Cimbri really looked like.[3]

If we can't say exactly *who* the Cimbri were, we also can't say exactly *why* they started migrating. The geographer Strabo says it was an "inundation of the sea" that forced them to relocate from their ancestral home on the North Sea. But whether it was ecological change, overcrowding, intertribal war, or a combination of those factors, by 120, a mass of two hundred to three hundred thousand Cimbri packed their bags and began walking south. By 113, the Cimbri had reached modern-day Slovenia, putting them just on the other side of the Alps from Italy. A local tribe warned the Romans of the sudden appearance of this new horde and asked the Senate for protection.[4]

Alarmed at the potential threat on their northern border, the Senate ordered consul Gnaeus Papirius Carbo—brother of the Gracchan land commissioner who had been driven to suicide—to take legions north to guard the frontier. Carbo placed his legions in the principal Alpine passes to make sure the Cimbri did not enter Italy. Whether it was the presence of the legions or because they never planned to enter Italy in the first place, the Cimbri kept moving west into what is today the Austrian Alps. After they bypassed his initial positions, Carbo reformed his legions and followed the Cimbri at a safe distance to monitor their movements and make sure they did not get any ideas about taking a left turn into Italy.[5]

Eventually, the Cimbri took notice of the Romans and sent ambassadors to meet with Carbo. The consul was surprised by their civilized manners and pleased when they said they sought no quarrel and were simply looking for an uninhabited territory to live in. In an apparent gesture of friendship, Carbo assigned some local guides to show the Cimbri the best route to Gaul—which he said would take them past the city of Noreia. But either because Carbo was genuinely suspicious of Cimbric intentions, or was spoiling for an opportunity to win a triumph, this gesture of friendship was a deadly ruse. Carbo instructed the guides to take the Cimbri on a circuitous route through the mountains while Carbo took his legions on a shortcut to Noreia. There Carbo's troops took up a hidden position and waited to pounce when the unsuspecting Cimbri finally arrived.[6]

Philosophers of war have maintained that victory in the field often goes to the general who is either able to choose the terrain of battle or maintain the element of surprise. At Noreia Carbo had both, but it did him little good because he dramatically underestimated the size of the enemy. When Carbo sprang his trap, the legions were quickly overwhelmed by the sheer number of Cimbric warriors, who smashed Carbo's army and forced them into a disorganized retreat. It was a humiliating defeat.[7]

Luckily for the Romans, the Cimbri did not follow up their victory by invading Italy. It really did seem like they were searching for a peaceful homeland to settle and had no wish to tangle further with the duplicitous and warlike Romans. But the fate of the two nations was now linked—the Battle of Noreia was only the beginning of the Cimbrian Wars.

E VEN BEFORE THE arrival of the Cimbri, the Senate was not thrilled about the state of their northern border, which now seemed to be under constant and perhaps fatal pressure from migrating hordes.

The trouble began on the Macedonian border in 114. The Scordisci, a Thracian tribe that dominated the Danube, began making incursions south into Roman territory. To stop the incursions, the Senate dispatched consul Gaius Porcius Cato, grandson of the legendary Cato the Elder, but Cato's army was crushed. With the Roman defenses in Macedonia shattered, the Scordisci overwhelmed the reserve garrisons and carved a wide swath of destruction. One scandalized Roman colorfully described the Scordisci invasion: "They left no cruelty untried, as they vented their fury on their prisoners; they sacrificed to the gods with human blood; they drank out of human skulls; by every kind of insult inflicted by burning and fumigation they made death more foul." This culminated with the sack of the Oracle of Delphi, one of the most famous and sacred institutions of the Greek world. Though known to hold a rich depository of treasure, the Oracle was protected by its universally recognized sanctity. But as the Scordisci recognized no such sanctity, they plundered Delphi at will.[8]

As the Scordisci had their way in Macedonia, the Senate was forced to send legion after legion for the next two years. One of the Metelli cousins led the Roman armies in 113 and the following year he was succeeded by our old friend Marcus Livius Drusus, the crafty tribune who successfully undercut Gaius Gracchus during their shared tribunate a decade earlier. Now a consul, Drusus successfully brought the conflict to a close, ending his year on campaign with a major victory that finally pushed the Scordisci out of Roman territory. The Scordisci remained a constant threat, however, so in 110 the Senate had to send yet another consul to aggressively patrol the Macedonian border against further invasion.[9]

With the Scordisci running amok in Macedonia and Greece, and the huge mob of Cimbri wandering around near the Alps, the Senate prioritized the stability of the northern border during these years. The crisis in the north certainly helps explain the Senate's anemic response to Jugurtha. Senatorial leaders like Scaurus hoped that negotiation and patience would bring order back to Numidia—which had, after all, been a faithful ally to Rome for nearly a century. What later Roman historians like Sallust blamed on scandalous bribery could simply have been the realistic recognition of the greater dangers in the north. Why send troops to Numidia when Italy itself was threatened by barbarian invasion?

The uncertain defense of the northern borders also had another impact on Roman politics: defeated commanders started facing legal prosecution for their failures. After his defeat at the hands of the Scordisci in 114, Cato was hauled before the Assembly and only narrowly avoided exile—the common belief being that Cato had only dodged prosecution by bribing the jurors. Less fortunate was Gnaeus Carbo. In 111, the Assembly called Carbo to account for provoking, and then losing, the Battle of Noreia. Marcus Antonius led the prosecution and easily secured a conviction. Like his brother, Carbo committed suicide rather than depart for exile. With both brothers now dead after being hounded by the refined optimate orators Crassus and Antonius, their sons would bear the optimates a special hostility in the years to come.[10]

DESPITE THE TROUBLE in the north, the people of Rome remained inflamed by the conduct of Jugurtha. After fleeing Rome in 111, Jugurtha returned to Numidia and raised an army. Unable to ignore Jugurtha's insulting behavior, the Senate sent more legions across the Mediterranean in 110. In response to the invasion, Jugurtha launched a yearlong campaign of evasion, delay, and trickery to bog the Romans down. Finally, in January 109, Jugurtha lured the legions into a trap. With the Romans hopelessly surrounded Jugurtha offered simple terms: leave Numidia within ten days or you will all die. Adding insult to injury, Jugurtha also demanded the defeated legionaries "pass under the yoke," a humiliating ritual of physically walking under a harness to acknowledge submission. The trapped Romans accepted the terms, passed under the yoke, and left Numidia.[11]

The humiliating defeat only confirmed the belief back in Rome that the pathetic campaigns in Numidia needed fresh leadership. In the elections for 109, the Assembly elected the sixth and final Metelli cousin to the consulship: Quintus Caecilius Metellus. Stern and disciplined, Metellus was both honest and intelligent, but an aristocratic pride defined his worldview. As the youngest of the Metelli, he was raised in a world where his brothers and cousins controlled the levers of power. He marched up the cursus honorum with ease, serving as quaestor in 126, tribune in 121, aedile in 118, and then praetor in 115. Politically rigid and unyielding, Metellus had little use for populare agitation because as a Metellan prince, his aristocratic connections were more than enough to secure his future prospects. After being elected consul, Metellus was assigned to take over the frustrating war in Numidia.[12]

With the previous year's army defeated, it was clear Metellus was going to have to raise more troops from a population already stretched thin by continued economic dislocation and war. The historical record is vague, but we know Metellus secured an exemption from various restrictions on conscription, including lifting the six-year maximum on service and broadening the age range from which he could draw. Both exemptions would have allowed Metellus to draw from experienced veterans who had already done their time—every one of which was worth five raw recruits.[13]

In his search for experienced soldiers, Metellus also made a point of enrolling the best officers he could find. The paucity of available talent goes a long way toward explaining what may otherwise be an inexplicable decision. Metellus asked Gaius Marius to serve as a legate. Though Marius had run afoul of the Metelli politically, there was no question that he was among the most capable officers in Rome. Marius did not hesitate to join the campaign. With the conflict in Numidia going so poorly and with the Senate clearly to blame, there would be plenty of opportunities for a mere novus homo to make a name for himself.[14]

Back in Numidia, Jugurtha was well informed of these developments and he did not like what he heard. Not only were the Romans preparing to come back, but his informants were clear that Metellus was not a man who could be bribed. So when Metellus and his army arrived in Africa in the spring of 109, Jugurtha abruptly changed tactics. He sent envoys offering to surrender to Metellus with only one string: that he and his children be spared. But Metellus was not going to be taken in by the wily king. Turning Jugurtha's tricks against him, Metellus bribed the envoys over to the Roman side. They were told to deliver a message of peace, but then to work secretly to arrest the king and deposit him at Metellus's feet. But Jugurtha was cautious to the point of paranoia and evaded the subsequent plots. Recognizing that there would be no negotiation, Jugurtha resolved to defeat the Romans in battle. Again.[15]

Jugurtha used his superior knowledge of the terrain to stay one step ahead of Metellus until he was able to lay an ambush in the late summer of 109. At the Muthul River, Jugurtha cut the Romans off from their source of water. But rather than forcing a quick surrender, Jugurtha found himself locked in a battle with Metellus that lasted all day. The legions managed to hold out until nightfall, at which point Jugurtha withdrew and the Romans built a network of fortified camps.[16]

The Romans spent the next few days in camp, where Metellus got troubling news. Jugurtha was riding around the countryside raising thousands more men from the surrounding communities to replace the men he had just lost. Despite the casualties the Romans had just inflicted, the Numidians would soon be back stronger than ever. With Jugurtha fielding an almost unlimited number of men, Metellus determined this was not a war that could be won by a series of battles. It would instead require a steady envelopment of the entire country to eliminate Jugurtha's access to men. The next phase of the war would offer few opportunities for glorious heroics, but Metellus was here to win the war.[17]

B ACK IN ROME, the ex-tribune Gaius Memmius used the debacles in Numidia to widen his crusade against senatorial misconduct. Just as Metellus left for Africa in 109, an allied tribune named Gaius Mamilius created a special tribunal later dubbed the Mamilian Commission to investigate corruption and treason. Memmius served as the principal prosecutor. Staffed by Equestrian jurors and run by populare leaders looking to settle old scores, the prosecution moved seamlessly from specific charges of bribery to a general attack on the Senate. Memmius and his fellow prosecutors "conducted the investigation with harshness and violence, on hearsay evidence and at the caprice of the commons."[18]

The first man hauled before the commission was Lucius Opimius, who had long been a bête noire of the populare—guilty of the uncompromising sack of Fregellae in 125 and the slaughter of the Gracchans in 121. Having avoided punishment for a decade, the time had come for Opimius to feel the wrath of the people. Opimius was charged with treason for his conduct leading the first embassy to Numidia. He was found guilty of accepting bribes from Jugurtha and exiled. Opimius departed Rome and "spent his old age in infamy, hated and abused by the people."[19]

Next up was the former consul Lucius Calpurnius Bestia, who had sailed off to Numidia in 111 to bring Jugurtha to heel and instead pocketed some cash and gave Jugurtha a slap on the wrist. The princeps senatus Scaurus personally defended Bestia before the commission, but Bestia too was convicted and exiled. Two men of consular rank had now been banished by the wrath of the populare.[20]

The commission then continued its general attack on the optimates who had failed Rome. Gaius Porcius Cato was prosecuted on trumped up charges—his real crime being his defeats in the north back in 114. And of course the officers who had led the campaign in Numidia that ended with the legions passing under the yoke were accused of treason and exiled. In the end, the Mamilian Commission convicted four men of consular rank in an unprecedented strike at the alleged authority of the Senate.[21]

The work of the Mamilian Commission was one of the key reasons that Sallust decided to write on the Jugurthine War: it marked the aggressive return of the populare as a force in Roman politics. A decade after the fall of Gaius Gracchus, the populare were returning with a vengeance. The populare assault on the Senate also cleared space for the rise of a new generation of novus homo. Men who could run for office and make their case on explicitly antisenatorial terms, to turn being novus homo from a negative to a positive. The chief beneficiary of this new environment would be Gaius Marius.[22]

T HE ROMANS WERE able to focus on the political drama swirling around Jugurtha in part because the northern border had remained relatively quiet. The Macedonian frontier was silent and the Cimbri had departed for parts unknown after the Battle of Noreia in 113. But four years after that last contact, the Cimbri reappeared. They had apparently failed to find a permanent home and were now descending south through the Rhône valley, ready to try their luck in southern Gaul again.[23]

With Metellus having departed for Numidia, the Senate ordered his colleague Marcus Junius Silanus to muster what forces remained in Italy. But with Metellus already requiring a special dispensation to raise recruits for Numidia, Silanus found himself drawing from an even thinner manpower pool. But the consul managed to dredge the last warm bodies out of that pool and march them through the Alps into Gaul. As the two sides squared off, a small party of Cimbric ambassadors traveled to Rome to say that "the people of Mars should give them some land by way of pay and use their hands and weapons for any purpose it wished." The Senate refused to grant the Cimbris' request—Rome made treaties with defeated enemies, not defiant tribes.[24]

After the Cimbri received their answer, Silanus encouraged the Cimbri to move along, but that provoked a battle. Details of the battle are non-existent and all we really know is the outcome: once again the Cimbri crushed the legions. The casualties were staggering. It was said that "after so many men had been killed, some were crying for sons or brothers; others, orphaned by the death of their fathers, lamented the loss of their parents and the desolation of Italy; and a very large number of women, deprived of their husbands, were turned into poor widows." But beyond the individual suffering, the Cimbric victory meant that the road to Italy was now clear.[25]

But, as before, the Cimbri showed no interest in pillaging Italy. Their new objective may have been to simply contain the Romans on the Italian peninsula as they set themselves up as the premier power in south-central Gaul. Their victories certainly upended the political situation in the region. Many of Rome's allies in Gaul tore up their treaties now that a bigger bully had moved onto the block.

Back in Rome, the plebs urbana were horrified by the failure of Silanus, and there was little happening in Numidia to take their minds off the looming menace of the Cimbri. Metellus's decision to seek a more methodical reduction of Numidia was militarily sound, but it fed the general belief that the only thing the nobles did in Numidia was drag their feet. Though Metellus was not actually dragging his feet, his image still took a hit back in Rome.[26]

In late 109, Metellus broke his army into smaller units and sent them out to ravage communities that remained loyal to Jugurtha. After he made a few brutal examples, communities started surrendering the minute the Romans arrived. To combat this war of intimidation, Jugurtha turned to guerrilla tactics. Allowing his peasant conscripts to go home, Jugurtha and his best cavalry units shadowed the legions wherever they went, harassing Roman communication and supply lines and picking off individual units if they ever strayed too far from the main force. They also rode ahead of the Romans to likely campsites, spoiling fields that might be used to feed Roman horses and poisoning any freshwater springs.[27]

But as weeks turned into months, the inhabitants of Numidia tired of the crisscrossing armies and blamed Jugurtha for provoking the Romans to war. Metellus attempted to exploit that resentment. He opened clandestine talks with Jugurtha's loyal lieutenant Bomilcar, who was last seen in Rome orchestrating the assassination of Massiva. After a mix of bribes and threats Bomilcar agreed to convince Jugurtha to surrender. Returning from the secret rendezvous, Bomilcar painted a dismal picture for Jugurtha: The Romans are going to win. The country is in ruins. The people are unhappy. It is time to give up for the good of all Numidia. Coming from such a close friend, Jugurtha relented and resigned himself to defeat. He sent an envoy to Metellus asking for terms of surrender.[28]

Metellus was not going to let Jugurtha off lightly. Jugurtha was to be stripped of his wealth and the means to make further war. He was to promptly deliver "two hundred thousand pounds of silver, all his elephants, and a considerable quantity of horses and arms." But with the darkness closing in, Jugurtha's survival instincts kicked back to life. When Metellus ordered the king to present himself in person, Jugurtha balked. The king refused the final order to surrender and instead rode deep into the interior of Numidia, far from the Romans. There, in distant seclusion, he could plot his return.[29]

Metellus was frustrated that his plan to end the war had been stymied at the eleventh hour, but he knew he had considerably weakened Jugurtha. Metellus was also gratified to learn shortly thereafter that the Senate had extended his command; he would have another year to capture the elusive king. But while Metellus focused on Jugurtha, an even greater danger lurked within his own ranks.[30]

GAIUS MARIUS HAD always kept his eye on the consulship. Though the path of his political career had been uneven, he felt that it was his destiny to one day achieve high office. He was now approaching his fiftieth birthday and continued to carry those ambitions of power. Marius was convinced that if given the chance he could outshine the stagnant optimates and become the most dominant man in Rome.

A year of fighting under Metellus had reminded everyone that Marius was an excellent soldier and popular with the men under his command. He was generous with spoils, mingled easily with the common legionaries, and joined in with camp labor. As Plutarch later wrote, "It is a most agreeable spectacle for a Roman soldier when he sees a general eating common bread in public, or sleeping on a simple pallet, or taking a hand in the construction of some trench or palisade. For they have not so much admiration for those leaders who share honor and riches with them as for those who take part in their toils and dangers." Marius personified this type of leadership.[31]

In early 108, Marius went to the port city of Utica to attend to some business and make a few necessary sacrifices to the gods. During these rituals, Marius asked a soothsayer to take stock of his own personal situation. The soothsayer told him "a great and marvelous career awaited him" and encouraged Marius to keep "trusting in the gods, to carry out what he had in mind and put his fortune to the test as often as possible." There was only one thing on Marius's mind at the moment, and the message from the gods could not be clearer. Marius resolved to return to the legionary camp and request Metellus grant him a leave of absence so he could return to Rome and run for the consulship.[32]

However, Metellus wasn't interested in letting Marius leave. He told Marius that such dreams were not for all men, that Marius really ought to content himself with the success he'd already won and not seek to rise above his station. But Marius refused to let it go, pestering Metellus until Metellus caustically put an end to the debate. "Don't be in a hurry to go to Rome," he said. "It will be soon enough for you to be a candidate when my son becomes one." Since Metellus's oldest son was then just twenty years old, the implication was clear: Metellus would never grant Marius's request for leave.[33]

Furious but undeterred, Marius activated the extensive network of support he had built up both back in Rome and among the soldiers and merchants in Numidia. Marius openly griped that Metellus was dragging his feet and that if he were in charge the war would be over in a matter of weeks. He also curried favor with the remnants of the Numidian royal family that had fled into exile. Another grandson of the long-dead King Micipsa named Gauda approached Metellus, requesting to be recognized as the rightful king when Jugurtha was dethroned. But Metellus refused to treat the young man with any royal honors. Marius tracked down the offended would-be king and promised that he would be king if Marius was in charge. Marius's politicking in Numidia led to a steady stream of letters back to Rome claiming that Metellus was turning into a slow-moving tyrant who was now too much in love with imperious power to end the war properly. Marius boldly claimed that if "but half the army were put in his charge, he would have Jugurtha in fetters within a few days."[34]

A S THESE POLITICAL machinations unfolded in the Roman camp, King Jugurtha was himself back to work—rebuilding his treasury, recruiting soldiers, and generally undermining the Roman occupation of Numidia. In the winter of 109–108, he made contact with the Roman-occupied city of Vaga and induced its people to revolt. With the revolt erupting on a holiday, the Roman garrison was caught off guard and slaughtered to a man. Well, *almost* to a man. The commander of the garrison, a well-liked officer named Titus Turpilius Silanus, somehow escaped unharmed.[35]

When word of the revolt reached Metellus, he raced his army to Vaga, overwhelmed its meager defenses, and sacked it mercilessly. The fate of the garrison commander Silanus, meanwhile, was still up in the air. Hauled before Metellus to explain how he lost the city but not his life, Silanus had no clear answers. In the closed-door deliberations that followed, Marius allegedly urged Metellus to sentence Silanus to death for treason. Metellus was fond of Silanus but ultimately agreed. Silanus was scourged and executed.[36]

But in the aftermath of the execution, Marius went around whispering that Metellus had done wrong by Silanus, and that his cruel punishment far outweighed the crime—doubly so because it was not even in Metellus's power as consul to hand down such a sentence without right of appeal to the Assembly. The incident was depressing to Metellus, especially because now his men doubted him and looked openly to Marius for leadership.[37]

Metellus likely hoped that all this carping and behind-the-back undermining of his authority would soon be irrelevant as his secret connection to the traitorous Bomilcar seemed about ready to bear fruit. But instead, Jugurtha discovered Bomilcar's treachery and executed his once faithful lieutenant. Metellus's latest plan to capture Jugurtha had failed, but it did help drive Jugurtha into paranoid isolation. From that point on Jugurtha "never passed a quiet day or night; he put little trust in any place, person, or time; feared his countrymen and the enemy alike."[38]

Since the failure to capture Jugurtha meant the war would continue, Metellus admitted that a disgruntled Marius would be more a hindrance than a help in the next campaign. So just twelve days before the consular election Metellus finally gave Marius leave to return to Rome. His hope was that even if Marius won election that the Senate would not appoint him to take over Metellus's command in Numidia.[39]

A FTER MARIUS DEPARTED, Metellus marched out to finish the war. At that point, Jugurtha's campaign was in dire straits. The king's increasing paranoia drove many former supporters away, and conscripts deserted almost as soon as they were pressed into service. In the closing months of 108, Metellus managed to chase Jugurtha all the way to the city of Thala, deep in the interior of Numidia. The city was supposedly impervious to siege as it sat atop the only source of freshwater for fifty miles. But thanks to a fortuitous rain that filled Roman water sacks, the legions were able to batter down the gates. The sack of Thala turned out to be a hollow victory, however: by the time the Romans entered the city, Jugurtha had already fled. Meanwhile, the leaders of Thala gathered up anything the Romans might seize as profitable plunder and loaded it into the main palace in the center of town. There they threw themselves one last grand banquet and afterward, set fire to the building, destroying everything in it, including themselves.[40]

Though the capture of Thala was not decisive, it did change the dynamic of the war. Thala had been Jugurtha's last great stronghold in

Numidia and its fall forced him out of his own kingdom entirely. Jugurtha kept constantly on the move, riding southwest into the wild territory beyond the reach of the "civilized" powers. It was there that he finally found refuge with a tribe of nomads inhabiting the Atlas Mountains. Thanks to the treasure he carried with him, Jugurtha convinced these nomadic horsemen to form the core of a new army.[41]

But the mercenary nomads alone would not be enough to continue the war with Rome, so Jugurtha also wrote to King Bocchus of Mauretania to propose an alliance. The Kingdom of Mauretania bordered Numidia to the west, covering the region of northwest Africa that roughly corresponds to modern-day Morocco. The two monarchs already shared a familial tie, though the exact nature isn't clear: some sources say Jugurtha married Bocchus's daughter; others say Bocchus married Jugurtha's daughter. Regardless, the king of Mauretania turned out to be amenable to a closer alliance as he had no love for the Romans or their habit of imperial expansion.[42]

The first joint operation of the new anti-Roman coalition was to attack the great city of Cirta. The city had been in Roman hands for many years now, and Metellus had used Cirta as the primary storehouse for his own treasury, baggage, and captured prisoners. Informed of the alliance between Jugurtha and Bocchus, Metellus decided not to rush out into battle, instead staying close to his defensive base, waiting for the kings to come to him. He sent out repeated letters of warning to Bocchus about getting mixed up with Jugurtha's inevitably doomed resistance. Bocchus wrote back hinting at a peaceful solution but always seeking leniency for Jugurtha. It is not clear whether Bocchus was stalling for time or genuinely trying to negotiate a settlement.[43]

It was while he corresponded with Bocchus that Metellus was hit with a broadside from Rome. Not only had Gaius Marius been elected consul, but the Assembly had voted to override the Senate's decision to keep Metellus in command of Numidia. Marius would soon be on his way to take over the job. Crushed and angry, Metellus was "more affected by this news than was right or becoming, neither refraining from tears nor bridling his tongue; although he had the other qualities of a great man, he showed little fortitude in bearing mortification."[44]

MARIUS'S CAMPAIGN FOR the consulship marked the culminating blow against the optimates in the Senate. What had begun with Memmius's attacks in 111, and then continued through the Mamilian Commission corruption trials in 109, now climaxed with the consular campaign of a proudly defiant novus homo. For Marius this day had been a long time coming.

Marius campaigned with a thunderous fury. In yet another clear break with mos maiorum, Marius routinely denounced Metellus for his conduct during the war. It was unheard of for a subordinate to criticize his general so openly, but Marius refused to be a slave to tradition—especially after Metellus tried to block him from the consulship. Above all, Marius made a single forthright promise: "If they would make him consul, he would within a short time deliver Jugurtha alive or dead into the hands of the Roman People." Not surprisingly, Marius was elected.[45]

After his victory, Marius's attacks on the Senate only intensified. He denounced the old nobles as men of lineage but not merit: "I personally know of men, citizens, who after being elected consuls began for the first time to read the history of our forefathers and the military treatises of the Greeks!" He said if they made mistakes that "their ancient nobility, the brave deeds of their ancestors, the power of their kindred and relatives, their throng of clients, are all a very present help." He himself could not "display family portraits or the triumphs and consulships of my forefathers; but if occasion requires, I can show spears, a banner, trappings and other military prizes as well as scars on my breast. These are my portraits." He then ended by saying triumphantly of the Senate that he had "wrested the consulship from them as the spoils of victory."[46]

But his election alone did not guarantee that he would take over the Numidian campaign. Indeed, the Senate had already determined Numidia would remain Metellus's province for another year. But as they had previously done for Scipio Aemilianus, the Assembly overrode the Senate and made Numidia Marius's province. The bonds of mos maiorum loosened still further.[47]

As he prepared to raise new legions, Marius ran into the same problem that had plagued Rome for a generation. As more and more families were pushed off their land, fewer and fewer men met the minimum property requirement for service in the legions. But while the consuls were forced to scrape the bottom of a very dry barrel looking for potential legionaries, tens of thousands of young men sat idle. The only mark against them was that they did not own land. So to fill his legions, Marius took a fateful step in the long history of the decline and fall of the Roman Republic—he requested exemption from the property qualification. Of this request to recruit from among the poorest plebs, Sallust says: "Some say that he did this through lack of good men, others because of a desire to curry favor ... As a matter of fact, to one who aspires to power the poorest man is the most helpful, since he has no regard for his property, having none, and considers anything honorable for which he receives pay." Any man, no matter how poor and destitute, could now serve in the army. With the promise of plunder and glory dangled before their eyes, poor men from across Italy rushed to sign up for Marius's open legions.[48]

Emergency suspension of the property requirements was not without precedent. An ancestor of the Gracchi had even led a legion composed of slaves and gladiators during the darkest days of the Second Punic War. But what makes this moment so important is that it marked a permanent transition from temporary armies conscripted from among the free citizens to professional armies composed of soldiers who made their careers in the army—whose loyalties would be to their generals rather than to the Senate and People of Rome. But Marius wasn't thinking about the grand sweep of history. For the moment, he just wanted to raise an army of men to go fulfill his promise to win the war.[49]

Eager to begin, Marius sailed for Africa before his new army was completely assembled. New cohorts of cavalry were still in the process of being raised, so Marius left his newly elected quaestor to finish the job. That quaestor's name was Lucius Cornelius Sulla.

CHAPTER 6

THE GOLDEN EARRING

Why, my son, do you so long for Ambition,
that worst of deities? Oh, do not; the goddess
is unjust; many are the homes and cities once
prosperous that she has entered and left to the
ruin of her worshippers.

EURIPIDES[1]

L UCIUS CORNELIUS SULLA WAS BORN IN ROME IN 138 BC. As
a Cornelii he belonged to one of the oldest patrician families in
Rome. But though he bore a noble name, and the easy arrogance
that went with it, Sulla's own particular branch of the family had long
since faded into obscurity. No one in his family had risen beyond praetor for three generations, and Sulla did not seem particularly primed to
restore the family to glory. As a young man he caroused with actors, po-
ets, and musicians—the bottom feeders of the Roman social order. He
and his friends drank and partied and lived their lives outside the stuffy
confines of the respectable classes. During his youth, Sulla also began a
romantic relationship with the actor Metrobius, who went on to become
his lifelong companion. Even as Sulla married, had children, and climbed
to the pinnacle of power, Metrobius remained by his side.[2]

Though Sulla was a carefree hedonist, he never neglected his studies.
He had great natural intelligence and received a good education. By the

time he was a teenager he was fluent in Greek and highly literate in art, literature, and history. Despite the low fortunes of his family, Sulla still spent his youth expecting to embark on a public career. But when his father died, Sulla discovered just how far the family fortunes had fallen. Sulla's father was bankrupt and left his son no inheritance. Sulla could not even afford to join the legions as a cavalry officer, the prerequisite to any political career. So rather than spending his twenties in the legions, Sulla continued his dissolute life in Rome, renting an inexpensive apartment and living his life in the pursuit of wine, women, and song.[3]

Sulla cut a striking figure on the streets of Rome, with sharp gray eyes and light reddish hair. Though plagued by breakouts of red splotches on his face, Sulla was a handsome and charismatic young man who commanded the attention of any room: "He was eloquent, clever, and quick to make friends. He had a mind deep beyond belief in its power of disguising its purposes, and was generous with many things, especially with money." He would never entirely leave his early life behind. The friends he made remained close at hand, and in the future, Sulla would live something of a double life: stern and composed while dealing with matters of business, and then, "once at table, he refused to be serious at all . . . he underwent a complete change as soon as he betook himself to good-fellowship and drinking."[4]

Around age thirty, Sulla secured an advantageous marriage to a woman called only "Julia," whom it is strongly suspected was a cousin of Gaius Marius's wife Julia—creating an attachment to Marius just as Marius's career was taking off. But though he was married, Sulla was not faithful. He was charismatic and indulged in numerous affairs, especially with older widows who were happy to help him maintain his libertine lifestyle. Sulla had a particularly prolonged affair with a woman known only by his pet name for her, "Nicopolis." She died around 110 BC and named Sulla as her principal heir. Around this time, his stepmother also died and similarly left him all her property. Suddenly Sulla had wealth to match his ambitions. The fact that he had started with so little and acquired so much later made his enemies sneer: "How can you be an honest man," they said, "when your father left you nothing, and yet you are so rich?"[5]

Sulla used his patrician advantage, plus a hefty fee, to bypass the required service time in the legion before standing for public office. Elected quaestor for 107, Sulla was attached to the command of newly elected consul Gaius Marius. The contrast between the two men was striking. As a novus homo, Marius had been forced to fight and scrape his way up the cursus honorum. He was not even allowed to stand for military tribune until he had spent a decade in the army. Sulla, on the other hand, walked out of the brothels, waived his patrician credentials, and purchased the job. Narrowing his eyes at this inexperienced dilettante, Marius ordered Sulla to stay behind in Rome to raise cavalry units, ensuring that he would not get in the way as Marius sailed for Numidia to finish the war against Jugurtha.[6]

WHEN MARIUS ARRIVED in Africa in early 107, Metellus was unable to overcome his rage at being cast aside, and so he refused the custom of personally handing over command to a successor. Instead, Metellus sent his second in command to greet Marius and hand over the army. Metellus, meanwhile, sailed back to Rome under a dark cloud of not entirely unjustifiable bitterness.[7]

But upon his return to Rome, Metellus found that his honor was not totally besmirched. Though Marius had seized the consulship, the Metelli were still powerful, and so the family arranged for Metellus to be met by jubilant crowds and induced the Senate to vote him a triumph. There was a ham-fisted effort to prosecute Metellus for the same charges of extortion and corruption that the Mamilian Commission had used so effectively, but it went nowhere. The jury refused to even consider the charges and Metellus was acquitted on all counts. The Metelli family then induced the Senate to award Metellus the title Numidicus for his work. Despite what he must have thought would be a lasting disgrace, Metellus Numidicus maintained his political stature and remained a powerful force in the Senate.[8]

Marius, meanwhile, had to make good on his promise to end the war quickly. But now that he was actually running the army and not just carping from the peanut gallery, he realized there was no magic strategy that would work better than what Metellus had already been doing. Jugurtha popped up and disappeared at will, and always danced just beyond the reach of the legions. During that first year, Marius managed to force a few encounters with Jugurtha, but the king always seemed to get away. So despite his promises of ending the war in a matter of days, Marius was still chasing the Numidian king as 107 gave way to 106.[9]

The Assembly kept its faith in him, however, and Marius managed to secure an extension for his command. But as he marched out in 106 he had a major problem on his hands: Jugurtha was nowhere to be found. The Numidian king's whereabouts during the entirety of 106 are unknown. We can say with a fair bit of certainty that he withdrew with his mercenary nomads across the Atlas Mountains to the southern desert country. Marius marched on the city of Capsa and then followed the mountains east, attacking cities and trying to force Jugurtha out of hiding. Finally, he reached the border between Numidia and Mauretania and found along the river Muluccha one of the last remaining strongholds Jugurtha could possibly rely on. Most importantly, it was where Jugurtha had dumped most of his remaining treasure before taking off across the mountains.[10]

SULLA HAD SPENT the beginning of the campaign in Italy gathering more cavalry. But with his units now filled, he joined Marius's army just as the siege of the fortress along the Muluccha began. Despite Marius's earlier doubts, Sulla turned out to be bright, talented, and a quick study. Sulla threw himself headlong into the soldier's life, never avoided hardship, and was soon regarded as the "best soldier in the whole army." Because he had spent his youth among the lower rungs of Roman society, Sulla had a natural rapport with the men. He laughed and joked with them, shared their toils, and was generous with favors and money without ever asking repayment—though the ever-cynical Sallust hints that this was just so Sulla could have as many men in his debt as possible. By the time the legions captured the fort of Muluccha, even Marius considered Sulla one of the best officers under his command.[11]

As the legions marched back to Cirta for the winter, the long-absent Jugurtha decided to finally strike. He had revived his alliance with Bocchus and the two massed an army and waited to hit the Romans by surprise. The legions narrowly escaped the ambush, though, thanks to a level-headed flanking move led by Sulla, which drove the combined Numidian/Mauretanian army into retreat. Two days later a second battle erupted, and this time the compact and disciplined legions scattered the Africans to the four winds. Bocchus fled back to the safety of Mauretania and Jugurtha disappeared yet again.[12]

A S MARIUS TIGHTENED the Roman hold on Numidia, the northern border once again began to crack. Roman authority in southern Gaul had been a relatively new phenomenon; it was not until the late 120s that the legions established a presence, and even then the province of Gallia Narbonensis was nothing but a thin strip of coastline connecting the Alps to the Pyrenees. The Romans had established their hegemony over the region after inflicting a string of defeats on the local Gallic tribes, but in the ruthlessly predatory world of war and politics, you were only on top if you could stay on top. The crushing defeats at the hands of the Cimbri in 113 and 109 crippled Roman prestige.[13]

The Cimbri themselves had gone back up the Rhône to central Gaul after destroying Silanus's legions in 109. But that only opened the door for other tribes to take advantage of the power vacuum. A tribe from modern Switzerland called the Tigurini took advantage of Roman setbacks and moved down out of the mountains. So as the newly elected consul Marius raised legions to go to Numidia in 107, his consular colleague Lucius Cassius Longinus raised legions to go to Gaul. It was this double threat that played a big part in the Senate dropping property requirements for service in the legions. Longinus's object was to defeat the Tigurini and repair the damage to the Roman reputation for invincibility that the Cimbri had so thoroughly spoiled.[14]

The Tigurini kept raiding west, however, and Longinus shadowed them all the way to the Atlantic Ocean. The Tigurini were aware the Romans were following them and at an opportune moment they laid a trap. The oblivious Longinus led his men directly into an ambush and died in the ensuing battle. Command of the defeated legions fell to a legate named Gaius

Popillius, who, like young Tiberius Gracchus in Spain, was forced to make a life or death decision on behalf of tens of thousands of men. Like Tiberius, Popillius chose life. After promising to hand over half their baggage and pass under the yoke, the battered Romans were allowed to depart.[15]

Back in Rome this defeat was greeted with the same angry shock that always greeted legions that surrendered. Upon his return to Rome, Popillius was charged with treason. He did not go quietly and snapped back at his accusers, "Now what should I have done when I was surrounded by so great a force of Gauls? Fight? But then our advance would have been with a small band . . . Remain in camp? But we neither had reinforcements to look for, nor the means to stay alive . . . Abandon the camp? But we were blocked . . . Sacrifice the lives of the soldiers? But I thought I had accepted them on the stipulation that so far as possible I should preserve them unharmed for their fatherland and their parents . . . Reject the enemy's terms? But the safety of the soldiers has priority over that of the baggage." The argument fell on deaf ears and Popillius was found guilty and exiled.[16]

But if there was one thing the Romans had never done, and would never do, it was give up a fight. They certainly did not give back territory they had already won. So even though they seemed to lose every army they sent north, in 106 the Senate dispatched the consul Quintus Servilius Caepio to do something—anything—to salvage the situation. Caepio had long been connected to the Metelli faction through the patronage of the influential optimates Scaurus and Crassus. In most ways Caepio was everything that was wrong with the Senate at the time. He was arrogant, greedy, self-glorifying, and singularly unable to put the Republic's interests above his own. And at his feet would be laid one of the greatest defeats in the history of the Roman Republic.

Before he left for the north, Caepio took care of some business on the optimates' behalf. Likely with support from Scaurus, Caepio carried a bill through the Assembly to roll back the power of the Equestrians. Ever since the experience with the Mamilian Commission, the nobles wanted to regain some control over the courts. Caepio's bill did not return the jury pool exclusively to the Senate but instead split it between senators and Equestrians. Speaking in defense of the bill, Crassus gave one of his most famous addresses, one that Cicero himself studied throughout his life. In it, Crassus called for the Assembly to "deliver us from the jaws of those whose cruelty cannot be satiated even with blood; suffer us not to be slaves to any but yourselves as a people, whom we both can and ought to serve." The bill passed.[17]

Arriving in Gaul for a campaign in 106, Caepio finally delivered some good news when he captured the city of Tolosa (modern Toulouse, in southwestern France). We might not know anything about Caepio's activities were it not for a famous scandal that soon passed into legend. Upon taking the city, Caepio's men stumbled across an incredible find: 50,000 bars of gold and 10,000 bars of silver. The fortune was soon identified as the missing treasure from a famous Gallic invasion of Greece way back in 279 that, much like the more recent incursions by the Scordisci, ended with the plunder of the Oracle of Delphi. But the sacred treasure had apparently carried with it a curse: "whoever touched a piece of gold from that sack died a wretched and agonizing death." As the Gauls were driven out of Greece they came to suspect that the tainted treasure was a part of their problem. According to legend, the Gauls dumped most of it in the lakes around Tolosa, but some of it wound up in a temple inside the city. This was the stash that Caepio's men discovered.[18]

But this is only half the story. Caepio ordered the sacred treasure boxed up and carried down south to the Massilia, where it could be shipped by sea to Rome, displayed in Caepio's inevitable triumph, and then deposited in the Temple of Saturn. But that's not what happened. While the treasure was being delivered, the convoy was set upon by a group of bandits and the gold was stolen. Few believed this was random chance—the common assumption was that Caepio had hired the bandits himself to steal the gold for him. If true, Caepio's double crime of plundering cursed gold from a sacred temple, and then conspiring to steal it all for himself, goes a long way toward explaining his unhappy fate. The historian Justin agreed that "this sacrilegious act subsequently proved a cause of ruin to Caepio and his army. The rising of the Cimbrian war, too, seemed to pursue the Romans as if to avenge the removal of that devoted treasure." But it could just have easily been that Caepio was a fool who provoked his own misfortunes without help from the gods.[19]

Down in North Africa, it did not take long after the battles at Cirta for King Bocchus to reverse course again and beg Marius for peace. Just five days after the dust had cleared, envoys from the Mauretanian king arrived in Cirta requesting Marius send trusted ambassadors to meet in person with Bocchus. Marius selected Lucius Cornelius Sulla to lead the embassy. Though he had only recently arrived, Sulla had already proven himself both eloquent and cool under pressure.[20]

Sulla made it clear to Bocchus the Romans were open to friendship with the Mauretanians. Though the king had joined Jugurtha's war, the Romans were a practical people. The last thing they needed was for the war in Numidia to keep expanding until it covered all of North Africa. Sulla told Bocchus that "we already have more than enough subjects, while neither we nor anyone else ever had friends enough." But he also reminded the king that while the Romans have "never been outdone in kindness; their prowess in war you know by experience." Bocchus took the hint. He asked permission to send an embassy directly to Marius to work out the preliminaries of a permanent peace. Sulla agreed and returned to Cirta to make his report.[21]

On their way to meet Marius, however, the small party of Mauretanian ambassadors was jumped by a gang of brigands. Taking a hasty flight and leaving all their baggage and papers behind, the envoys arrived at Cirta looking like refugee peasants rather than royal agents of a great king. But Sulla secured further a diplomatic trust between the two powers by graciously welcoming them into the city and refusing to doubt for a minute their pitiful story. The ambassadors were apparently surprised to discover that the corrupt and treacherous Romans were in fact quite civilized and generous.[22]

After hearing the ambassadors out, Marius called a war council in early 105 that voted to send the Mauretanian ambassadors on to Rome with a recommendation that the Senate conclude a peace. The Senate concurred and decreed: "The Senate and People of Rome are wont to remember both a benefit and an injury. But since Bocchus repents, they forgive his offence; he shall have a treaty of friendship when he has earned it." The king was delighted to find the Romans so amenable to a peace. He sent a message back to Marius requesting that Sulla—who had displayed generous wisdom thus far—serve as Roman representative. With Sulla's help the king could begin the practical process of aligning Mauretanian and Roman interests. Marius agreed.[23]

Escorted by Bocchus's son to ensure safe passage, Sulla and his bodyguards were not sure whether they were being led into a trap. Their fears peaked when scouts suddenly arrived and alerted the party that Jugurtha himself was camped just two miles ahead. Sulla and his companions braced for treachery, but Bocchus's son swore his father's good intentions. The prince promised to march side by side with Sulla the whole way. Jugurtha could not risk the prince's life, as it would permanently sever any chance he had at reforming the alliance with Bocchus. So in dramatic fashion the party continued riding past Jugurtha's camp. Though the tension in the air must have been impossibly thick, the Numidian king simply watched them pass.[24]

The final act of the Jugurthine War played out as a game of high stakes negotiations between Sulla and Bocchus on the one hand, and Bocchus and Jugurtha on the other. Bocchus and Sulla met openly in the Mauretanian court, where the king told Sulla that he had not made up his mind how to proceed. He requested Sulla give him ten days to compose a final answer. But this was merely a trick played on Jugurtha's spies, who dutifully raced to the Numidian camp and reported that Jugurtha had ten days to change Bocchus's mind.[25]

But in the middle of that same night, Bocchus summoned Sulla for the *real* meeting. Bocchus told Sulla that he would never cross the Muluccha River that marked the border with Numidia, and that all that he had— soldiers, ships, and money—was at Rome's disposal. Sulla accepted all of this with calculated regard. He told Bocchus that the Romans felt no gratitude for the king's pledges, as they had already defeated the Mauretanians in battle. If Bocchus wanted to earn his treaty of friendship there was only one way to do it: hand over Jugurtha.[26]

The next day Bocchus summoned a courtier he knew to be in touch with Jugurtha and passed along a message for the Numidian king. Bocchus said he was about to make a peace with Rome—what could Jugurtha offer to make him change his mind? A reply came back quickly from Jugurtha. The Numidian king promised Bocchus anything he wanted to restore the alliance; for starters, Jugurtha would hand over nearly a third of Numidian territory. Jugurtha also proposed that Bocchus kidnap Sulla, and then together they could ransom him to the Senate and force the legions to withdraw from Africa entirely. Bocchus agreed to meet Jugurtha at a secluded location outside of the city.[27]

With both sides having made their pitches, Bocchus found himself with an ulcer-inducing decision to make: betray his fellow king to the Romans and possibly risk the wrath of his subjects, or seize Sulla and risk the wrath of the legions. The king stayed up the whole night before the rendezvous with Jugurtha deciding what to do.[28]

The next day Bocchus, Sulla, and a small party of retainers rode out toward the secluded spot. Bocchus was about to double-cross either Sulla or Jugurtha, and to Sulla's satisfaction, Jugurtha drew the short straw. Bocchus's men surrounded the clearing and when Jugurtha appeared the men sprang out of the ambush. Jugurtha's few remaining retainers were killed and the king himself was seized and handed over to Sulla. Sulla dutifully delivered Jugurtha in chains to Marius. Twelve years after Jugurtha had begun all this by assassinating Hiempsal, and seven years after the Senate had been forced to declare war following the massacre at Cirta, the war with Jugurtha was over.[29]

B UT THIS HAPPY news was about to be blotted out by an unfathomable disaster in the north. The Cimbri had first arrived in 113, defeated the Romans at Noreia, and then moved on. After a four-year hiatus, they had come down the Rhône river in 109 and defeated the Romans again. Now, after yet another four-year cycle, the Cimbri came back around in 105, once again migrating down the Rhône toward the Mediterranean coast. The Senate was understandably spooked by the return of this enemy that had bested them twice.[30]

Though now widely suspected of playing a role in the disappearance of the Tolosa gold, the Senate extended Caepio's command in the north and kept his army intact—two full Roman legions plus twice as many Italian allies and Gallic auxiliary forces—bringing his combined numbers up to somewhere around thirty-five thousand. To double the number on the northern front the Senate instructed one of the consuls for 105, Gnaeus Mallius Maximus, to gather an army of equal strength. This time the Cimbri must be destroyed. It was a good thing the property requirements had been dropped or Rome might not have been able to muster the strength to put the sixty to eighty thousand men through the Alps while simultaneously maintaining the legions in Numidia.[31]

Gnaeus Mallius was not just any newly elected consul, though. He was, like Marius, a novus homo. Between 191 and 107 only three confirmed novus homo had been elected consul. But in the rising tide of populare agitation, the Senate could not stop a string of novus homo from entering office. In the fourteen years between 107 and 94, five novus homo would be elected consul, and Gaius Marius himself would become far and away the most dominant leader in Rome. When Mallius drew Gaul as his province, the Senate was once again forced to trust a new man with the safety of Rome.[32]

In the Roman military hierarchy, no one outranked a consul, so when Mallius arrived in Gaul it was his right to supplant Caepio as commander in chief. But Caepio, being the arrogant noble that he was, greeted the novus homo Mallius with nothing but dismissive insolence. He claimed to be operating in a separate geographic province on the other side of the Rhône and insisted on maintaining autonomy on his side of the river. This lack of unity between the two senior commanders—which all the sources lay squarely at Caepio's feet—was the principal cause of their shared demise. There was not one 60,000-strong Roman army. There were two 30,000-man armies—and the Cimbri would fatally exploit the difference.[33]

In early October 105, a forward patrol from Mallius's legions scouting the approach of the Cimbri unexpectedly ran right into the main body. The patrol was surrounded and destroyed. Realizing the Cimbri would be arriving any minute, Mallius begged Caepio to cross the Rhône and join their armies together. Caepio mocked Mallius, saying that he would be happy to cross the river and help the frightened novus homo consul, who was obviously quaking in his boots over nothing. The two Roman armies converged near Arausio on the east bank of the Rhône, but out of a mixture of hubris and spite, Caepio still refused to join his army to Mallius's.

Caepio even blew off envoys from the Senate who begged him to submit. Caepio not only refused, he camped with his army situated between his colleague Mallius and the Cimbri. The long-held suspicion is that Caepio's grand plan was to bring the Cimbri to battle first and force Mallius to play a supporting role, embarrassing the new man and capturing all the glory for himself. When ambassadors from the Cimbri came to make their request for land, Caepio roundly abused them and sent them packing.[34]

We do not know whether Caepio then marched out to instigate battle or whether he waited for the Cimbri to come to him, but it's clear he provoked the disaster to come. He never once seemed to realize that the Romans were about to face hundreds of thousands of Cimbric warriors and that even combined, the Romans would be outnumbered. When the battle began, it is likely that Caepio's forward army was overwhelmed by the first wave. Pushed backward, Caepio's forces would have run into Mallius's army and created a confused tangle without form, direction, or unity of purpose. This frustrated mob of confused legionaries was then surrounded by the Cimbri and pinned against the Rhône. With nowhere to go and all order lost, the Cimbri consumed the trapped legions like acid eating through flesh.[35]

By nightfall, the Romans were not just defeated, they were annihilated. The sources place the total dead at somewhere between 60,000 to 80,000 legionaries plus another 40,000 camp followers. Everyone agrees that almost no one made it out alive. There were some survivors who got away—both Caepio and Mallius made it back to Rome, as did a young officer named Quintus Sertorius, who was able to swim across the river to safety (he would go on to become one of the greatest generals in Roman history). Many more Romans were presumably taken as slaves. But, taken together, it is clear that the Battle of Arausio was one of the single greatest disasters in the history of Rome from its founding in 753 BC to the fall of the west in AD 476. All now seemed lost in Gaul.[36]

But a funny thing happened on the way to Armageddon—the Cimbri again withdrew. The ancient historians never spend much time trying to explain the motives and actions of the Cimbri, so it's left to modern historians to speculate that in all likelihood the Cimbri were never interested in invading Italy, but instead simply wanted to keep the violent and aggressive Romans bottled up on the Italian peninsula. So after demonstrating to the Romans three times in a row that they best not mess with the Cimbri, the tribe withdrew again and migrated west toward Spain.[37]

The panic in Rome must have been severe. With the elections for next year's consulship approaching, there was no question who the people thought could stave off the end of Roman civilization, which appeared to be the stakes. The Assembly did not want another incompetent Carbo, or overmatched Silanus, or fatally arrogant Caepio. The people wanted Gaius Marius. The Assembly tossed aside two more pieces of mos maiorum to get their wish. Roman law still forbade a man from serving a second consulship within ten years of his first election, and a candidate had to be physically present in Rome to stand for election. The Assembly ignored both rules and elected Marius in absentia to his second consulship in three years. Marius settled loose ends in Numidia and prepared to return to Rome.[38]

O N JANUARY 1, 104, Gaius Marius celebrated the beginning of his second consulship with a triumph. Not since the glory days of the conquest of Carthage and Greece had a triumph been this spectacular. Aemilianus's parade after Numantia (a parade Marius himself would have marched in) was a famous disappointment. Since then it had been a string of victories against various Gallic and Thracian tribes whose spoils paled in comparison to the treasures Roman consuls had once returned from campaign with. But Marius's triumph was of "great magnificence." Treasure, slaves, and wondrous ornaments of the exotic African kingdom paraded to wild cheering from a population still reeling from the disaster at Arausio just three months earlier.[39]

The crown jewel of Marius's triumph was King Jugurtha himself. The last time Jugurtha was in Rome he had bribed senators, defied the Assembly, and ordered an assassination. He managed to upend domestic Roman politics and stay one step ahead of the legions for a decade. Now he was bound in chains like a common criminal and forced to march alongside his two sons, facing the humiliation of being the object not of awe and fear, but mockery and ridicule. At the end of the triumphal parade, Jugurtha was tossed into a prison cell so roughly that the gold earring he wore—the last piece of gold he had to his name—was ripped clean out of his ear. There was no more bribery. No more cunning plans. The Romans left him to die in a dungeon pit naked and starving: "He himself, too, conquered and in chains, saw the city of which he had vainly prophesied that it could be bought and would one day perish if it could find a purchaser. In Jugurtha it had a purchaser—if it had been for sale; but once it had escaped his hands, it was certain that it was not doomed to perish." After six days of defiant resistance, Jugurtha finally dropped dead on the floor.[40]

But Marius was not able to enjoy his triumph in peace. Men who disdained the usurping novus homo praised the young noble Sulla as the *real* captor of Jugurtha. According to military and political tradition, the man who held imperium over a province received all credit and all blame for the fortunes of war. It was how it had always been done. It was mos maiorum. But enemies of Marius encouraged Sulla to tell his story. The proud and ambitious Sulla was all too happy to play the game and went so far as to cast as his personal seal an image depicting the capture of Jugurtha. Marius was not amused. "This was the first seed of that bitter and incurable hatred between Marius and Sulla, which nearly brought Rome to ruin."[41]

CHAPTER 7

MARIUS'S MULES

The generals of this later time . . . who needed
their armies for service against one another, rather
than against the public enemy, were compelled to
merge the general and the demagogue.

PLUTARCH[1]

THE MEN WERE GETTING RESTLESS. FOR THREE DAYS, THEY had sat in their camps along the Rhône river in southern Gaul, surveying a vast horde of barbarians. Eager to fight after nearly two years of anticipation, they could not understand why Marius did not give the order to attack. Was this not what they had been waiting for? Was this not what they had been training for? For three days, they endured the ferocious war cries and taunts from the enemy. They endured repeated attacks on the walls. They endured the enemy ravaging the countryside. But Marius refused to let them attack.[2]

The men's indignation at their commander's inaction soon turned to disgust. "What cowardice has Marius discovered in us that he keeps out of battle," they asked. "Does he fear the fate of Carbo and Caepio, whom the enemy defeated? Surely it is better to do something, even if we perish as they did, rather than to sit here and enjoy the spectacle of our allies being plundered." But Marius held fast, saying there was far more at stake than pride. "It was not," he said, "triumphs or trophies that should now be the object of [your] ambition, but how [you] might ward off so great a cloud and thunder-bolt of war and secure the safety of Italy." Instead of fighting, he ordered his soldiers to man the walls and observe the enemy. He told them to study their weapons and watch how their horsemen rode. Marius wanted his men to grow accustomed to the frightening war cries and painted faces of these northern warriors so that the legionaries understood they were facing ordinary men, not demons from the underworld.[3]

On the fourth day, the great mass of barbarians offered one last attack, coming hard at the walls of the Roman camps. They were predictably repulsed. Deciding these Romans would never come out of their hiding place, the barbarians elected to pull up stakes and keep moving. In a great procession, they marched past the Romans camps—an entire nation of men, women, and children continued their migration south down the Rhône. As the horde passed they shouted a final taunt at the Romans, asking if they had any messages for their wives, "for we shall soon be with them." When the last of these northerners had passed and traveled a safe distance down the river, Marius finally ordered his men to break camp and follow.[4]

G AIUS MARIUS HAD not lingered long in Rome after celebrating his triumph over Jugurtha in January 104 BC. The disaster at Arausio was still just a few months old, and though the Cimbri had gone west, there was nothing to guarantee they would not turn around and come back. But Marius could not simply race north to take command of the legions in southern Gaul because there *were* no legions in southern Gaul— they had been wiped out at Arausio. Having left most of his Numidian forces behind in Africa to secure the post-Jugurtha peace, Marius was going to have to build a whole new army from scratch.

The core of this new army was a reserve legion that had been conscripted by the previous year's consul, Publius Rutilius Rufus. When his ill-fated colleague Mallius had gone off to battle the Cimbri, Rutilius had stayed behind in Rome to continue raising reinforcements. Not wanting these reinforcements to sit idle, Rutilius kept them busy with a training regimen adapted from the gladiatorial schools. The men engaged in hand-to-hand combat, calisthenics, and physical conditioning. When Marius inherited this small force in early 104 he found it to be one of the best-trained groups of soldiers he had ever commanded.[5]

To build around this core, Marius canvassed for new recruits. As with the Numidian campaign, Marius secured an exemption from the property requirements and drafted men of every class and background. He had little difficulty raising recruits. Men who had watched their friends and neighbors win riches and fame in North Africa now wanted in on the action. Where once the hopeless underclasses had been left behind by the Roman conquest of the Mediterranean, they now stood to profit along with the nobility. We do not know exactly how many men Marius took with him to Gaul, but it was perhaps as many as thirty thousand Romans plus forty thousand Italian Allies and foreign auxiliaries. One thing we know for sure, however, is that Marius made sure Sulla stayed by his side. Though Marius was annoyed that Sulla happily took credit for capturing Jugurtha, he could not deny that Sulla was among the most talented officers in Rome. Having finished his term as quaestor, Sulla joined Marius as a legate and became his chief lieutenant in Gaul for the coming campaign.[6]

After Marius arrived in Gaul, he moved west beyond the frontier base at Aquae Sextiae and built up a fortified position along the Rhône river, probably near modern-day Arles. If the Cimbri came back from Spain along the southern coast or once again descended through the Rhône valley, they would have to pass through Marius's army. After settling in, Marius began to train his legions, expanding the program pioneered by Rutilius the year before. Though the men trained with a sense of urgency, as it turned out the Cimbri would not return for two full years. But this reprieve did not mean the Republic was able to enjoy a moment's peace; while the northern frontier was quiet, the island of Sicily was seized by another violent slave insurrection.[7]

THIRTY YEARS HAD passed since the great slave rebellion had erupted on Sicily in the 130s. After the slave armies of "King Antiochus" were finally defeated, the Senate had introduced a few reforms to mitigate

some of the worst abuses of the slaves. But as the years passed, and memories of the First Servile War faded, most Roman owners slipped back
into their old brutal habits. But the next slave rebellion was not merely
a reaction to abusive treatment; it was also driven by an unkept promise
that came directly from Marius.[8]

As Marius filled out his new army, he called for foreign auxiliaries.
But King Nicomedes III of the allied Kingdom of Bithynia replied that
the publicani tax farmers had been arresting and selling his subjects
into slavery, so he could not meet his obligation. Closer to home, the
Italians echoed the same complaint. The publicani tax farmers had apparently been seizing and enslaving anyone who fell short of meeting
their tax obligations. Since this practice now affected Rome's ability to
fill the legions, the Senate issued a decree that henceforth no citizen
of an allied nation, Italian or otherwise, could be held in slavery in a
Roman province. They further decreed that any man, woman, or child
so held was to be emancipated immediately. Ironically this decree of
emancipation would end up triggering the second great slave revolt in
Roman history.[9]

To enforce the decree in Sicily, a praetor named Publius Licinius Nerva
set up a tribunal in 104 to go through the records and determine who
among the hundreds of thousands of slaves on the island qualified for
release. In the first week, the tribunal was able to identify and emanci-
pate eight hundred slaves. But with their profits on the line, a coalition
of Sicilian estate owners confronted Nerva and demanded he shut down
the tribunal. Using a mixture of bribes and threats, the owners convinced
Nerva to turn away future slaves petitioning for release.[10]

But by that point, the rumors of emancipation had taken on a life of
their own. Every slave in Sicily now believed their ticket to freedom was
in the mail. When the tribunal shut down after liberating just a few hundred men, slaves on estates across the island boiled with rage. Down on
the southwest coast, an armed revolt broke out and a few hundred slaves
occupied the heights of Mount Caprianus. Within a week, the rebel force
was up to two thousand. A hastily raised Sicilian militia was sent to subdue to the slaves, but this militia dropped their weapons and ran at the

first whiff of battle. Word of this victory spread and in no time the slave army had grown to more than twenty thousand.[11]

After this initial uprising, the Second Servile War followed the same course as the First Servile War. In fact, its course is *so* similar that some scholars believe ancient historians simply copied and pasted details of the second revolt to fill out the lost details of the story. So once again a Syrian slave prophet gathered the rebels and recast himself as a king—though this time his name was King Tryphon rather than King Antiochus. Then—as before—a second revolt broke out on the other side of the island, this one led by a Cilician named Athenion. There was once again hope among the local Sicilians that the two slave armies would destroy each other, and once again deflation when King Tryphon and Athenion joined forces. But though all of these details are suspiciously similar, the Second Servile War was not an invention—it was a very real uprising that consumed Sicily for the next three years.[12]

MEANWHILE BACK IN Rome, the populares who had kept the Senate under siege and carried Marius to two consulships continued to feel their oats. In fact, the reelection of Marius was not the only unprecedented result of the election of 105. Joining Marius in the consulship was another novus homo named Gaius Flavius Fimbria. Never in Roman history had two novus homo served as colleagues in the consulship.[13]

The populare also filled the lower rungs of the magistracies. Though the evidence is thin, 105 was almost certainly the year Gaius Memmius— agitating tribune in 111 and principal prosecutor during the Mamilian Commission in 109—was elected praetor. Enemies of the optimates like Lucius Cassius Longinus* and Gnaeus Domitius Ahenobarbus were elected tribunes and would soon use their positions to prosecute grudges both personal and political. 105 was also the year another ambitious novus homo took his first step up the cursus honorum. More radical and with fewer scruples than the Gracchi, Lucius Appuleius Saturninus was

* No relation to the Lucius Cassius Longinus who was killed fighting the Tigurini in 107.

elected quaestor and would shortly be at the center of a political move-ment that almost toppled the old senatorial order completely.[14]

So while Marius was off preparing a defense against the Cimbri, this cohort of populares launched an offensive against the Senate. The now much-despised Caepio was obviously a prime target. The Assembly had already stripped Caepio of his consulship in the aftermath of Arausio, and now the tribune Longinus passed a law that expelled from the Senate any man who had had his imperium revoked by the Assembly. Booted from the Senate, Caepio then had to answer for the missing Tolosa gold. But much to the populares' frustration, the ensuing trial proceeded with plenty of senators on the jury. Caepio was found not guilty of stealing the treasure. His acquittal only fueled populare wrath.[15]

The tribune Ahenobarbus then settled a personal grudge against Scau-rus, who he believed blocked his chance at a priesthood. After tying up Scaurus in court with frivolous lawsuits, Ahenobarbus carried a law open-ing the college of pontiffs to popular election. Until now, the vacancies in a priesthood had been filled by the senior pontiffs, allowing the optimate nobility to keep the priesthoods as their own special preserve. Now priests would be elected by popular vote. The case of Ahenobarbus also demon-strates how difficult it is to separate the personal from the political in the Late Republic. Likely driven by a personal grudge, Ahenobarbus rammed through a bill that further strengthened the power of the Assembly and weakened the nobility.[16]

Also during this year of populare ascendency, another young tribune named Lucius Marcius Philippus introduced a bill aimed at wholesale land redistribution. We don't know the details of Philippus's bill, but we know that in the midst of debate over this legislation, Philippus made his famous observation that "there were not in the state two thousand people who owned any property." The anti-populare Cicero goes on to note that Philippus's speech "deserves unqualified condemnation, for it favored an equal distribution of property; and what more ruinous policy than that could be conceived?" The legislation did not pass, but the fact that it was even introduced is proof that gains made during the Gracchan era had been reversed by the turn of the century.[17]

But while some of these populare attacks were carried out by ambitious men of noble rank simply looking to inflict as much damage as possible on their political rivals, many more were real populare radicals looking to burn down the world.

WHILE ALL OF this played out in Rome, Marius remained on alert in Gaul. While he waited, he introduced an array of strategic and logistical reforms that revolutionized how the Roman army functioned in the field. In the long arc of Roman military history, the last great transformation of the legions had occurred back in the 300s during the Samnite Wars. Fighting in the broken hill country of central Italy, the Romans abandoned the rigid Greek phalanx and developed more flexible formations. The organization of the legions then remained largely unchanged all the way down to the final conquests of 146. The years after 146 saw the legions transform once again, and the ancient sources credit Marius with many of the innovations that turned the legions as they had existed in the third century BC into the armies Pompey and Caesar would lead as they completed the conquest of the Mediterranean in the first century.[18]

The most important of Marius's innovations was a heavy emphasis on the physical conditioning of the soldiers and the speed of their maneuvers. Concluding that the endless baggage trains that followed any Roman army hindered the mobility of the legions, Marius decreed that his men would now carry their own gear—their weapons, blankets, clothes, and rations would be hoisted on their own backs. Observing these self-sustaining soldiers, old-school officers took to derisively calling the men "Marius's Mules." But it was effective: speed and cohesion became vital assets to the legions. Marius also promoted a pan-legionary esprit de corps by ending the practice of each legion having its own animal symbol, ordering instead that the eagle—a bird that had special meaning for Marius—be the universal symbol of the legions.[19]

Marius also introduced tactical improvements to the weaponry his soldiers carried, most prominently developing a new type of spear. The standard weapon carried by every soldier was usually hurled at the enemy at the outset of any battle. But the hurled weapons were often then picked up and chucked back at the Romans. So Marius developed a new type of spear using lead to join the steel tip to the wooden shaft. When it hit its mark, the soft lead would buckle and bend and leave the spear of no use to the enemy, who now also had to disentangle themselves from the awkwardly protruding projectile.[20]

But though he is often credited with every military reform that took place during these years, Marius was not solely responsible for the changing face of the legions. He is, for example, often credited with changing the basic tactical unit of the army from the small *maniple* to the larger *cohort*. Since the larger tactical squares allowed for stiffer resistance to a mass barbarian charge, it became standard among historians to place the adoption of the cohort in the midst of the Marian reforms. But as it turns out there is not one shred of evidence to support the claim. So while Marius is critical to the transformation of the legions, it is important to remember he was also just one man working inside a much larger process.[21]

Marius wound up spending the entirety of 104 waiting for a Cimbric invasion that never materialized. But unwilling to allow any other man to take over the Gallic frontier, the Assembly once again bucked mos maiorum by electing Marius to a second consecutive consulship for 103. Only a few scattered times in the whole history of the Republic had a man ever served two consulships in a row—the last time being during the Second Punic War when the great Quintus Fabius Maximus served as consul in both 214 and 215. But Caepio and Mallius's inability to work together meant that Rome could not risk another such division of authority. So the Assembly elected Marius to a groundbreaking second consecutive consulship—his third consulship in six years.[22]

While Marius waited patiently for the return of the Cimbri, he spent a great deal of time rebuilding Roman alliances in Gaul. He sent men under cover to gather intelligence on the local tribes, to learn what they wanted, what they feared, what their internal rivalries were. Then he dispatched Sulla on a diplomatic circuit to offer each tribe a unique package of carrots and sticks that would bring them back into the Roman fold. By the end of 103, the Romans once again had a network of allies they could count on when the Cimbri came back. *If* the Cimbri came back.[23]

By now, Marius had himself internalized the conviction that he must remain consul until he defeated the Cimbri, but since they kept not showing up, it seemed like the emergency atmosphere that had propelled him to consecutive consulships was fading. At risk of losing the coming consular election, Marius returned to Rome and forged an alliance with the unscrupulous young politician Saturninus to help maintain his iron grip on the consulship.

L UCIUS APPULEIUS SATURNINUS had been elected quaestor along with the other populare nobiles in the election of 105. Assigned to Ostia to monitor the grain supply, Saturninus took over just as the Second Servile War shut down the supply line from Sicily. Due to the crisis, the Senate took the extraordinary step of stripping Saturninus of his responsibilities. The princeps senatus Scaurus assumed his post for the duration of the year. Though the historian Diodorus attributes Saturninus's humiliating censure to "laziness and his debased character," it is just as likely that even the most active and virtuous quaestor would have been unable to cope with such a dire situation.[24]

Spurred by the insult, Saturninus returned to Rome and ran for tribune. Cicero, who held Saturninus in disdain, said that "of all the factious declaimers since the time of the Gracchi, he was generally esteemed the ablest: and yet he caught the attention of the public, more by his appearance, his gesture, and his dress, than by any real fluency of expression, or even a tolerable share of good sense." But his performance was good enough—Saturninus won a tribunate for 103.[25]

Though a man like Marius used populare rhetoric to fuel his political rise, he also burned to be accepted by the nobility, to be recognized as their equal. Saturninus, on the other hand, was a bomb-thrower. Like many popular revolutions in history, the men who unlock the door are not always the same men who come bursting through. The men who had run populare programs the year before, like Ahenobarbus, Longinus, and Philippus, were all from ancient noble families who, like Marius, saw populare rhetoric as a path to power. Saturninus, on the other hand, really did seem to want to just burn the whole thing down.

Now a tribune, Saturninus joined with fellow populare Gaius Norbanus to bring the despised Caepio back to trial. Two of their optimate-aligned colleagues tried to veto the trial, but with respect for mos maiorum running dangerously low, Norbanus instigated a riot that physically drove the rival tribunes out of the Assembly. Caepio was duly prosecuted, convicted, and sentenced to exile. Violence once again proved to be the last word in Roman politics.[26]

But Saturninus did not stop with Caepio. The tribune turned his attention to the unfortunate Mallius. Until now Mallius had been a martyr of the populare, the novus homo who had been betrayed by an arrogant noble. But Saturninus was now wielding a more indiscriminate weapon and Mallius too was prosecuted, convicted, and sentenced to exile.[27]

After securing these convictions, Saturninus then passed a law establishing a new permanent court that would deal with cases of *maiestas*, crimes that damaged the prestige of the state. This law took the ad hoc corruption tribunals and made them a permanent fixture of public life. Any noble who took a wrong step could now expect to find himself brought before the new court and prosecuted before a panel of Equestrian jurors on the flimsiest of pretenses. The new court would not exactly be the Revolutionary Tribunal that became such a feared tool during the French Revolution. But it was close.[28]

Having established a means of destroying his enemies, Saturninus looked to consolidate his own base of popular support. He identified the veterans of the Numidian war as the perfect foundation. Many of the men who had served in Numidia were now back living in the vicinity of Rome and were a political force waiting to be organized. Saturninus began working the veterans, letting it be known that he planned to introduce a bill to award allotments of land in North Africa to every man who had fought Jugurtha. Unlike the Gracchan allotments, Saturninus's allotments were meant to be a retirement bonus. The land would be a veteran's to dispose of as he saw fit: he could keep it or sell it. The new land-for-veterans scheme was a novelty when Saturninus pitched it, but it set a precedent for the future that a legionary could expect land when he was discharged from service.[29]

But Saturninus's land-for-veterans proposal was as much about currying favor with Marius as building a political army. Nearing the end of his second consecutive consulship, Marius wielded enormous influence. Saturninus wanted to exploit that influence. He calculated that Marius would be well disposed toward a program to enrich the Numidian veterans. But in addition to taking care of Marius's soldiers, Saturninus also orchestrated some mutually beneficial political theater in the Forum. Marius wanted to be reelected consul, but having already served twice in a row, another campaign might seem arrogant and vain. So Marius returned to Rome in the lead-up to the election for 102 and announced that he was not interested in another consulship and that the people should elect another man. Right on cue, Saturninus accused Marius of treason for leaving the citizens of Rome defenseless and roused his audience to demand that Marius take back the consulship. Marius was reelected overwhelmingly and in January 102 entered an unprecedented third consulship in a row, now his fourth in total.[30]

WHILE ALL OF this was unfolding, the slave uprising in Sicily continued to rage. Ironically triggered by the urgent need to fill out the armies in Gaul, the Senate now had to redirect legionaries to deal with the revolt. In 103, the beleaguered Senate instructed praetor Lucius Licinius Lucullus to raise as many men as he could and go take back Sicily. No doubt able to draw from southern communities terrified of the rebellion spreading to the mainland, and augmented by Sicilians with nothing left to do but fight, Lucullus cobbled together a force of about seventeen thousand men. Spooked by the arrival of this army—a real army this time—King Tryphon and Athenion marched out to confront Lucullus, hoping their superior numbers would carry the day. But their nearly 2 to 1 numerical advantage was not enough. In the ensuing battle the slaves broke and fled, leaving behind a reported twenty thousand dead.[31]

But despite his victory, Lucullus made no concerted effort to consolidate his position. It was not until nine days later that Lucullus finally led his forces to the fortified slave capital of Triocala. Lucullus made one attempt to capture the city, but when it proved too tough, the praetor withdrew back to Syracuse. Lucullus's baffling conduct caused a scandal back in Rome, where he was condemned as man who "either through sloth and negligence, or corrupted by bribes, neglected entirely the proper conduct of his duty." Instead of crushing the revolt, Lucullus had allowed it to persist. So in early 102, the Senate dispatched a replacement to take over the campaign.[32]

Feeling slighted after losing his command, Lucullus made a shocking announcement to his troops. He said that they had done their duty to the Senate and People of Rome and were hereby discharged. In addition to demobilizing the seventeen thousand men he had arrived with, Lucullus also "burned his palisades and fortification works, so as not to leave to his successor any useful resources for the conduct of war. Because he was being accused of dragging out the war, he believed that he could exonerate himself by ensuring the humiliation and failure of his successor." Having left his successor with no army and no fortifications, it should come as no surprise that upon returning to Rome, Lucullus was brought up on charges and exiled.[33]

W HILE SICILY CONTINUED to burn in the spring of 102, the moment Gaius Marius had been waiting for in Gaul finally arrived: the Cimbri were coming back. Marius's intelligence network was strong and he was informed early of their imminent return. He also learned that at least three other tribes had joined them in a grand anti-Roman alliance. Besides the Cimbri themselves were the Teutones and the Ambrones, both of which we can also trace back to the North Sea. Also joining the alliance were the Tigurini, who once again sought to take advantage of perceived Roman weakness.[34]

Marius was also told that the objective of the anti-Roman alliance was to break into Italy on two fronts. The Teutones and Ambrones would move down the Rhône valley and enter Italy from the northwest while the

Cimbri would swing east and enter Italy from the northeast, near where they had first clashed with Caepio at Noreia. The Tigurini's job would be to secure the passes through the Alps. The division of the invasion meant the Romans would have to divide their own defenses. While Marius remained in southern Gaul to face the Teutones and Ambrones, his consular colleague Quintus Lutatius Catulus headed to northeastern Italy to prevent the Cimbri from passing through the Alps.[35]

Having scouted the landscape of southern Gaul for over two years, Marius knew exactly where he wanted to place his fortified camps for first contact with the enemy. Situated on high ground next to the Rhône, the camps would be nearly impregnable. When word came that the Teutones and Ambrones were about to appear, Marius led his legions north and built their camps. We have already seen what happened when first contact came. Marius refused to let his men leave the camps and forced them to wait until the great horde had moved on. When the Teutones and Ambrones departed, Marius finally ordered his men to break camp and follow. The antsy legionaries were baffled by their general's seeming lack of nerve. They did not yet realize that Marius was executing a carefully laid-out plan.[36]

Using the superior speed of his legions, Marius raced along parallel to the barbarian horde until they all reached another location he had carefully selected near Aquae Sextiae. With the Teutones and Ambrones camped beside the river, the legions occupied a clearing in the forest that overlooked the barbarians' camps. Marius told his thirsty troops that "they could get water there, but the price of it was blood." The battle began with a preliminary engagement that saw Marius isolate and eliminate thirty thousand Ambrones. Then, a few days later, Marius arrayed his troops at the crest of a long slope and forced the Teutones to charge up to meet them. But as soon as contact was made the legions drove them right back down the hill. As the Teutones fell back under heavy assault, Marius ordered a hidden reserve unit to burst out of the woods into the exposed Teutone rear. By the end of the battle, Marius and his legions were not just victorious; they destroyed an entire branch of this two-pronged invasion of Italy.[37]

The casualties of the Battle of Aquae Sextiae were massive: somewhere between one hundred and two hundred thousand dead, including plenty of civilians caught up in the bloody chaos. Rather than fall into slavery, mothers "dashed their children upon the rocks and then took their own lives by the sword or by hanging." It was later said that the local inhabitants of the region "fenced their vineyards round with the bones of the fallen, and that the soil, after the bodies had wasted away in it and the rains had fallen all winter upon it, grew so rich and became so full to its depths of the putrefied matter that sank into it, that it produced an exceeding great harvest in later years."[38]

W HILE MARIUS WON the greatest battle of his career to date, he did not have long to bask in the glow of victory. Reports came through that his colleague Catulus was having a hell of a time over in northeastern Italy. Catulus was an upstanding optimate senator, but he was more scholar and statesman than soldier. Catulus was "a man eminent for all the politer virtues, for wisdom and for integrity," but revealed himself to be "too sluggish for arduous contests." Marius read alarming reports from the east about failures to hold the Alpine passes.[39]

Catulus may not have been an experienced general, but he did have by his side the supremely talented Sulla. Chafing under years of subordination to Marius, Sulla managed to get himself transferred to Catulus's command for the campaigns of 102. Sulla did signal work as the legions awaited the Cimbri, arranging alliances with native tribes and organizing stable supply lines. But with only about twenty thousand men at their disposal, no amount of preparation was going to make a difference against hundreds of thousands of Cimbri. An initial clash in the mountains proved that the numerical superiority of the slow-moving horde was too great. The Romans were forced into a fighting retreat.[40]

In danger of being enveloped in the mountains and destroyed like every other Roman army that had fought the Cimbri, Catulus declared the Alpine passes indefensible and pulled his legions out of the mountains, falling all the way back to the Adige River in northern Italy. It may have been a sound strategic judgment, but when Catulus abandoned the mountains he allowed the Cimbri an uncontested passage into Cis-alpine Gaul. After a decade of knocking on the door, the Cimbri were finally in Italy.[41]

To hold the line, Catulus ordered heavily fortified camps built on both the near and far sides of the Adige, with a bridge connecting the two. But when Cimbric scouts located the Roman camp, their chiefs de-vised a clever strategy. A detachment of Cimbri headed downriver and began to construct a dam, "tearing away the neighboring hills, like the giants of old, carrying into the river whole trees with their roots, frag-ments of cliffs, and mounds of earth, and crowding the current out of its course." Meanwhile, a second detachment went upriver and constructed floating projectiles, "heavy masses" that swept along the swift current and "whirl[ed] down the stream against the piles of the bridge . . . which made the bridge quiver with their blows." With the banks of the river now flooding from the dam and the bridge being blasted with repeated projectiles, Catulus and his army began to suspect this was not going to end well.[42]

With the Roman camps flooded and broken, the Cimbri launched an all-out attack. By all accounts, the men holding the forward camp fought valiantly, but the legions on the far side of the river saw the situation as hopeless and ran. One cavalry detachment did not stop riding until they got all the way back to Rome—a story we know because among the riders was the son of Marcus Aemilius Scaurus. When the young officer arrived in Rome, the princeps senatus refused to acknowledge him and cast him out of the family for his cowardice. After surviving the war with the Cim-bri, the young man committed suicide in disgrace.[43]

Catulus's own conduct during the battle became a matter of fierce de-bate. According to Catulus himself, when he discovered his army in flight, he sacrificed his own reputation for that of his men: "For finding that he could not persuade his soldiers to remain, and seeing that they were mak-ing off in terror, he ordered his standard to be taken up, ran to the fore-most of the retiring troops, and put himself at their head, wishing that the disgrace should attach to himself and not to his country, and that his soldiers, in making their retreat, should not appear to be running away, but following their general." But it is more likely that Catulus was trying to put a positive spin on a disorganized flight south.[44]

But even though the road to Rome now lay open, the Cimbri remained in the north. Apparently they fell under "the influence of a milder climate and of an abundance of drink, food, and baths." They had always been looking for a home—perhaps this was it. But they may also have lingered because they were waiting to reunite with the Teutones and Ambrones, who should be coming through the western Alps any day now. They did not yet realize their cousins had already been wiped out.[45]

CHAPTER 8

THE THIRD FOUNDER OF ROME

Freedom, democracy, laws, reputation, official position, were no longer of any use to anybody, since
even the office of tribune, which had been devised
for the restraint of wrong-doers . . . was guilty of
such outrages and suffered such indignities.

APPIAN[1]

WITH THE CIMBRI OCCUPYING CISALPINE GAUL AND
slaves still rampaging through Sicily, politics in Rome took
a radical turn. The emergency atmosphere allowed Saturni-
nus and his cronies to push the political envelope. They had already reintroduced violence when the tribune Norbanus forced the prosecution of
Caepio with the help of an angry mob. Now, after helping Marius secure
reelection, Saturninus had at his disposal a small army of Marius's ex-
soldiers ready to flex their electoral and physical muscle.

Joining Saturninus at the head of this new populare political army was
Gaius Servilius Glaucia. Glaucia was despised by most of his fellow senators. Cicero calls him "the most abandoned wretch that ever existed." Cicero also later said that though he does not recommend vulgar metaphors,
it would have been accurate to call Glaucia "the shit of the Senate." But
even the dismissive Cicero admitted Glaucia was "keen and artful, and

excessively humorous; and notwithstanding the meanness of his birth, and the depravity of his life, he would have been advanced to the dignity of a consul." But Glaucia would not advance to the dignity of a consul— instead the depravity of his life would lead to his ruin.[2]

To give their coming takeover of Rome a veneer of moral authority, Saturninus and Glaucia invoked the memory of the now legendary Gracchi brothers. Saturninus displayed busts of the martyred Gracchi in his home and spoke of the martyred brothers in his speeches. So important was owning the Gracchan legacy that Saturninus appeared in the Forum one day with a young man who he claimed was the long lost son of Tiberius Gracchus. The young man was about the right age, and Saturninus demanded he be officially registered in the census and recognized as the legitimate heir of the Gracchi.[3]

Anyone who knew the Gracchi family personally knew Saturninus was spinning a transparent fiction. Sempronia—the Gracchi's still-living sister—refused to receive this alleged nephew, whom she had never met. But this was an age when a lie was not a lie if a man had the audacity to keep asserting the lie was true. For Saturninus the only thing that mattered was planting a seed in the minds of potential supporters that a son of the Gracchi sat in Saturninus's inner circle.[4]

But the presentation of this lost Gracchi was also a trap for Saturninus's optimate enemies, especially Metellus Numidicus. After being stripped of the Numidian command Metellus had returned to Rome and spent the next five years registering his disapproval of all populare measures. But though his name was sneered at in the streets, Metellus still commanded a large following, and his reputation among his fellow optimates was unimpeachable. So in the same election for 102 BC that returned Marius to his third consecutive consulship, Metellus was elected censor. The sudden appearance of "Tiberius Gracchus the Younger" shortly after Metellus entered office cannot have been a coincidence.[5]

The principal job of the censor was to maintain the citizen rolls, and Metellus predictably refused to acknowledge the legitimacy of the Gracchan imposter, setting off a firestorm in the streets. Then Metellus went even further: accusing Saturninus and Glaucia of crimes against the public morality, he announced his intention to expel both from the Senate. In no time, Saturninus and Glaucia organized a mob to protest Metellus's conduct. The proud Metellus tried to stand firm against this angry rabble but was eventually forced to take refuge in a temple on the Capitoline Hill to escape the insults and bricks spewing from the crowd. After the mob dispersed, Metellus's cousin and fellow censor convinced him to stop flagrantly poking the hornet's nest and leave Saturninus and Glaucia in the Senate. But despite this concession, both censors refused to recognize Tiberius Gracchus the Younger. But that hardly mattered—the damage was done.[6]

Shortly after this incident, emissaries representing King Mithridates of Pontus arrived in Rome. Pontus was a far-off kingdom on the Black Sea coast, and Mithridates had recently slit the throat of the king of neighboring Cappadocia and placed his son on the throne. The Pontic envoys requested the Senate recognize the transfer of power. As would befit a delegation of this kind, the Pontic ambassadors arrived in Rome loaded with gifts, and Saturninus was able to revive that old antisenatorial theme of elite corruption by foreign powers. Reminding everyone of Jugurtha's scandalous bribes, Saturninus lambasted both the Senate and the Pontic ambassadors for corruption and tried to physically intimidate the ambassadors into leaving the city.[7]

The physical intimidation was too much for the Senate to bear, and Saturninus was brought up on charges of violating the sanctity of a foreign embassy. Facing a capital charge, Saturninus used exaggerated theatrics to mobilize sympathy in the streets. "Throwing off his rich apparel, putting on poor and sordid clothes, and allowing his beard to grow, he ran up and down to the tumultuous throngs of people throughout the city . . . begging with tears that they would assist him in his present calamities." Saturninus claimed the charges were trumped up and he was really being prosecuted for "the good will he bore the people." When the day of the trial finally arrived, an angry mob packed the Assembly, making it difficult—even unsafe—to continue. Saturninus was released before the trial even began.[8]

The Gracchi are often pointed to as the arch-masterminds of mob tactics and unscrupulous populist politics. But their activities had mostly been driven by a genuine desire to reform the Republic. The violence that surrounded their lives came unexpectedly, without prior forethought, and was an unwelcome intrusion. Saturninus, on the other hand, was the first to show the demagogues of the future generations just how far cynically manipulated mob violence could push a man's career forward. And Saturninus was only getting started—his powerful new political ally, Gaius Marius, was about to return home in complete triumph.

THE SITUATION IN the north following Catulus's defeat was drastic but not dire. Marius had already wiped out the Teutones and Ambrones, and though the Cimbri now squatted in north Italy they showed no signs of continuing south. Marius entered his fourth consecutive consulship in January 101 and spent the winter transferring as many troops as possible from Gaul to Italy. Massing all available forces on the south bank of the Po River, Marius combined his Gallic army with Catulus's remaining legions and assumed overall command. Marius kept both Catulus and Sulla in positions of leadership, but there would be no repeat of the fatal disunity at Arausio. Marius was in sole command. In the spring of 101, he led 50,000 men across the Po River to confront 200,000 Cimbri.[9]

When the legions appeared on the horizon, Cimbric ambassadors rode out to greet the Romans. The Cimbri were confident and demanded the Romans cede territory in Cisalpine Gaul. The ambassadors reminded Marius that the Teutones and Ambrones would be crossing over into Italy soon and the Romans couldn't hope to withstand their combined might. At this, Marius burst out laughing and said, "Don't trouble yourself about your brethren, for they have land, and they will have it forever—land which we have given them." The Cimbri refused to believe Marius's claim to have wiped out their allies, until Marius ordered the shackled kings of the Teutones paraded through the camp. Incensed, the Cimbric ambassadors withdrew. A few days later one of their principal chiefs rode to the Roman camp to settle a simple question with Marius: when and where the two armies would meet in battle.[10]

On the third day following this meeting, the Romans and Cimbri lined up for battle on the Raudian Plain. Marius led the left wing of the legions, with Catulus in the center and Sulla on the right. Across the plain the Cimbri arrayed a massive infantry that allegedly spanned more than three miles across, with a cavalry detachment alone numbering fifteen thousand. Though a fog in the morning covered everything with a hazy mist, Marius made sure his army faced west so that when the sun rose and burned off the fog, the Cimbri would be staring directly into the sun. This position also put the legions upwind from the enemy—both the sun and the wind would become key factors in the battle to come.[11]

In their memoirs, both Sulla and Catulus claimed that once the Battle of the Raudian Plain began, Marius became confused in the rising dust cloud, and when he advanced, he missed the Cimbri completely, leaving Catulus and Sulla to do the real fighting. But this is fairly obviously propaganda. Most likely Marius deployed the same strategy he used at Aquae Sextiae: pin down the main front line of the enemy and then deliver a deadly flanking shot. Catulus and Sulla did indeed fight a heated battle while Marius disappeared into the dust, but far from missing the enemy, he was off delivering the fatal blow to their exposed flank.[12]

For the Cimbri the battle turned into a rout. The blinding sun gave way to a huge cloud of dust that blinded them, and they found themselves under relentless attack from multiple sides. Their warriors began to flee but their own mothers and wives would not allow them to escape. Standing behind the front line, "the women, in black garments, stood at the wagons and slew the fugitives—their husbands or brothers or fathers, then strangled their little children and cast them beneath the wheels of the wagons or the feet of the cattle, and then cut their own throats." The Battle of the Raudian Plain spelled the end of the Cimbri—they left 120,000 dead on the plain and the survivors were enslaved. As is so often the case in Roman history, repeated defeats in battle could be endured as long as the Romans won the war.[13]

When news of the victory reached Rome, no one could now deny the magnificent supremacy of Gaius Marius, Rome's invincible general. At the pinnacle of his fame, power, and prestige, even "the first men in the state, who had until then envied the 'new man' who had reached so many important posts, now admitted that the state had been rescued by him."

Marius was hailed as "the Third Founder of Rome," elevating him to a hyper-elite pantheon of heroes that included only Romulus himself and the legendary Marcus Furius Camillus, the man who had brought Rome back from the brink of extinction after the traumatic sack by the Gauls in the 380s. Not even Scipio Africanus, who had delivered Rome from Hannibal, earned such an honorific. But strangely Marius himself refused to assume the standard triumphant cognomen and he never became known as "Marius Gallicus" or "Marius Cimbricus." Instead he retained the two simple names he had been born with: Gaius Marius.[14]

T HE ALMOST UNBELIEVABLE news that Rome was free of the threat of the Cimbri was soon matched by good news from Sicily. Marius's consular colleague in 101 was Manius Aquillius, one of his longtime protégés. Son of the disgraced organizer of Asia, the younger Aquillius had served as one of Marius's chief lieutenants in Gaul. As consul in 101, he was tasked with finally ending the Second Servile War. Aquillius brought a professional bearing to the conflict and set about restoring order to the island.[15]

The job was not going to be easy. Following Lucullus's unconscionable dismantling of the Roman forces in early 102, his replacement could do nothing to stop the slave armies for the whole next year. At some point during that year, however, "King Tryphon" died and Athenion took over as supreme leader of the slave forces. With the slaves ascendant, lawlessness again spread to the native Sicilians: "For since there was at this time complete anarchy . . . and no Roman magistrate exercised any jurisdiction, all ran wild and committed many great enormities with impunity, so that all places were full of violence and robbery, which pillaged the possessions of the rich." Those who had once been "pre-eminent amongst their fellow citizens for their wealth and distinction, by a sudden change of fortune were . . . treated with the greatest contempt and scorn."[16]

By the time Aquillius arrived in the spring of 101, Athenion had extended his dominions as far as Messana (modern-day Messina) on the northeast tip of the island. Aquillius arrived with cohorts of veterans from Marius's Gallic army and was quick to challenge the slaves to a battle, during which he allegedly killed Athenion in single combat. This heroic embellishment probably traces back to Aquillius's own reports of the war, but whether it was in dramatic single combat or a more routine clash of armies, Athenion died in the fighting and just ten thousand surviving rebels fell back to the fortress at Triocala.[17]

But unlike Lucullus, Aquillius pursued the survivors and captured the slave capital of Triocala. Rounding up the last of the rebels, Aquillius shipped them all to Rome, where he planned to make them fight against various wild beasts for the amusement of the Roman citizens. But once these final rebels arrived in Rome and learned their fate, they committed mass suicide rather than be used as human props in the arena. It was the final bloody act of the Second Servile War that left Sicily depopulated and despoiled.[18]

B ACK IN ROME, jubilation reigned. With all their enemies finally dead or in chains, the Romans commenced with a nonstop victory party. The Assembly declared fifteen days of thanksgiving after news of Marius's victory over the Cimbri and then prepared for his great triumphant return to the city. But Marius would not celebrate this triumph alone; he instead invited Catulus to share the stage with him. Joint triumphs were not unheard of, but they were incredibly rare—a triumph was a political expression of singular achievement. The point was to own the spotlight, not share it. Friendly sources paint this as an act of generous magnanimity. But hostile sources say Marius knew Catulus had *really* won the battle over the Cimbri and feared a revolt from Catulus's legions if their commander was left out.[19]

The sources also diverge on Marius's subsequent campaign for a sixth consulship in 100. Friendly sources say the voters justly rewarded Marius for his service—a victory lap to enjoy. Hostile sources say that with the military crisis over, the voters were ready to end the run of consecutive consulships. These latter sources claim Marius spread lavish bribes in order to win reelection. But it's doubtful such underhanded tactics were necessary. The Third Founder of Rome enjoyed unprecedented fame, wealth, and power. He won reelection easily. He would now be consul for a fifth consecutive year.[20]

While it appeared as though Marius only wanted to use his fifth consulship to ensure that his Gallic veterans would get the same land bonus as his Numidian veterans, he came to office in January 100 flanked by populare radicals who had a much more aggressive agenda. Saturninus won another term as tribune and artfully controlled the Assembly. His partner Glaucia was elected praetor, giving him wide jurisdiction over the courts. Another close ally named Gaius Saufeius was elected quaestor, giving this radical clique access to the state treasury. Marius's consular partner Lucius Valerius Flaccus, meanwhile, could not be counted on to stand in their way and is described as "more a servant than a colleague."[21]

Saturninus's campaign for tribune had already set the tone for the coming year. With every indication that Saturninus planned to use his term to drive Metellus Numidicus into exile, the optimates backed a young ally named Nonius to run for tribune and stop him. When it appeared that Nonius might indeed win election, the radical populares did not even wait for the vote. An armed gang, most likely drawn from the more unscrupulous corners of Marius's veterans, jumped the unfortunate Nonius and beat him to death. With the bonds of mos maiorum shredded, Saturninus paid no immediate price for this preemptive political assassination. After pushing Nonius's body aside, Saturninus easily won election. All of this set the stage for the year 100—a year that very nearly saw the fall of the Republic.[22]

During this fateful year it becomes difficult to disentangle who was using whom—but it appears Saturninus was now pursuing a more overtly sinister version of Gaius Gracchus's program. Saturninus, Glaucia, and their cronies—who still included the phony son of Tiberius Gracchus—tried to revive the old Gracchan coalition of plebs urbana, rural peasants, Equestrians, and populare nobles looking to stick it to their optimate rivals. But Saturninus's coalition was also now joined by Marius's veterans, who would provide much needed muscle. Where Gaius Gracchus had been pulled into violence against his will, Saturninus pursued it without compunction. Where Gaius sought to restore the balance of the Polybian constitution, Saturninus wanted to truly crush the Senate and use Marius's veterans to rule the city with an iron fist.

ONCE SATURNINUS TOOK up the office of tribune, he pursued a dizzying slate of reforms aimed at overwhelming the power of the optimates in the Senate. The seeds of the new antisenatorial coalition had been sewn long before the fateful year of 100. At some point prior to taking up his praetorship—probably during an otherwise unrecorded term as tribune—Glaucia put forward a new law returning control of the Extortion Court to the Equestrians, reversing the temporary restoration of senatorial power engineered by the now exiled Caepio in 106. But Glaucia's law not only returned the jury pool of the Extortion Court to the Equestrians, it also expanded the scope of the charges to include not just magistrates accused of extortion but also anyone who benefited from the crime, opening up literally any citizen to prosecution at the hands of the Equestrian jurors. Glaucia also curtailed an oft-used ploy of delaying trials with procedural tactics. Glaucia meant for the court to be a hammer against the nobility and he did not want the jurors to be able to avoid delivering a blow out of pity or empathy. This was no time for either.[23]

This pro-Equestrian measure already in place, Saturninus entered the tribunate of 100 and offered the plebs urbana an expanded grain dole. This was an especially provocative measure, since the Senate had recently decreed that given the chaos in Sicily, anyone proposing subsidized grain was acting against the public interest. Saturninus gleefully took up the challenge. One of his fellow tribunes vetoed the bill, but Saturninus simply ignored him. A veto had once been enough to grind the entire Republic to a halt; now it was simply wadded up and tossed aside. The provocative grain dole was especially offensive to young Quintus Caepio, whose father had been exiled by Saturninus's gang three years earlier. As quaestor for 100, the younger Caepio had been the one to recommend to the Senate that the treasury could not afford further grain subsidies. With both his father's honor and his own now spit upon by Saturninus,

Caepio lost his temper and led a gang of his own to the Assembly. This mob destroyed the planks and urns used for voting, but the vandalism only delayed passage of the bill. The damage was repaired and the Assembly voted the unaffordable grain dole into law.[24]

With the Equestrians and plebs urbana placated, Saturninus moved on to the real meat of his program: an ambitious set of colonies and land grants for Marius's Gallic veterans. Having already established land grants in Africa, Saturninus now proposed new plots elsewhere in the empire. He staked the people's claim to all the territory the Cimbri had recently occupied and said the Assembly had the right to distribute it to the men who had fought for it. Saturninus also proposed land in southern Gaul and Sicily be distributed to Marius's veterans. The rural poor—from whom Marius had recruited his soldiers—flooded into Rome to pass the bill overwhelmingly.[25]

Saturninus's growing coalition also included the Italian Allies, because *all* of Marius's veterans would qualify for the land grants, not just Roman citizens. Marius himself was a provincial Italian who hailed from a city that had only been fully enfranchised a generation before he was born. He was, and always remained, thoroughly pro-Italian in his politics. During the course of the wars he frequently doled out citizenship for acts of valor, even going so far as to enfranchise an entire cohort of Italians from Camerinum after the victory against the Cimbri. When his arbitrary—and possibly illegal—enfranchisement of his soldiers was challenged, Marius caustically retorted that "the clash of arms had prevented his hearing the voice of the law."[26]

But while on the dusty plains of battle it was impossible to distinguish Roman from Italian, back in Rome the citizens knew the distinction well. As usual they grumbled at the land being offered to mere Allies. This cleavage in Saturninus's coalition allowed the optimates to finally rally opposition. Tapping into the resentful pride of the plebs urbana, the optimates formed gangs of their own that disrupted Saturninus's activities wherever they could. Violent street clashes became a routine matter of state.[27]

But despite these clashes, Saturninus pushed through the bill allotting land to Marius's veterans. Aware that it might be repealed when he left office, Saturninus inserted a clause requiring every senator to swear an oath that they would never repeal the law upon pain of banishment. With this oath, Saturninus and Marius had laid another trap for the hated Metellus Numidicus. Marius personally addressed the Senate and registered his approval of the law, but expressed misgivings about the oath, providing cover for more conservative senators like Metellus who were aghast at the requirement. But just hours before the deadline to take the oath, Marius abruptly changed his mind. He told his fellow senators he was going to swear the oath and walked over to the Temple of Saturn for the ceremony. Without time to think, the other senators had only minutes to choose between taking the oath and going into exile. They all chose to swear the oath—even optimate stalwarts like Scaurus and Crassus. The only one who refused was Metellus Numidicus. Saturninus's supporters menaced him to the point of riot, but announcing that he could not abide such violence on his own account, Metellus accepted exile. "For," he said, "either matters will mend and the people will change their minds and I shall return at their invitation, or, if matters remain as they are, it is best that I should be away." Saturninus duly carried a law prohibiting any Roman from offering Metellus fire, water, and shelter. Throngs of tearful friends and clients accompanied Metellus Numidicus to the gates of Rome to watch him depart for exile.[28]

But as they celebrated finally nailing Metellus, Saturninus and Glaucia were about to discover that their marriage of convenience with Marius had come to an end. With land for his veterans secured, and his old nemesis Metellus finally dispensed with, Marius had nothing further to gain from backing the radicals. His labors complete, Marius could now move on to consolidate his own position inside the nobility and transition to life as a powerful elder statesman. But for Saturninus and Glaucia, all these laws were just the beginning. As they pushed forward, Marius drew back, and the stage was set for a final bloody confrontation.

WITH THE ELECTIONS for 99 approaching, Saturninus and Glaucia planned to push their agenda even further. Saturninus ran for reelection as tribune and was joined by the "son" of Tiberius Gracchus. In a shot across the bow, Marius ordered the fake Gracchus arrested for fraud and tossed in prison. The fake Gracchus was later sprung from jail and Saturninus won reelection; but it was obvious Marius was no longer on their side.[29]

This political break was confirmed when the consular election began. Three men emerged as frontrunners. The popular orator Marcus Antonius, recently returned in triumph from his suppression of Cilician pirates, had the full backing of the optimates; his election was nearly guaranteed. The leading contender for the other spot was Gaius Memmius. Having built his own career railing against the corrupt nobility during the Jugurthine War, Memmius was a powerful populare candidate who threatened to leave no space for the third man in the ring: Gaius Servilius Glaucia.[30]

The threat of Glaucia winning a consulship was obvious to all. If he combined consular power with Saturninus's control of the Assembly, there was no telling what damage they could cause together. Luckily there was a solution. As a sitting praetor, Glaucia's candidacy was technically illegal, and as consul Marius had the right to disqualify him from the election. Continuing his pullback from his old allies, Marius declared Glaucia's candidacy invalid. Marius's move against Glaucia was rich in irony, as he himself had blown through all existing prohibitions during his streak of consulships. But as befitted the age, Glaucia ignored the disqualification and continued to canvass for votes, precipitating a crisis in Rome not seen since the days of the Gracchi.[31]

When election day came, the voters filed through the stalls and dropped their ballots in the urns. As expected, the herald soon announced that Marcus Antonius had secured election to one of the consulships. Voting then continued to fill the second spot. The moment it looked like Memmius was going to win, Saturninus and Glaucia directed a gang of supporters to crash down on the stalls, smash the voting urns, and break up the election. In the ensuing riot, the unfortunate Memmius was cornered on the rostra and beaten to death with an "unshapely bludgeon." After a life spent attacking the optimates, Memmius was finally done in by the populare he had always courted. The revolution was devouring her children.[32]

With the election now thrown into bloody confusion, Marius called the Senate to an emergency session. After a quick debate, the Senate resolved to follow the precedent established a generation earlier. They instructed Marius to do what was necessary to preserve the state. This was the same senatus consultum ultimum they had issued to Opimius during the showdown with Gaius Gracchus. But this latest senatus consultum ultimum came with a troubling new twist. When Opimius marched on the Aventine in 121, neither Gaius Gracchus nor Fulvius Flaccus held a magistracy—they were private citizens being punished by a sovereign consul. But in 100, Saturninus was a sacrosanct tribune and Glaucia a praetor. Could they be dealt with as brutally as the Gracchans?[33]

With Rome in chaos and the rule of law already breaking down, Marius did not much quibble over the legality of his orders. Calling on a mix of volunteers from the plebs urbana and his own veterans, Marius prepared to restore order by any means necessary. Now under serious attack, Saturninus, Glaucia, Saufeius, and the faux son of Tiberius Gracchus led a party of armed followers up the Capitoline Hill and occupied the principal citadel of Rome. But Marius did not follow Opimius's reckless example. Instead, he deployed the same professional competence that had always served him so well. He systematically cut all the water pipes servicing the Capitoline and then told the renegades that they were surrounded, had no hope of escape, and now faced slow death by dehydration. He waited as the heat of the day did its work, and then promised to protect the rebels if they would surrender.[34]

Saufeius apparently proposed rejecting the offer and burning down the capital and all its sacred temples. But Saturninus and Glaucia refused this last desperate act of destruction. They surrendered. Marius afforded the praetor Glaucia the dignity of being placed under house arrest, but led Saturninus and the rest of his gang into the Senate house and locked them up until he could figure out how best to process them. But the plebs urbana answered the question for him. Whether with Marius's tacit approval or without (the former far more likely), a mob broke into the Senate house and dispensed exactly the kind of justice Saturninus himself had built a career on. Using roof tiles, the mob stoned the unarmed prisoners to death.

Saturninus soon lay dead on the floor of the Senate. Glaucia didn't fare much better. He was dragged from his home and murdered in the street. So, just like their more noble forbears, the Gracchi, the latest group of populare agitators ended as a bloody pile of bodies being pushed into the Tiber River.[35]

W ITH THE RADICALS safely dumped in the Tiber, the Senate set about picking up the pieces. They knew they could not repeal *every* piece of legislation that had been voted through during the populare swing of 104 to 100. The land and colonies for Marius's veterans was left in place. The election of priests would remain, as would the jury pool drawing from the Equestrian class only. But other legislation—including probably the expanded grain dole—was never implemented.

The fall of the populares also meant that the men they had exiled were now allowed to return. Chief among the exiles was Metellus Numidicus. As soon as Saturninus was dead, Metellus's son began a tireless campaign to have his father recalled to Rome; so tireless were his efforts that he soon earned the cognomen "Pius" for his filial devotion. But though Saturninus and Glaucia were dead, Metellus still had enemies. One of the tribunes in 99 had been expelled from the Senate by Metellus and nursed a grudge. This tribune spent his entire year in office vetoing any attempt to bring Metellus back. But once his term expired, the Assembly voted to recall Metellus from exile. The tribune who had opposed the Metellans was made to pay a heavy price for his obstruction. After leaving office, he was jumped by an armed gang and murdered. Even though the storm had passed, a complete return to normalcy was out of the question.[36]

Just as Metellus Numidicus returned, Marius himself decided it would be prudent to absent himself from Rome for a while. As the glow of his military victories faded, his fellow Romans were left with a general unease about the methods and tactics he had used to control events at home. So Marius found a pretext to travel east in the summer of 98 and made a long circuit of the Aegean. He returned to Rome a year later, bought a house near the Forum and a villa in the country. Between these two homes, Marius settled into retirement. Like many old war horses, Marius was uncomfortable being put out to pasture and soon found himself burning to get back in the game: "As excellent a general as he was, he was an evil influence in time of peace, a man of unbounded ambition, insatiable, without self-control, and always an element of unrest." This insatiable craving for more glory led to Marius's ruin, and in the years to come he would put "the ugliest possible crown upon a most illustrious career in field and Forum . . . driven by the blasts of passion, ill-timed ambition, and insatiable greed upon the shore of a most cruel and savage old age." [37]

CHAPTER 9

ITALIA

Though we call this war a war against allies in
order to lessen the odium of it, if we are to tell
the truth it was a war against citizens.

Florus[1]

Q uintus Poppaedius Silo hailed from the Marsi
tribe of central Italy. Long respected for their martial valor, it
was said that no Roman consul had ever celebrated a triumph
over the Marsi, or without the Marsi. Silo himself was a veteran of the legions, almost certainly fighting in the armies of Gaius Marius against the
Cimbri. A leader of wealth and standing at home, Silo also had plenty of
friends in Rome and spent a great deal of time in the city. But though Silo
was thoroughly integrated into the Roman system and had shed blood
defending the Republic, he was still not technically an equal citizen—a
fact that was becoming intolerable.[2]

In the summer of 91 BC, Silo paid a call to his old friend Marcus Livius Drusus, the son of the man who had so thoroughly stymied Gaius
Gracchus in 122. Drusus the Younger was now tribune and furiously
stirring up a political storm of his own. Silo traveled to Rome to implore
Drusus to rethink some of his proposals. Drusus planned to revive the
old Gracchan-style land commission, which threatened Italian communities with arbitrary confiscation of property. Silo said the Italians

would only accept land redistribution if a bill finally delivering equal citizenship came with it.* Drusus agreed that the time had come to finally settle the matter once and for all. He promised to take the Italian citizenship bill to the Assembly.[3]

In return for this promise, Silo pledged to support Drusus without reservation. He said, "By Capitoline Jupiter, Vesta of Rome, Mars the patron of the city, Sol the origin of all the people, Terra the benefactress of animals and plants; by the demigods who founded Rome, and the heroes who have contributed to the increase of its power, I swear that the friend or the enemy of Drusus will also be mine; I will not spare my life or my children or my parents, if the interests of Drusus and those who are bound by the same oath require it. If, by the law of Drusus, I become a citizen, I will regard Rome as my homeland, and Drusus as my greatest benefactor. I will communicate this oath to the largest possible number of my fellow citizens. If I keep my oath, may I obtain every blessing; and the opposite, if I violate my oath." This was not an idle promise. In less than a year, Quintus Poppaedius Silo would be leading the Italians to armed insurrection.[4]

U NTIL THE AGE of the Gracchi, the Italian Allies had prized their autonomy inside Rome's Italian confederation. The complaints they lodged in the Senate usually had to do with the fact that too many of their citizens were migrating to Rome—often to avoid being conscripted into the legions. Meanwhile, the Senate and People of Rome were long concerned that waves of migrants would disrupt their own collective stranglehold on power. Elites in both Rome and the Italian cities often worked together to force the migrants to return to their original homes.[5]

But there was one persistent complaint lodged by both rich and poor Italians alike: arbitrary abuse at the hands of Roman magistrates. Gaius Gracchus highlighted a case in which slaves carried a Roman magistrate

---

* It was on this visit that Silo infamously hung four-year-old Cato the Younger out the window in an attempt to convince little Cato of the need for Italian citizenship. Cato the Toddler demurred. See Plut. Cato Min. 2.

in a litter. A local Italian peasant "asked in jest if they were carrying a corpse." The insulted magistrate ordered the peasant beaten to death. In another case, the wife of a magistrate was angry some public baths had not been cleared for her solitary use. As punishment, "a stake was planted in the forum and ... the most illustrious man of his city, was led to it. His clothing was stripped and he was beaten with rods." The longstanding protection from arbitrary arrest, flogging, and execution enjoyed by even the poorest Roman citizen did not apply to the Italians. It was an indignity felt acutely by all classes.[6]

After 146, the benefits of being an independent Ally started to pale in comparison to the benefits of being a citizen of Rome. The Italians voiced new complaints about the lack of equality in the late 130s, as the Gracchan land commission set to work divvying up ager publicus. The various Italian cities had to rely on the generous patronage of Scipio Aemilianus to protect them from the land commissioners. In 125, Fulvius Flaccus presented a bold solution to the problem: citizenship in exchange for land. This was a deal many Italians were ready to take—especially among the wealthy landowners who would be the ones able to take advantage of the benefits of citizenship. These wealthy Italians would have been happy to give up a few iugera of land in exchange for full access to Rome's legal and political system.[7]

After the failure of Flaccus's controversial bill triggered the revolt of Fregellae, the Senate took the opportunity to introduce a practical compromise. Adept at the game of divide and conquer, the Romans introduced a new policy of *civitas per magistratum*. Under this new arrangement, Italians holding Latin Rights who were elected to local magistracies were individually awarded Roman citizenship. The elites loved the new arrangement and after one last push by Gaius Gracchus to enfranchise all the Italians in 122, the issue went dormant for a generation.[8]

Gaius Marius reintroduced the Italian question during the Cimbrian Wars. Marius was long a champion of the Italian cause. He had fought alongside them his whole life. He himself hailed from a provincial Italian city. When the Italians complained about harassment by the tax farmers, Marius pushed the Senate to stop Italian enslavement. Out on campaign,

Marius routinely exercised his power as consul to reward exemplary Italian soldiers with citizenship. Coming from all classes, these enfranchised soldiers returned to their home cities with extra rights and privileges. As they remingled with friends and family who did not enjoy the same rights, the seeds of discord took root.[9]

The rest of the Italians were encouraged to think that broader rights might be on the way when the census of 97 came around. With the right of civitas per magistratum floating around, many affluent Italians residing in Rome passed themselves off as former magistrates and enrolled as citizens. The Marian censors were intentionally lax with checking credentials, and when the census was complete, many in the Senate were suspicious and wanted to take another look at it. As was now the established pattern, the Romans always dangled the possibility of citizenship only to snatch it away.[10]

In 95, the great orator Lucius Licinius Crassus won the consulship. Upon taking office, he proposed forming a commission to clean up the citizenship rolls. In true optimate fashion the inquiry was premised on the unobjectionable argument that citizens should be counted in the census and noncitizens should not. This made perfect sense to the citizens of Rome who voted in favor of the inquiry. But as a necessary prelude to the work, Crassus and his consular colleague Mucius Scaevola carried a further bill expelling all Italians from the city. This recurring expedient was usually only deployed around elections, but this time it was meant to make sure only true Roman citizens were counted as Roman citizens.[11]

All of this seemed perfectly reasonable to the Romans, but it put in motion the wheels of the Social War. The group hardest hit by the purge and expulsion were men of Equestrian rank—men with financial means and business connections in Rome who nonetheless had not yet found their own path to citizenship. It would be this class of disgruntled Equestrians who would be the iron backbone of Italian rebellion. They returned home to their native cities, mingled with the veterans of the northern wars, and began to plot revolution.[12]

For the Senate, however, this was not simply a matter of keeping clean books. Maintaining a tight lock on citizenship meant keeping a tight lock on the Assembly. Above all, they feared that the Roman leader who finally delivered citizenship to the Italians would have client rolls that dwarfed his rivals, destabilizing the political balance in the Senate. This was the same threat once posed by the Gracchan land commission. The short-sighted obsession with the petty dynamic of electoral politics led to the most unnecessary war in Roman history.

B ECAUSE HISTORY HAS a sense of humor, a completely unrelated conflict in Asia triggered the final showdown over Italian citizenship. The province of Asia had been at the forefront of Roman politics in the 130s and 120s and then, much like the Italian question, had gone dormant. After Asia was incorporated into the empire, Rome's attention diverted to Africa and Gaul for the next twenty years. Asia had been left to just hum along. And there was no reason not to let it hum: it was generating the massive profits funding those wars in Africa and Gaul. Cicero later said, "Asia is so rich and so productive . . . it is greatly superior to all other countries." Taxes that had once been owed to King Attalus now formed a steady stream of wealth that poured directly into the Temple of Saturn.[13]

But with just a handful of staff running the provincial government, the business of handling the Asian taxes fell into the unsupervised hands of the publicani, who routinely extorted more money than was owed. Since the men who owned the publicani companies sat in the jury pool of the Extortion Court, there was no one to complain to. Policing themselves, the publicani operated with impunity.

But now that peace had returned to the Republic, the Senate wanted to go back to running their empire rather than just saving it from ruin. After helping clean up the citizenship rolls in 95, Mucius Scaevola led an old-style senatorial embassy to Asia to investigate how the province was running and make any appropriate reforms. It had been twenty-five years since anyone had really checked to see how things were going. Accompanying Scaevola was another ex-consul, Publius Rutilius Rufus, the consul for 105 who had introduced new training techniques for the soldiers. Considered the preeminent stoic intellectual of his generation, Rutilius was an optimate of the first order and above reproach.[14]

When this embassy arrived, it turned out things were not going well at all. Everyone in Asia complained about publicani abuse, and the benevolent Scaevola doled out clemency left and right: "Whenever any who had been oppressed by those tax-gatherers appealed to him, he commissioned upright judges, by whom he condemned them in every case, and forced them to pay the penalty imposed upon them to the persons they had injured." Scaevola stayed in the province about nine months arranging a revision of the provincial tax system. He then returned to Rome, leaving Rutilius in charge of settling the details. The reforms imposed in Asia were broadly popular, and it looked like Scaevola and Rutilius had settled Roman administration in Asia for a generation.[15]

Back in Rome, the publicani companies were not happy about any of this. When Rutilius returned in 92, he was indicted in the Extortion Court. The charges were ludicrous. Rutilius was a model of stoic probity and would later be cited by Cicero as the perfect model of a Roman administrator. In the face of this farce, Rutilius refused to even offer a defense so as not to acknowledge its legitimacy. He refused requests by both Crassus and Antonius to let them defend him. With the angry publicani controlling the jury, the outcome was in little doubt. Convicted of extortion, Rutilius thumbed his nose on the way out the door. He settled in the Asian city of Smyrna, to sit among the people who allegedly hated him, but who actually loved him.[16]

Optimates in the Senate like Scaurus, Crassus, and Scaevola were scandalized by all this. Their attempt to rein in the publicani had backfired and now one of the best men in Rome had been banished. The optimates concluded that taking back control of the Extortion Court was the only sure guard against future persecutions. This looming showdown over the courts would spiral out of control and make 91 another year marked by political violence—marks coming with predictable regularity. First 133, then 121, then 100, and now 91. Violence had become a routine part of the cycles of Republican politics.[17]

THE MAN AT the center of the latest crisis was Marcus Livius Drusus. Not unlike the Gracchi, Drusus was an ambitious young noble on the make. He was one of the most talented orators of a new generation that had grown up on the speeches of Crassus and Antonius. He carried himself with the arrogant confidence of a young man who expected the world to come to him. He loved being the center of attention, and when an architect once boasted that he could build a wonderfully secluded house that provided security and discretion, Drusus said, "If you possess the skill you must build my house in such a way that whatever I do shall be seen by all."[18]

Drusus did not traffic in populare circles—he was a scion of the optimate and raised to be a talented, if arrogant, future leader of the nobility. His father, Drusus the Elder, had fully ingratiated himself with the optimates for his attacks on Gaius Gracchus, and later shared a censorship with Scaurus in 109. It is not surprising that Scaurus tapped the son of his old colleague to carry a package of bills to the Assembly to restore judicial power to the Senate.[19]

Knowing that transferring the jury pool back to the Senate would trigger Equestrian resistance, Drusus and the optimates planned to build the same coalition pioneered by Gaius Gracchus, except use its power this time to build the Senate up rather than tear it down. First, Drusus proposed enlarging the Senate from three hundred to six hundred men. That way even if "the Senate" controlled the courts, it would only be after it was augmented by three hundred prominent Equestrians. This was a provocative proposal, as existing senators might not like to see their prestige watered down—nor be happy about the arrival of uncouth commoners. But the senatorial prohibition on engaging in commerce meant if a potential new senator was a merchant, he would have to either give up his trade or decline admission. Either way, the new senators would all be landed gentry like the old senators, with only the men of business left out in the cold.[20]

As the Equestrians were quite capable of mobilizing public support for their interests, Drusus was ready with a slate of programs to feed the old Gracchan coalition. For the plebs urbana, Drusus proposed a new subsidized grain dole. For the rural poor, Drusus proposed an agrarian law that was modeled on the original *Lex Agraria* of Tiberius Gracchus. This was all very popular with the Roman voters, but put the Italians on alert. They had successfully deflected the Gracchan commission; now it appeared Drusus was coming back for another pass. This was the issue that led Silo to visit his friend Drusus, where each wound up pledging their lives, their fortunes, and their sacred honor to the cause of Italian citizenship.[21]

But though Drusus's intention was to make everyone happy by promising everyone everything—he boasted that "he had left nothing for anyone else to distribute"—this time the people dwelt on the downsides. Neither rural farmers nor senatorial elites liked subsidizing grain for the plebs urbana. The old senators were wary of adding three hundred new members and diluting their own power. The Equestrians worried they were about to be shut out of power altogether. And of course, nearly all Romans from every class and occupation opposed Italian citizenship.[22]

D RUSUS AND HIS optimate backers also faced stiff opposition from one of the consuls for the year, Lucius Marcius Philippus. Philippus was an old rival of Scaurus and Crassus going back to the crisis years of 104–100. Philippus was the one who said there were only two thousand men who owned property in Italy while proposing a radical land redistribution bill of his own. In fine Roman fashion, now that a similar bill was being proposed by his enemies, Philippus opposed it vehemently. He was backed by the publicani, who rightly felt threatened by Drusus's package of laws. On the day of the vote, Drusus had done his work well and it looked like everything was going to pass. But then, Philippus marched into the Forum and tried to shut down the Assembly. One of Drusus's men "seized him by the throat and did not let go until blood poured into his mouth and eyes." Philippus managed to get away but he was furious at the maltreatment of a consul.[23]

Given the state of the historical record, it is hard to know exactly which of his reforms Drusus managed to enact. We know he carried the land bill and grain bill, as well as the jury reform. But either because it never made it to the rostra or was voted down, the Italian citizenship bill never materialized. It appeared that the Italians were about to have their prize snatched away. Again. The Italian veterans who had served together under Marius got together with the disgruntled Equestrians who had been kicked out of Rome in 95. Their mutual grumbling turned awfully seditious.[24]

Even before the bill was dropped, a violent splinter faction of Italians formed a plot to assassinate the consul Philippus and his colleague Sextus Julius Caesar* at the Latin Festival. Drusus successfully warned the consuls in advance and they left the festival alive, but it raised the uncomfortable question of how Drusus had come to hold such dangerous knowledge in the first place—who was he in league with? But as late as September 91, it seemed like Drusus still had the support of most of the Senate; the steady hands of Scaurus and Crassus kept most of the senators with him.[25]

While they kept a firm hand on current events, a group of optimate grandees met at Crassus's villa in September 91 to discuss loftier subjects. Among the small party were Crassus's old friends Antonius and Scaevola along with two promising students: Publius Sulpicius Rufus and Gaius Aurelius Cotta. Old Scaurus was not present, but as fit his persona, he was known to be off at his own estate, "somewhere in the vicinity."[26]

We know about this dinner party because it is the setting of one of Cicero's most important dialogues, *On the Orators*. Cicero learned of the gathering years later from one of the participants and used it as the setting for a wide-ranging dialogue on the history, theory, and practice of oratory. Fascinating as the details of this discussion are, the more relevant point is why Cicero chose that time and place to set his dialogue. Cicero enjoyed placing characters at the moment of maximum experience and wisdom—the moment before death. And death hung over the men gathered at Crassus's villa. Within a few years, nearly every one of them would be dead. Cicero did not just set *On The Orators* at the end of his heroes' lives; he set it on the brink of a civil war that, unbeknownst to all of them, was just weeks from breaking out.[27]

The only one of the group not to die violently was the host, Lucius Crassus, who had the good sense to die before any of the fighting started. With Philippus once again raising hell in the Senate about annulling Drusus's laws, Crassus rose in defense and delivered yet another long and

---

* Uncle of THE Julius Caesar.

eloquent address that returned the Senate to its senses. But likely already sick from some unspecified ailment, the exertion of the speech drove Crassus to bed, and a week later he died. He was not yet fifty. Cicero said of Crassus's sudden death:

> This was a melancholy occurrence to his friends, a grievous calamity to his country, and a heavy affliction to all the virtuous part of mankind; but such misfortunes afterwards fell upon the commonwealth, that life does not appear to me to have been taken away from Lucius Crassus by the immortal gods as a privation, but death to have been bestowed on him as a blessing. He did not live to behold Italy blazing with war, or the senate overwhelmed with popular odium, or the leading men of the state accused of the most heinous crime . . . or, finally, that republic in every way disgraced, in which, while it continued most flourishing, he had by far the preeminence over all other men in glory.[28]

With his rivals distracted by the death of their friend, Philippus pounced. He induced the Senate to nullify Drusus's laws, either on a religious pretext or for the violence inflicted on Philippus personally at the Assembly. And though he is often cast along with the other radical tribunes in Roman history, Drusus was not ready to take the same plunge as his predecessors Saturninus and the Gracchi brothers. He accepted his fate and did nothing to veto the annulment. Though he did say: "Although I have the power to oppose the decrees of the senate, I will not do so, because I know that the guilty will soon receive their punishment."[29]

It is difficult to tell when exactly the Italians reentered the picture, but with the final annulment of Drusus's laws, word surely went out that the time had come for action. It did not take long for Quintus Poppaedius Silo to rally ten thousand men to join him in a demonstrative march on Rome. When they neared the city one of the praetors went out to meet the Italians and said: "Whither do you go, Poppaedius, with so great a company?" Silo responded, "To Rome, for I have been summoned by the tribunes of the plebs, to share in the citizenship." The praetor responded, "You may obtain what you seek far more easily, and much more honorably, if you do not approach the Senate in a hostile manner; for the Senate will not be compelled, but entreated and petitioned, to bestow such a favor upon the Latins, who are their allies and confederates." Silo turned around and went home, but this was the beginning, not the end.[30]

After the Italians went home, someone decided Marcus Livius Drusus was going to pay for the trouble he had caused. We don't know who plotted his death, whether it was Italians believing he had betrayed them or someone nursing a personal grudge. But someone wanted Drusus dead. The tribune grew suspicious and started conducting business in his home, which he thought would protect him. But as he shooed out callers at the end of one evening, Drusus suddenly cried out in pain thanks to a knife lodged in either his hip or groin (depending on the visual you'd prefer). Still brimming with pride despite his failures, Drusus died saying, "O my relatives and friends, will my country ever have another citizen like me?" The killers were never found and no inquest was made into the murder. Everyone just wanted to forget about this whole nasty business and let things get back to normal. But things were a long way from normal.[31]

THE CITIZENS OF Rome did not know what they were getting into when they rejected the Italian citizenship bill. Given the surprise they all showed when the Social War erupted under their feet, they were clearly oblivious to the ramifications of dropping the bill. For the Romans, it was just another rejection in a long series of rejections of Italian citizenship. No big deal. But for the Italians it was the last straw.[32]

Ignorant of the hornet's nest they had just bashed with a stick, it slowly dawned on the Romans that something might be wrong. At the very least, Silo and his march of ten thousand men was enough to put the Senate on notice that *something* was happening out there. So after Drusus's murder, the Senate dispatched agents to various Italian cities to take the temperature of the Allies. Most of these agents reported no trouble at all—at least on the surface. But in the city of Asculum, located on the far side of the Apennines northeast of Rome, a report came in that Roman citizens had been seized as hostages. A praetor hurried to the city to investigate. With the residents of Asculum on the verge of revolt anyway, they attacked the praetor and murdered him. Then the insurrectionaries rampaged through the city killing any other Roman citizen they could find. These murders marked the beginning of the revolt of Asculum and the beginning of the Social War.[33]

The speed with which the revolt spread is a testament to how long the Italians had been planning. A wide crescent covering most of east-central Italy erupted in a massive coordinated insurrection involving at least a dozen Italian tribes. The Latins remained steadfast with Rome, and the Umbrians and Etruscans kept aloof, but east-central Italy departed the Roman confederation en masse. Two principal tribes led the revolt. First were the Samnites in the south, who had chafed under Roman domination for hundreds of years and who now took the opportunity to bloody a few noses. Joining them were the Marsi in the north, among whom Silo was a principal leader. Contemporary Romans considered the Marsi to be the main drivers of the revolt and often referred to the war as the Marsic War. It was not until later that it became known as the War Against the Allies, which is how *socii*, the Latin word for "Ally," led to the Anglicized name for the conflict: the Social War.[34]

Rebel leaders from across this central Italian crescent of insurrection met in the city of Corfinium. They rechristened the city Italia and established a capital. Roman historians would describe the Italians forming a government modeled on the Roman structure of consuls, praetors, and a Senate. But in realty the structure was far more decentralized. Individual tribes operated under their own leaders, who communicated with each other via a collective war council in Italia. That council presented to Rome its central demand: Either we are equal citizens in the Republic or we are independent. The choice was *civitas* or *libertas*.[35]

With the Senate not realizing yet the scope of the crisis they were falling into, they rejected the ultimatum out of hand. So the Italian armies gathered under their local generals and launched a simultaneous uprising in late 91. Since all the Italian generals were intimately familiar with both Roman politics and war, they knew exactly what to hit first. Going all the way back to the tribal wars of the early Republic, the Romans planted Latin colonies in the backyards of defeated enemies. These communities remained outposts of Roman military authority. The first thing the Italians did was attack these Latin colonies, then seize control of the roads to cut off Rome's ability to communicate outside their own sphere in Latium. It was a simple and effective strategy that caught the Romans with their togas down.[36]

T HE POPULATION OF Rome was dumbfounded as each scrap of news from outside Rome revealed yet another city or tribe in revolt. The Senate scrambled to organize a response to the crisis. They ordered provisional governors to stay at their posts until further notice, and then assigned every consul and praetor for the year 90 to the province of Italy. It was a concentration of sovereign magistrates on the peninsula not seen since the Second Punic War.[37]

But before they could wage a war, the Roman leadership had to spend valuable time establishing which of them was to blame for the insurrection. A tribune named Quintus Varius Hybridia proposed a commission to purge those who had supported Italian citizenship and thus "incited the Italians" with false promises and selfish demagoguery.[38] Tribunes loyal to the men who might be targeted by the commission tried to veto the bill, but as was now painfully routine, a violent mob menaced the tribunes into fleeing the Assembly. The bill passed, and it was time to go head-hunting.[39]

Staffed by an all-Equestrian jury and led by ex-consul Philippus, the Varian Commission attacked its enemies with reckless abandon. At least a half-dozen prominent senators were prosecuted, including Scaurus and Antonius. The old optimates avoided conviction because they were, after all, some of the most powerful men in Rome. But their less august friends did not fare so well. Among those exiled was Gaius Aurelius Cotta, one of the young men at Crassus's house that fateful night in September 91. His exile is probably the reason he lived through the civil wars.[40]

But though Scaurus was not convicted by the Varian Commission, the princeps senatus had come to the end of the line. Now past his seventieth birthday, the old master of the Senate had lived long enough to see the Metellan faction he had led for nearly thirty years disintegrate around him. Metellus Numidicus was dead as were most of his brothers and cousins. Of the next generation, only Numidicus's son Metellus Pius showed promise. With Crassus unexpectedly dead, and their shared protégés all targeted and exiled, the faction splintered. Other families sensed the weakness of the Metelli and closed in for the kill. As the historian Velleius Paterculus notes: "Thus it is clear that, as in the case of cities and empires, so the fortunes of families flourish, wane, and pass away." While Scaurus lived, the Metellans remained a dominant power in Rome, but the old man followed his friend Crassus and died in early 89.[41]

W HILE THESE POLITICAL prosecutions unfolded, the campaign season arrived in the spring of 90, and the Romans were ready to start a counteroffensive in multiple theaters. Consul Lucius Julius Caesar[*] was assigned to the Samnites in the south, while Publius Rutilius Lupus operated in the north against the Marsi. Meanwhile, proconsul Sextus Caesar was dispatched across the Apennines to Asculum. Spread out beneath the senior magistrates were an array of legates and praetors who operated with an unusual amount of independence. Among them were the men who would define the next violent phase of Roman politics: Metellus Pius, Pompey Strabo, Cinna, Quintus Sertorius, even old Marius came out of retirement. But no one used his service in the Social War to better political advantage than Lucius Cornelius Sulla.[42]

Sulla had stayed on the sidelines during the explosive political battles of 104–100 that climaxed with Saturninus's insurrection. When things started getting back to normal in 99, Sulla made a bid for praetor but was rebuffed by the voters, the story being that the voters were not happy Sulla was trying to skip out on being aedile. He was still old friends with King Bocchus of Mauretania and the people wanted Sulla to throw some fancy African-themed games. But wanting to get on with his career, Sulla promised to throw the desired games if he was

---

* Elder cousin of THE Julius Caesar.

elected praetor. Running again the next year, he was elected. The games were magnificent.[43]

After his year in Rome, the Senate ordered Sulla to Cilicia to keep an eye on the pirates preying on Mediterranean shipping. But while in the east, he was ordered on a delicate mission. For the last few years the kings of Pontus and Bithynia had fought over the border kingdom of Cappadocia. An interminable round of squabbling between the Pontic king Mithridates VI and the Bithynian king Nicomedes III led the Senate to throw up their hands and order both Nicomedes and Mithridates to confine themselves to their own kingdoms. Cappadocia would henceforth be free of foreign tribute and govern themselves. By "govern themselves" the Senate of course meant Cappadocia would be ruled by a pro-Roman puppet king. For this job they selected a pliant young noble named Ariobarzanes. Sulla was instructed to guarantee the new puppet king's peaceful ascension to the throne.[44]

Sulla successfully installed Ariobarzanes and then traveled even farther east to settle a border dispute with the Armenians. The trip made Sulla the first Roman ambassador to formally sit down with envoys from the Parthian Empire, the heirs of the great Persian Empire in the far-off Iranian highlands. Rome and Parthia were destined for endless rounds of conflict in Syria and Mesopotamia once the Romans enveloped the Mediterranean, but at this point the Romans hadn't even moved beyond the Aegean Sea. At this first summit, however, Sulla gave the Parthians a taste of Roman manners. He laid out the chairs with himself in the middle facing the other two, making Parthia the equal not of Rome but Cappadocia. When the Parthian king found out his ambassador took this inferior seat, he had him put to death.[45]

After this successful tour, Sulla returned to Rome, and in the summer of 91 welcomed a visit from old friend King Bocchus. Bocchus brought along some magnificent works of art, which he offered for display on the Capitoline Hill. One of the pieces depicted Bocchus handing Jugurtha to Sulla—the same scene depicted on Sulla's seal. Furious at this insulting reminder that Sulla had *really* ended the Jugurthine War, Marius complained, and when rebuffed, led a party of friends up to tear the new installation out. The civil war between Marius and Sulla nearly broke out right then. But when the Social War erupted over the winter of 91–90, the two men set aside their differences. It would be the last time they fought on the same side.[46]

THE CAMPAIGNS OF 90 showed just how much more prepared the Italians were than the Romans. In the south, consul Lucius Caesar led an army thirty thousand strong into an ambush and was forced into a chaotic retreat. It wasn't until he received reinforcements from Gaul and Numidia later in the year that he was able to recover. While his campaign stalled, a Cretan mercenary approached the consul and offered his services. The Cretan said, "If by my help you defeat your enemies, what reward will you give me?" Caesar replied, "I'll make you a citizen of Rome." The Cretan scoffed: "Citizenship is considered a nonsense amongst the Cretans. We aim at gain when we shoot our arrows . . . so I have come here in search of money. As for political rights, grant that to those who are fighting for it and who are buying this nonsense with their blood." The consul laughed and said to the man, "Well, if we are successful, I will give a reward of a thousand drachmae." A Cretan could be bought for a thousand drachmae, but the Italians demanded the Romans pay in blood.[47]

Though the war in the south did not start well, at least Lucius Caesar lived. In the north, his colleague Lupus would not be so lucky. Lupus seemed well positioned to succeed; he was Gaius Marius's nephew and called his uncle to serve as a legate. But though he had an invaluable asset inside his command tent, Lupus did not use it. Marius advised his nephew to drill the new recruits before marching into battle, but Lupus was impatient and brushed off the recommendation. An entire detachment of his army was subsequently lost on patrol, and then when the Romans reached the Tolenus River, the Marsi ambushed Lupus's main army. Marius was downriver when he noticed the bodies floating by and rushed up to help. He found his nephew dead and the army in shambles. Marius took charge of the situation, regrouped the survivors, and built a strong camp. For the first time in a more than a decade, Gaius Marius was in command of an army.[48]

But Marius had plenty of enemies in the Senate who did not want him back in command of an army. So they dispatched Quintus Caepio to share the command in the north. The son of the infamous Caepio who caused the catastrophe at Arausio, Caepio the Younger was himself a tempestuous and abrasive young man. He arrived in the north without any interest in listening to the advice of Gaius Marius. Like his father before him, this arrogant disdain led him to ruin.[49]

After Caepio joined the campaign, the Marsic leader Silo boldly approached the Roman camp and requested an audience. Silo told Caepio the war was hopeless and he was ready to defect back to the Romans. As a show of good faith he offered to personally lead Caepio to the location of the Marsic army. He also presented two babies he claimed were his children and bid them to Roman custody. Caepio and a small party followed Silo to reconnoiter the spot. But as soon as they were a suitable distance removed from the Roman camp, Silo's men jumped Caepio in the darkness and killed him. The fate of the babies remains unknown.[50]

After assassinating Caepio, Silo tried to goad Marius into a fight just as the Teutones had taunted him at Aquae Sextiae. Silo said, "If you are a great general, Marius, come down and fight it out with us." But as always, Marius was smart and did not take the bait. He said, "If you are a great general, force me to fight it out with you against my will." Marius would later be accused of timidity in his old age, but from the arc of his career, we know Marius wouldn't be caught dead fighting a battle not of his own making. Gaius Marius was never considered a brilliant general in the mold of Alexander, Hannibal, or Scipio Africanus, but he was so careful in his preparations and so steady in executing his plans that he won wars no one else could win. Near the end of the year he did it again—Marius scored Rome's first victory against the Marsi.[51]

Meanwhile out in Asculum, where this had all started, the proconsul Sextus Caesar maneuvered his way toward the city. His principal legate was a rising novus homo who was attached to the command because his family estates were principally held in the region: Gnaeus Pompeius Strabo. Rendered in English as Pompey Strabo, he was the father and precursor of Pompey the Great, though at the moment his son was just a teenager preparing for his first campaign. Eventually the legions began a siege of Asculum, but over the winter Sextus Caesar himself succumbed to a camp illness and died. His legate Pompey Strabo was suddenly in charge.[52]

All these defeats and deaths of commanders came as troubling news back in Rome. As the year 90 proceeded, "many were the slaughters, sieges, and sacking of towns on both sides, during this war, victory hovering sometimes here and sometimes there . . . giving no assurance to either party which of them she favored." With casualties running high, the Senate passed a decree that all war dead would be buried where they fell rather than be brought back to Rome. They hoped to avoid scaring potential new conscripts. This was no time to discourage enlistment.[53]

HAVING NOW PROVOKED the Italians to war, the Senate suddenly woke up to the fact that they were about to lose control of the whole peninsula. The question of Italian citizenship had been floating around for fifty years, and was rejected every time it arose. But with the mortal necessity of making sure no other Italians went into revolt, the Romans finally relented. The Italians could have their citizenship.

After the consul Lucius Caesar returned to Rome to oversee the elections for the next year, he carried a bill through the Assembly: the *Lex Julia*. The *Lex Julia* offered full Roman citizenship to any Italian who had not yet taken up arms. The newly enrolled would enjoy the rights of full citizens, including protection from arbitrary abuse and the ability to vote in the Assembly. But even though it was pitched as full citizenship, the Senate could not resist a subtle catch. The entire population of Italy would be lumped into ten new tribes who would always vote last in the Assembly. With voting only proceeding until a majority of tribes agreed, the final tribes were rarely called on to vote. The Senate was willing to enfranchise the Italians, but not to let them take over the Republic. But that was for a later debate—for now the word spread that the Romans had caved and it was *civitas* for everyone.[54]

After Lucius Caesar promulgated the *Lex Julia*, he presided over the consular elections for 89 that saw Pompey Strabo elected. A severe and ambitious *novus homo*, Strabo was not particularly liked by his colleagues, but his military talent was undeniable. Strabo was cut from the same mold as Marius, an ambitious novus homo provincial who was raised to be a soldier, and disdained the pampered old men of the Senate. Strabo also had ancestral ties to Picenum, which would allow him to use his personal influence to end the war. But before he left, Strabo carried a bill through the Assembly that unilaterally conferred Latin Rights on all communities in Cisalpine Gaul north of the Po River. There had been heavy Italian migration to the region after the Cimbrian Wars, but most of the population lacked any formal rights at all. Not only would the *Lex Pompeia* prevent the war from spreading north, it gave Strabo himself a wide base of support to draw on, not only to prosecute the war against Asculum, but also to be ready for whatever happened next.[55]

Once Strabo returned to Asculum, a rising tribune named Gnaeus Papirius Carbo helped pass a further law called the *Lex Plautia Papiria*. Young Carbo was the son of the Carbo hounded to suicide by Antonius in 111, and the nephew of the Carbo hounded to suicide by Crassus in 119. It is not surprising that young Carbo bore a special hatred for such leisurely optimate scum. Just getting started in politics, Carbo passed the *Lex Plautia Papiria*, a law extending citizenship even to Italian communities still under arms. The law said that "if any men had been enrolled as citizens of the confederate cities, and if, at the time that the law was passed, they had a residence in Italy, and if within sixty days they had made a return of themselves to the praetor," then they would receive full citizenship. The *Lex Julia* and *Lex Plautia Papiria* combined to do the trick and prevent the Italian rebellion from spreading—but that did not mean there were not still plenty of Italian rebels.[56]

T HOUGH 89 WENT better than 90 for the Romans, the year still began with another dead consul. Lucius Porcius Cato* arrived to take over the troops under Marius in early 89, and like Lupus and Caepio was dismissive of the old man. Cato forced Marius to resign his legateship by claiming Marius was in poor health. But Cato promptly led his

---

* Uncle of Cato the Younger.

men in disastrous attack on a Marsic camp and was swiftly killed in the fighting.[57]

But elsewhere things went better. A nascent rebellion in Umbria and Etruria fizzled out between the promise of citizenship and a sharp campaign from the new consul Pompey Strabo—aided now by both his teenage son Pompey and a young staff officer named Marcus Tullius Cicero. Strabo then returned to Asculum and continued the siege. The Italians mustered an army numbering in the tens of thousands to dislodge Strabo, but Strabo would not be dislodged. After the last relief effort failed, despair in the city led the Italian commander in charge to lose faith in his countrymen. He threw himself a great banquet and at the end drank a goblet full of wine and poison.[58]

Its capacity to resist exhausted, Asculum finally surrendered in November 89. Strabo was not forgiving in victory. When he entered the city he had "all the leading men beaten with rods and beheaded. He sold the slaves and all the booty at auction and ordered the remaining people to depart, free indeed, but stripped and destitute." But though the sack of Asculum was expected to raise funds for the wider war, Strabo kept control of most and embezzled the rest, earning him the enmity of all sides. Everyone was soon calling Strabo the "Butcher of Asculum."[59]

The remaining rebels had counted on a quick strike to bring the Romans to their knees, but instead now faced a prolonged war. The offer of citizenship was not coming after a clear defeat—which left many Italian leaders suspicious of Roman intentions. But with the legions pressing on all sides, the Italian government decamped Italia and moved deep into Samnite territory, a region of implacable ancestral hostility to Rome. They still had plenty of men and strategic strong points, but the rebellious crescent was collapsing. Of the remaining leaders, the old Marsic general Silo was put in overall command of what was left of the Italian armies. They still had fifty thousand men under arms but could expect no further help with the promise of enfranchisement now spreading across Italy.[60]

Down in the south, Sulla finally emerged with an independent command. He was ordered to march down the coast through Campania to return wayward towns to the fold. Sulla ended up outside the gates of insurgent

Pompeii* and laid a siege. An Italian army rushed to the aid of Pompeii and defeated Sulla in their first encounter. But Sulla regrouped and sent the Italians running to the safety of nearby Nola. For his heroics during this campaign, Sulla's men awarded him the prestigious grass crown for saving a legion in battle. Now brimming with confidence, Sulla led his forces back to Pompeii and captured it. Then he turned and plunged into the territory of the Hirpini. After using a massive bonfire to torch the principal city of Aeclanum, the rest of the Hirpini surrendered and Sulla moved into Samnium, where he took the city of Bovanium. It was a run of success that made Sulla hugely popular in Rome just in time for the consular elections.[61]

B Y THE END of 89, the Social War was winding down, but the two years of conflict had devastated the population of Italy. Though ancient numbers are almost always inflated, allegedly three hundred thousand people died in the conflict, Romans and Italians being indistinguishable after funeral pyres turned their bodies to ash.[62]

Economically, the war was a disaster and crippled Italian productivity even more than the invasion of Hannibal. The lands of rich and poor alike were ruined by either plunder, neglect, or intentional destruction. Senators were cut off from their Italian estates—which would have been seized and ransacked by insurrectionary Italians. Every corner of Italy reported grain shortages and famine by the spring of 88, a famine compounded by the plebs urbana in Rome who, "like an insatiable stomach that consumes everything and yet remains always hungry . . . more wretched than all other cities that she was making wretched, left nothing untouched and yet had nothing."[63]

The chaos of the Social War also triggered a monetary crisis. As the war progressed counterfeit coins flooded the market and led families to hoard coins they knew to be good, steadily reducing the amount of good money in circulation. With the monetary market tightening and their interests in Asia threatened, the publicani bankers called in debts. But creditors were unable to meet their debts because their estates had been

---

* Yes, THAT Pompeii.

ruined in the war. Even the Republic itself was short of cash and forced to auction off land known as the "treasures of Numa," which had been set aside to fund the high priesthoods.[64]

In the midst of this crisis, a praetor named Asellio sought to ease the burden of debt for the dispossessed upper classes. He allowed debtors to sue creditors, and in the flurry of lawsuits, ruined debtors started securing exemptions from repayment. The publicani bankers, now facing ruin themselves, blamed Asellio for their misfortunes. One day, while he was offering a sacrifice in the Forum, a small gang started throwing rocks at him. Asellio fled into a nearby tavern but was cornered. An assassin slit his throat. Appian said of the incident: "Thus was Asellio, while serving as praetor, and pouring out libation, and wearing the sacred gilded vestments customary in such ceremonies . . . slain in the midst of the sacrifice." Nothing was sacred anymore.[65]

A S ACTIVE HOSTILITIES became limited to a few remaining rebel strongholds, the rest of Italy began to see what the *Lex Julia* meant in practice. A census coincidentally arrived in 89 but there had not been enough time to think through the details of who would be enrolled and who would not. This was a huge decision, as the number of incoming Italians would potentially double the citizen population. If the Italian population was distributed evenly into the thirty-five tribes they would swamp Roman voices in the Assembly. The Senate already kept the plebs urbana and *all* freedmen buried in the four urban tribes, with the rural tribes easily dominated by rich citizens who could afford to travel to Rome for elections. It wouldn't take much for the Italians to seize control of the Assembly if only a few motivated new citizens endured the expense of travel to Rome to participate in politics. So the censors "accidentally" broke a religious rite necessary to ratify the census. It had to be tossed out.[66]

The last remaining rebel armies remained intractably armed in Apulia and Samnium. With the deadline to register as a citizen long since passed, these remaining rebels could not expect the same generosity their cousins were now promised. And some among them like Silo had likely concluded that he was never going back to the Romans. The last remnants of Italia had fled south to Samnium, where they regrouped around Silo. With about thirty thousand men still under arms, Silo raised twenty thousand more. Far from preparing for a last stand, Silo reinforced Nola and recaptured Bovanium, entering the city in grand triumph to reassert Italian dignity. He still believed he could win.[67]

The Roman forces in the region were now led by Metellus Pius. The two armies finally ran into each other in Apulia in early 88, and though the ensuing battle killed only six thousand men, Silo was among them. After his death, a few Samnites and Lucanians would continue to resist, but the death of Silo marks the official end of the Social War. Down in Apulia the last remnants of the resistance cast about for aid to carry on their cause, and at least one faction looked to the aggressive power of King Mithridates of Pontus. But by then Mithridates of Pontus was already locked in his own mortal struggle with Rome.[68]

CHAPTER 10

THE RUINS OF CARTHAGE

Envoys met him on the road and asked him why
he was marching with armed forces against his
country. "To deliver her from tyrants," he replied.

APPIAN[1]

THE KINGDOM OF PONTUS STRETCHED ACROSS WHAT IS
today the Black Sea coast of Turkey. In the 500s BC the Greeks
had planted a ring of colonies around the Black Sea that were
later absorbed into the Hellenic kingdoms that emerged after the death
of Alexander the Great. The first King Mithridates of Pontus hailed from
the mountainous interior of Anatolia, but in the 280s he expanded his
domains north to the shores of the Black Sea. His successors continued
this expansion, culminating with the capture of the Greek city of Sinope
in 183. Hemmed in by east-west-running mountains, the new Kingdom
of Pontus occupied the fertile and mineral-rich strip of land between the
mountains to the south and the coast to the north. Mixing Greek and
Persian elements, the Pontic kings took advantage of the soil, metal, and
trade connections they now controlled. But in the mid-second century,
Pontus remained a minor eastern kingdom in a world full of minor eastern kingdoms.[2]

Mithridates VI was born in Sinope fifty years after it became the capital of Pontus. The eldest son of the king, Mithridates was expected to one

day reign over Pontus, but his path to power would not be easy. Like any self-respecting Hellenic king, his father was assassinated by poison in 120, leaving a power vacuum in the kingdom. With Mithridates still a minor, his mother, Queen Laodice, stepped in and took over as regent. But contrary to all parental morality, Laodice clearly favored her younger son. The teenage Mithridates dodged an assassination attempt by his mother and ran away from the palace. According to legend, Mithridates embarked on a seven-year-long training montage—hunting, swimming, reading, studying the people, learning fifty languages—until he had become the embodiment of the ideal prince. At the end of the heroic montage, Mithridates returned to Sinope in 113 and evicted his wicked mother and brother, both of whom soon died of "natural causes."[3]

Upon his ascension to the throne, Mithridates built up a mercenary army to further project Pontic authority. In the 110s, he answered a call for help from Greek cities in the Crimea, on the other side of the Black Sea, who were under attack from raiding Thracians. Mithridates expelled the Thracians and won the justifiable submission of the Crimean communities. Now joined under his benevolent protection, Mithridates controlled the entire circuit of Black Sea trade—with Russia to the north, Persia to the east, Greece and Italy to the west, and the entire Mediterranean to the south. Mithridates controlled access to wealth, resources, and manpower that would make his Black Sea empire one of the strongest powers Rome ever encountered.[4]

Early in his career, Mithridates allied with his neighbor King Nicomedes III of Bithynia to divvy up territory in Anatolia. Roman ambassadors ordered them to desist, but with Roman attention tied up with Jugurtha and the Cimbri, there was little the Romans could do. Eventually, Mithridates and Nicomedes had a falling out over control of Cappadocia, which bordered both kingdoms and served as the overland trade link between the Black Sea and the Mediterranean. In 101, Mithridates personally slit the throat of the king of Cappadocia and placed his own son on the throne. This was the settlement Mithridates wanted ratified when his ambassadors were abused in Rome by Saturninus.[5]

With Mithridates now commanding an international reputation, Gaius Marius made a point to meet the Pontic king on his circuit of the east in 98. After a conference, Marius told Mithridates, "Either strive to be stronger than Rome, or do her bidding without a word." Some say Marius already had his eye on a future war with Mithridates, but for the moment Pontus was just another random eastern kingdom. There was no reason for Marius to suspect what would become obvious a decade later: that Mithridates VI was not just Mithridates VI—he was Mithridates *the Great*.[6]

A few years later, Mithridates's ambitions provoked the Senate to intervene in Cappadocia when they ordered Sulla to place the client king Ariobarzanes on the throne. But despite this minor setback, Mithridates recovered. Not only did he secure a marriage alliance with the powerful King Tigranes I of Armenia, but his old rival Nicomedes III died in 94 leaving a mere boy on the Bithynian throne. With the Romans mired in the Social War, Mithridates induced Tigranes to invade Cappadocia while he invaded Bithynia. Both the puppet king Ariobarzanes and the boy king Nicomedes IV fled to Rome.[7]

THE REFUGEE KINGS of Cappadocia and Bithynia arrived in Rome just as the Social War was breaking out. The Senate had more important things to worry about than who controlled a few dusty goat paths in Anatolia, so they ignored the entreaties of the two young kings. To gin up interest in their plight, the kings promised lavish indemnities in exchange for help, so the Senate relented and sent an embassy to escort Nicomedes and Ariobarzanes back across the Aegean. The man they selected for the job was Manius Aquillius, Marius's former lieutenant and victor of the Second Servile War.[8]

When the Romans arrived, Mithridates and Tigranes withdrew back to their own kingdoms rather than tangle with the Romans. Reinstalling the two kings, Aquillius leaned heavily on them to make good on the lavish promises they had made back in Rome. The kings sputtered about poverty, but Aquillius told them all wealth they ever needed was in Pontus for the taking. A charitable reading of Aquillius pushing the kings to invade Pontus is that he believed Mithridates an empty shirt. So far any time the Roman gaze turned to him, the Pontic king averted his eyes and retreated to his den. But it has also been suggested that as a close friend and ally of Marius, Aquillius was deliberately provoking Mithridates so Marius could lead the eastern command he coveted. Of course, it's also possible Aquillius was just being stupid.[9]

In the spring of 89, Nicomedes IV invaded Pontus. But Mithridates was not an empty shirt, and the Pontic army sent the Bithynians limping home in a broken heap. Mithridates complained to Aquillius about the encroachment, but got no response. So the king concluded that Rome planned to use its client kingdoms to squeeze Pontus off the map. But Mithridates had no intention of being squeezed off the map. After years of careful groundwork, the king of Pontus was ready to reveal the full potential of his Black Sea empire.[10]

To get Aquillius's attention, Mithridates sent armies into Cappadocia and once again chased Ariobarzanes out of the country. Then he fortified the frontier with Bithynia and sent an embassy to Aquillius in Pergamum. These ambassadors read aloud a list of all Mithridates's foreign alliances, and gave a full accounting of the resources at his disposal—from the size of his treasury, to the number of men he could conscript, to the number of ships in his fleet. The ambassadors then said that if Rome was not careful they risked losing their dominions in Asia. It was not a declaration of war. But it was an invitation for a declaration of war.[11]

With only a single legion of true Roman soldiers at his disposal, Aquillius had to rely on local conscripts to guard the border with Pontus. But what these conscripts lacked in skill, they made up in abundance. Within a few months, Aquillius could call on four armies of 40,000 soldiers each. One army was led by Nicomedes IV, and the other three by subordinate Roman praetors. But though Aquillius soon had 150,000–200,000 men guarding every pass in and out of Bithynia, that did not mean he was a match for Mithridates. With his legitimacy based on military strength from the beginning, Mithridates's core Pontic army was trained, disciplined, and experienced. Around this core, Mithridates could call in new conscripts of his own from across the known world. In this first campaign, Mithridates marched against Aquillius with 150,000 men. At their height, the Pontic armies would bulge to 250,000 infantry and 40,000 cavalry.[12]

When Mithridates advanced on Bithynia, he crushed Aquillius's con-scripts "guarding" the passes. All four armies disintegrated and the Roman officers evacuated the mainland to the island city of Rhodes. Aquillius himself retreated to Pergamum and evacuated to the island of Lesbos. As if this land invasion was not enough, Mithridates also sent a war fleet through the Bosporus. The Romans had hired a Greek navy to block the straights, but they too disintegrated upon contact with the enemy. Now Pontic forces controlled both the land and the sea. If Aquillius had really come to provoke Mithridates into a war, he had done a fine job.[13]

Mithridates proceeded to envelope the entire province of Asia. Being an enlightened model of an ideal king, Mithridates knew exactly how to introduce himself. He announced that he was here to liberate the people of Asia from the yoke of the Roman oppression. A generation of pub-licani abuse in Asia gave Mithridates the perfect propaganda tool: he declared a five-year tax holiday and canceled all outstanding debts owed to Italians. Then, when Mithridates promised leniency to the people of Lesbos in exchange for handing over Aquillius, the people complied. Now a prisoner, Aquillius became a frequent target of humiliating jokes in Mithridates's court.[14]

W HILE AQUILLIUS LOST control of Asia, his patron Marius stewed back in Rome. After being shunted aside during the Social War, Marius had gone home and watched with increasing bitterness as the next generation of rising stars took over. Pompey Strabo was building a pow-erful base in Picenum and Cisalpine Gaul. Down in the south, Metellus Pius—son of Marius's late rival Numidicus—would soon be consul. And then there was Sulla, whose success ate at Marius most of all. Sulla's ex-ploits in Campania and Samnium were added to the list of heroic deeds on Sulla's resume that went all the way back to his capture of Jugurtha in 105. As the Social War wound down, Sulla's star burned hotter than any man's in Italy.[15]

Casting a dejected eye on the situation in Italy, Marius looked further afield for a chance to quench the thirst for glory, and spied the deterio-rating situation in Asia. But if Marius really thought he could secure an eastern command, he was deluding himself. He was almost seventy years old. The Romans did not send seventy-year-olds to run their wars. To prove he could handle the job, Marius came down to the Campus Martius daily to exercise and display his physical prowess. He cut a comic, and somewhat pathetic, figure going through his regimen. Crowds gathered to watch, some cheering him on but most "moved to pity at the sight of his greed and ambition, because, though he had risen from poverty to the greatest wealth and from obscurity to the highest place he knew not how to set bounds to his good fortune." On top of his age, Marius had already been maneuvered out of commands during the Social War, so why on earth he thought anyone would let him take five legions to Asia is a mystery. Marius was never in serious consideration for the job. The men who *were* in serious contention were off waging the Social War, not doing jumping jacks in the Forum.[16]

The consular elections in 89 were delayed until the end of the year due to the ongoing war. By then Rome probably knew about Mithridates's capture of Cappadocia and provocative letter to Aquillius. A consulship now meant a chance to run a great war in the east, and candidates came hard for the job, "every one striving to be general in the war against Mithridates, lured on by the greatness of the rewards and riches to be reaped in that war." When the elections finally came at the end of December, there was intense jockeying for the command. Sulla and his close friend Quintus Pompeius Rufus (whose son had recently married Sulla's daughter) ran as a team, with Gaius Julius Caesar Strabo Vopiscus trying to push his way in between them.[17]

But Vopiscus was trying to cut in line. He had never served as praetor and was thus ineligible. With the elections approaching, the old optimate faction in the Senate sought to block Vopiscus, who was a notoriously unstable populare. To deny Vopiscus the consulship, they turned to newly enrolled tribune Publius Sulpicius Rufus. Sulpicius seemed like the perfect guy for the job: "a man of eloquence and energy, who had earned situation by his wealth, his influence, his friendships, and by the vigor of his native ability and his courage, and had previously won great influence with the people by honorable means." Sulpicius had grown up at the feet of the Metellan optimates and was one of the young students present for the dialogue at Crassus's villa in September 91. Sulpicius vetoed Vo-piscus's request for a dispensation. But since the word of a tribune wasn't what it used to be, it took a few rounds of street clashes before Vopiscus conceded defeat.[18]

Sulla and Pompeius won the consulship and Sulla received the east-ern command—one of the signs he took to mean that fortune favored his every undertaking. Far from allowing his pride to reject the idea that his accomplishments were the result of luck, Sulla embraced Fortuna as his personal deity: "Being well endowed by nature for Fortune rather than for war, he seems to attribute more to Fortune than to his own ex-cellence, and to make himself entirely the creature of this deity." Shortly after his election he received another fortunate break—securing a new marriage to Metella, the widow of Scaurus. With this marriage, Sulla took the reins of the old Metellan faction and began to re-form it in his own image.[19]

B UT AFTER PAVING the way for the election of Sulla and Pompeius, the tribune Sulpicius turned on his optimate friends. The old Metel-lan faction seemed to be entering permanent eclipse. Crassus had died in 91. Scaurus died in 89. And of course, the cohort of six Metellan cousins had now come and gone, leaving behind only their uneven sons to carry the mantle. Despite the recent marriage of Sulla and Metella that might revive the family's fortunes, Sulpicius decided to throw in his lot with Marius. Where once Sulpicius had followed the optimate path to power, he now embraced the populares.[20]

For this betrayal, Sulpicius is roundly denounced in the sources "so that the question was not whom else he surpassed in wickedness, but in what he surpassed his own wickedness. For the combination of cruelty, effrontery, and rapacity in him was regardless of shame and of all evil." Cicero later wailed, "For why should I speak of Publius Sulpicius? Whose dignity, and sweetness, and emphatic conciseness in speaking was so great that he was able by his oratory to lead even wise men into error, and vir-tuous men into pernicious sentiments." But it would not be until the early months of 88 that Sulpicius's betrayal revealed itself.[21]

Sulpicius's turn against the optimate was not entirely unpredictable. He was known to be an "admirer and an imitator of Saturninus, except that he charged him with timidity and hesitation in his political measures." Any man who believed Saturninus timid must have had a ferocious spirit. But in Sulpicius's final analysis, it was not courage that Saturninus lacked, but organization. The Gracchi, Saturninus, and Drusus had all relied on random mobs raised in an emergency to fight their battles. So Sulpicius's great contribution to Roman politics was the invention of the professional street gang. Surrounding himself with three hundred armed men of Equestrian rank whom he called the Anti-Senate, Sulpicius also kept thousands of mercenary swordsmen on retainer. If Sulpicius gave the word they would be ready to fight.[22]

But beyond his alliance with Marius, Sulpicius saw that his real path to power went through the Italians. In early 88, he proposed a law to recall the men exiled by the anti-Italian Varian Commission. And with the question of civitas for the Italians settled, Sulpicius announced his intention to give them full *suffragium* to go with it. Rather than bury the Italians in new tribes that voted last, or lump them into the four urban tribes, Sulpicius planned to disperse them equally throughout the 31 rural tribes. If Sulpicius carried this measure, the Italians could command majorities in the Assembly. Sulpicius would not just win a new host of grateful clients, he would control the Assembly itself.[23]

Both the Senate and the plebs urbana were threatened by Sulpicius's proposal. Old noble patrons, working merchants, and common artisans alike could see the Roman voice in government was about to be diminished and wanted the Italians kept separate, "so that they might not, by being mingled with the old citizens, vote them down in the elections by force of numbers." Having surrendered the issue of citizenship, the Romans built a new line at suffrage. Sulpicius's proposal led to clashes in the streets between angry plebs urbana and the Anti-Senate.[24]

With these riots breaking out, Sulla was at his camp at Nola. As soon as he heard the news, he hurried back to Rome. When he reached the Forum, Sulla and his colleague Pompeius staged a dramatic intervention. Tribunician vetoes not being what they once were, they decided to see how Sulpicius liked a taste of full consular authority. Standing on the rostra of the

Temple of Castor and Pollux, Sulla and Pompeius used their religious authority to declare a *feriae*, a holiday that triggered the cessation of all public business. Sulpicius did not care for this taste of this consular authority, but instead of meekly submitting, his Anti-Senate pulled out hidden weapons. With the crowds hostile and the threats getting specific, Sulla and Pompeius retreated from the rostra. The consuls got away but Pompeius's son was not so lucky. An outspoken defender of his father, the younger Pompeius went too far, and Sulpicius's gang killed him on the spot.[25]

Sulla found the closest safe haven near at hand: Marius's house at the foot of the Palatine Hill. What was said between the two men is unknown, but Marius must have told Sulla the only way he was getting out of this alive was to rescind the feriae and allow the vote on Sulpicius's laws to proceed. Left with no other choice, Sulla agreed. It would be the last time they were in the same room together.[26]

Emerging from his consultation with Marius, Sulla remounted the rostra and withdrew the holiday decree, allowing public business to return to normal. Then he departed the Forum. Cleared of these distractions, Sulpicius convened the Assembly and carried his bills on Italian suffrage. Then he tossed in the surprise kicker, something no one was expecting. He convinced the Assembly to withdraw Sulla's appointment to the eastern command and transfer it to Marius. Already on his way back to the army, Sulla had no idea he had just lost his job.[27]

THE SIX LEGIONS Sulla led during the Social War were still camped outside Nola. This army had been fighting under Sulla for a year, and he had earned their devoted loyalty. Sulla always had an easygoing rapport with common soldiers. Though he had the unmistakable air of an arrogant aristocrat, he never shirked his duty or let his men down. And now that he had been elected consul, he was about to lead them east to pacify some wayward king on the far side of the Aegean. Fighting a civil war in your own backyard is neither fun nor profitable, but conquering a rich eastern kingdom sounded mighty fine indeed. So as the soldiers sat around Nola waiting for Sulla to come back, they dreamed of the campaign to come.[28]

When Sulla returned a few days later he likely did not ride with his usual resplendent vigor. He was still consul, and still slated to run the eastern war, but he had been embarrassed in the head-to-head confrontation with Sulpicius and Marius. He had been forced by violence to humiliate himself and withdraw his own decree. Sulla's agitation turned to fury when a messenger arrived bearing the incredible news: The Assembly had stripped Sulla of the eastern command. Gaius Marius would now lead the expedition.[29]

The shock of the revelation cannot be understated. Old Marius's pathetic pursuit of the command was well known. His calisthenics out on the Campus Martius were a joke, not a prelude to getting the job. Especially not after Sulla had won the consulship *and* drawn the Mithridatic command. But after years of enduring Sulla's arrogant vanity, Marius was finally ready to get his revenge. His plan was to bury Sulla under a wave of humiliations from which Sulla could not recover. Following either the letter of the law or the unwritten codes of mos maiorum would be the end of Sulla; if he wanted to survive he was going to have to break both.

This news of the change in command would have been impossible to contain. Restless shockwaves rippled through the camps at Nola. What happened next? Was Sulla still their commander? Were they still going east? Then the notice went around that Sulla planned to address his troops. Throughout Roman history, generals had addressed their troops only to discuss military business—usually matters of pay, discipline, and strategy. Now for the first time, a Roman general delivered a political speech to his men. Sulla described what had happened back in Rome, told them about his maltreatment at the hands of Marius and Sulpicius, and then revealed the latest outrage: he had been stripped of the eastern command. The soldiers were outraged—not only at the treatment of their chief, but also out of fear that they would be left behind. Marius had his own vast recruiting network of veterans, friends, and clients to draw on. The troops under Sulla's command were likely to be left in Italy and miss out on the riches they had already spent in their minds.[30]

Believing he had successfully euthanized Sulla's political career, Marius began the process of taking over the legions and sent two military tribunes to Nola with orders to remove Sulla from command. These two guys—whose names are unrecorded—became unfortunate early casualties of the Civil War. Assuming command of the army was supposed to be a matter of routine paperwork, but when the two officers arrived they were seized by Sulla's inflamed legions and stoned to death.[31]

With his men ready to follow him anywhere, Sulla took a conference with his senior officers and made his audacious proposal. If Sulpicius and Marius were going to run roughshod over consular authority, then they were going to have to live with the consequences. Sulla told them he was going to lead his six legions back to Rome. Almost to a man his officers refused to participate in any such march. Never before had a Roman general marched legionaries against Rome itself. So left with only a quaestor and some centurions, Sulla led his legions onto the Via Appia and began a slow march on Rome.[32]

SULLA WAS NOT in any great hurry. He hoped the very fact of his approach would have the intended effect of forcing Marius and Sulpicius to back down. Unlike Marius, whose entire career was built on careful planning, Sulla was likely improvising each step and trusting himself to the goddess Fortuna. He later said, "Of the undertakings which men thought well-advised, those upon which he had boldly ventured, not after deliberation, but on the spur of the moment, turned out for the better." For now it was enough that his army was moving toward Rome—what he would do when he got there was anyone's guess. Including Sulla himself.[33]

Sulla's march triggered a flurry of activity in Rome. Sulpicius used his own considerable powers as tribune, combined with Marius's new military authority, to seize control of the situation. Partisans of Sulla were identified and assassinated, while the Senate was cowed into submission by Sulpicius's Anti-Senate. Those who managed to dodge the assassins, including the consul Pompeius, slipped out of Rome for the safety of Sulla's army. On the other side, many soldiers—either for personal or patriotic reasons—refused to help Sulla conquer Rome. They deserted the march and raced ahead to Rome. This created a whirlwind of movement,

as families coming to and from Rome jammed the streets, both sides carrying exaggerated rumors and reports about the situation in the old camp.
Marius is murdering everyone! Sulla wants to raze Rome! Needless to say,
it was not a time for careful contemplation.[34]

The old guard in the Senate found themselves adrift in this chaotic
storm. Certainly not friends with Marius and Sulpicius, they were now
equally horrified that Sulla was marching six legions against Rome.
So a moderate faction of senators attempted to find a way to broker a
peace. They dispatched two praetors to Sulla's approaching army, but
with both linked to the Marians, Sulla scoffed at their demands. The
praetors themselves were then severely maltreated. Though they got
out alive, Sulla's men smashed their symbols of office and tore off their
togas. They returned to the Senate in a pitiful state. The Senate then
sent another group of envoys who asked Sulla why he was marching his
army against his own country, to which Sulla responded: "To deliver her
from tyrants."[35]

When Sulla arrived at the outskirts of Rome he invited the Senate to
further talks. The Senate's representatives revealed that they had already
decreed Sulla be given his command back. But everyone knew their decree
was useless if Sulpicius controlled the Assembly. To bridge the impasse,
Sulla said he was prepared to meet Marius and Sulpicius out on the Campus Martius and would pitch camp until a summit could be arranged.[36]

But as soon as the envoys left Sulla told his men to suit up for battle. Word had already reached him that his friends inside the city were
turning up dead. He also learned that Marius and Sulpicius were arming
their supporters, promising freedom to slaves and gladiators who fought
for them. The tales coming out of the city were more exaggerated than
Sulla realized at the time. The call for slaves to join turned up a pitiful
response; six veteran legions were marching on Rome—any slave who
joined Marius would likely enjoy his freedom for all of five minutes before dying in the service of another man's ambitions. But not knowing
how weak the Marians really were, Sulla wanted to quickly secure a decisive victory. He ordered one of his legions forward to capture and hold
the Esquiline Gate.[37]

Marius and Sulpicius were alerted that Sulla's men were moving and they prepared their own forces for battle. The two sides clashed in the forum of the Esquiline Hill. Marian partisans beat back the encroaching legionaries and pelted them from rooftops with tiles. Appian says that after a generation of street fights, this was "the first fought in Rome with bugle and standards in full military fashion, no longer like a mere faction fight. To such extremity of evil had the recklessness of party strife progressed among them." With fighting under way, Sulla turned up personally with reinforcements and used archers with flaming arrows to drive the Marians off the roofs.[38]

The Marians could hold against a single legion but never six, and they fell back as Sulla entered the city. Marius took temporary refuge in the Temple of Tellus and called for the citizens of Rome to join him in this patriotic defense against Sulla's treacherous invasion—but his call went unheeded. To the plebs urbana, this was a grudge match between nobles that they wanted no part of. With Sulla seizing control of the main streets, Marius, Sulpicius, and their chief accomplices fled the city.[39]

SULLA MARCHED THROUGH Rome following the path of Roman triumphs toward the Capitoline Hill. With a last clutch of Marians having captured the Capitoline Hill, Sulla led an entire legion across the Pomerium, the sacred inner boundary of Rome, within which no citizen was to bear arms. One of the last and most sacred lines of mos maiorum had been crossed.[40]

Sulla was now left in the awkward position of being the first Roman to ever conquer Rome. He went out of his way to deflect the odium, singling out men under his command caught looting and punishing them for all to see. After a nervous night during which both he and Pompeius stayed up until dawn crisscrossing the city to make sure everything was under control, Sulla called for a public meeting the next morning in the Forum.[41]

When the crowd assembled, Sulla told them that his anger was only directed at a few select enemies. To prove his point, he announced the names of just twelve men he now considered enemies of the state. Marius and Sulpicius were at the top of the list. As public enemies, these twelve could now be killed on sight. But Sulla stressed that other than those twelve men, the rest of the population could expect no further trouble— even if they had taken part in the fighting. Sulla just wanted things to go back to normal.[42]

But by "normal" Sulla did not just mean the way things had been the day before. He wanted the Romans to return to their roots. He said that the Republic had fallen into a terrible state of disrepair and needed to return to the virtuous constitution of their elders. A bill presented to the Assembly should first gain approval from the Senate. Voting should be heavily tilted toward major landowners. Taking a page from Drusus's re- forms, Sulla proposed adding three hundred Equestrians to the Senate to bulk up their numbers and make the institution robust and powerful again. But before he got those wider reforms dispensed, Sulla addressed more specific business. He announced that every law passed since Sulla and Pompeius declared the holiday was null and void. Sulla and Pom- peius would still be consuls. Sulla would still have the eastern command. The plan to disperse the Italians throughout the thirty-one rural tribes would disappear into thin air.[43]

Under the watchful eye of the Sullan legions, the Assembly turned Sulla's suggestions into law. But after the reforms passed, Sulla sent his men back to Nola to prove that he was not a tyrant or a king. The Senate was, by now, convulsed with mixed emotions. Sulla was clearly acting as their savior and benefactor, but they bristled at Sulla's pretensions to now be the patron of the Senate—as if they were now his clients. And crossing the Pomerium with an entire army was unforgivable sacrilege.[44]

But Sulla studiously maintained that he was following a chain of prec- edent that linked Opimius in 121, to Marius in 100, to Sulla here in 88. What he had done was no different than what they had done: he took extraordinary consular action to quell a violent political faction. But of course, both Opimius and Marius had operated under the senatus con- sultum ultimum. The Senate had passed no such decree this time. Sulla acted under his own authority only. Legal scholars in the Senate were vexed, but Sulla's legions spoke for themselves.

THE RUINS OF CARTHAGE

I N THE AFTERMATH of their defeat, the inner-circle Marians bolted out of Rome in every direction. Sulpicius ran for the coast but never made it outside the vicinity of Rome. Within a day of taking flight he was betrayed by a slave and executed the moment he was apprehended. Sulla later thanked the slave and said the man "deserved freedom in return for his services in giving information about the enemy." But as soon as the manumission was complete Sulla "decreed that he should be hurled from the Tarpeian Rock because he had betrayed his master."[45]

Marius, meanwhile, fled that night to one of his estates twelve miles outside the city with his son, grandson, and a small party of loyal partisans. Knowing they could not stay in the area they agreed to sail for North Africa, where they would take refuge in the veteran colonies set up in the wake of the Numidian war. These communities had been planted more than fifteen years ago, but hopefully they would remember their former general and patron.[46]

The next morning Marius and his party set sail from Ostia. Marius's ship was not quite one hundred miles down the Italian coast when storms threw her against the shore near the city of Terracina. With the ship wrecked, the party had to continue on foot. Knowing Terracina was currently run by one of his enemies, Marius led the party along the coast toward the city of Minturnae, where Marius said he had friends. On the way, some shepherds told them the countryside was lousy with Sulla's cavalry patrols. Unable to complete the trip before nightfall, Marius and his beleaguered compatriots spent a miserable night hiding in the woods without food or shelter.[47]

The next morning, Marius led the party back to the shore to continue the walk to Minturnae. While they walked, Marius lifted their spirits by telling them a story from his childhood. When he was a boy he saw an eagle's nest fall from a tree. Gathering the nest in his cloak, he saw that it contained seven tiny eagles. As an eagle traditionally lays no more than two eggs, the unprecedented little flock was a fabulous find. His parents took the birds to a local seer to inquire if it had any special meaning. The seer was amazed and said their son would "be most illustrious of men, and was destined to receive the highest command and power seven times." Now on the run and condemned as enemies of the state, Marius reminded his friends that this could not possibly be the end for he had only been consul six times and was yet destined for one more. Somehow, some way, he would be consul again.[48]

But just miles from Minturnae, they were spotted by a cavalry patrol. With nowhere to turn, someone in Marius's party saw two ships sailing close to shore. Without waiting for permission from the sailors, the fugitives jumped in the water and swam. Most of the party reached one boat, forced the sailors to take them on board, and used very colorful threats to force the captain to sail them away. The older and slower Marius meanwhile dragged himself aboard the second boat and presented himself to the dumbfounded captain.[49]

The cavalry detachment hailed the captain from shore and said the wet old man on his boat was the fugitive Gaius Marius. The captain now faced the dilemma Marius would impose on everyone he met during his ordeal: hand over Marius and risk the wrath of his friends, or protect Marius and risk the wrath of his enemies. The captain decided he could not hand Marius over and sailed away. Not immediately following the boat that had sped off with Marius's companions, the captain steered the craft to the mouth of a nearby river. The captain told Marius to go ashore, rest, and gather some provisions from the trip. As soon as Marius disembarked the captain sailed away. His solution to the dilemma was to set Marius down and run away.[50]

The abandoned Marius sat for a time and contemplated his sorry state. Then he picked himself up and moved inland, tromping through swampland, still aiming for Minturnae. With night falling, he ran into a peasant and begged shelter for the night. The peasant complied, but then a cavalry patrol rode up and banged on the door. While the frightened peasant confessed everything, Marius tore off his clothes and dove into a nearby swamp. He hid in the murky water with "his eyes and nostrils alone showing above the water." But the patrol found him anyway. Gaius Marius, six-time consul and Third Founder of Rome, was dragged out of the swamp "naked and covered with mud." Then he was led into Minturnae by a rope around his neck.[51]

Though it had only been five days since Sulla had captured Rome, word had already spread that the fugitive Marius was to be killed on sight. But the leaders of Minturnae anguished over the dilemma of what to do with him. After placing Marius under house arrest they brought out a slave and ordered him to go kill Marius. According to the story, this slave was either Gallic or Cimbric and thus likely made a slave by Marius himself. Overawed rather than filled with vengeance, the slave refused. He said, "I cannot kill Gaius Marius," and ran out of the room.[52]

Unable to kill Marius, the leaders of Minturnae decided to put him on a boat: "Let him go where he will as an exile, to suffer elsewhere his allotted fate. And let us pray that the gods may not visit us with their displeasure for casting Marius out of our city in poverty and rags." From the mainland, he sailed to the island of Aenaria, on the north end of the Bay of Naples, where he reunited with the men he had been separated from. Finally able to point themselves toward Africa, they sailed around Sicily, eventually putting in at Eryx on the northeast coast for supplies. But the quaestor in Eryx had been alerted to Marius's general route and pounced as soon as the Marians put ashore. After a bloody battle on the docks that left sixteen dead, Marius and his remaining men cut loose their ship and put back out to sea.[53]

Finally, Marius landed on the island of Cercina off the coast of Africa. One of his veteran colonies had been established on the island after the Numidian war and he was welcomed into the homes of the inhabitants. The governor of Africa, meanwhile, had been told Marius was likely heading toward him and now faced the great dilemma of the fugitive Marius. The governor's duty was clear—he must arrest Marius and kill him. But the province was full of Marius's veterans. If the governor killed Marius, he was likely signing his own death warrant.[54]

After a few days, Marius crossed to the mainland and was greeted by an official bearing a decree from the governor: "The governor forbids you, Marius, to set foot in Africa; and if you disobey, he declares that he will uphold the decrees of the senate and treat you as an enemy of Rome." Dejected, Marius sat brooding. When the official finally asked for Marius's reply, the old general said, "Tell him, then, that you have seen Gaius Marius a fugitive, seated amid the ruins of Carthage." Not far from where Scipio Aemilianus had once wept tears of dread foreboding, old Marius now sat and "as he gazed upon Carthage, and Carthage as she beheld

Marius, might well have offered consolation the one to the other." He did not fight the decree and returned to Cercina.[55]

MEANWHILE, FAR OFF to the east, Mithridates had completed the envelopment of Anatolia. Because he needed the entire region to be united in opposition to Rome, the Pontic king ordered a blood pact. As spring gave way to summer in 88, Mithridates sent out a letter to every Asian city now under his dominion. As a sign of mutual solidarity the local magistrates were to wait thirteen days after receipt of the letter and then apprehend and murder every Italian in their jurisdiction—including women and children.[56]

Under the circumstances, there was little anyone could do but comply. No one was going to risk the wrath of Mithridates just to save a few Italians they didn't really like anyway. So on the thirteenth day after receiving the letter, every city across Asia arrested and systematically executed all resident Italians. Informers were offered a share of confiscated Italian property, leading neighbor to betray neighbor. Each city soon had a pile of bodies. In total, the dead numbered as many as eighty thousand people. Mithridates himself undertook the central sacrifice of this gruesome pact. Bringing out the captured Manius Aquillius, Mithridates ordered molten gold poured down his throat. There was no going back now. The massacre of the Italians was an act of calculated genocide to bind the eastern cities against Rome. Each was now individually complicit in the murder of Romans. It was now either fight and win with Mithridates, or face the vengeance of Rome alone.[57]

CHAPTER 11

THE SPIKED BOOTS

Prosperity tries the souls of even the wise; how
then should men of depraved character make
a moderate use of victory?

SALLUST[1]

B ACK IN ROME, SULLA PRESIDED OVER THE CONSULAR ELEC-
tions for 87 BC and used them as an opportunity to further
demonstrate he was not the tyrant his enemies made him out to
be. Having already ordered his troops to vacate the city, Sulla now publicly refused to interfere with the election. Even as men hostile to him
stood for the consulship.[2]

Chief among these candidates was Lucius Cornelius Cinna. Cinna
burst onto the historical stage here in the consular election for 87, and for
the next four years would hold a dominant position in Roman politics.
But about this man who is so critical to Roman history, we know almost
nothing. Here is what we *do* know: He came from the same patrician
Cornelii family as Sulla, but the "Cinna" branch left almost no trace. His
father was probably the consul for 127, but we cannot be sure. Cinna
himself was probably elected praetor for 90 or 89, and served as a legate during the Social War. But that is all we know. The rest of Cinna's
life—his family, his rise up the cursus honorum, his campaigns, success,
failures—has been lost to history.[3]

We can, however, speculate with some confidence that Cinna was born no later than 130, probably a few years earlier. This meant he was hitting his twenties just as the Cimbri were appearing in Gaul and Jugurtha was running loose in Numidia. Fulfilling his ten years of military service during this period, Cinna likely either served in Numidia or on the recurring campaigns against the Cimbri. But though these campaigns are well documented by Roman historians, and featured major figures like Marius and Sulla, Cinna is never mentioned. His name never appears, even in passing. Given his later political leanings, though, it seems likely he served in the north under Marius and alongside the Italians whose cause he would later champion.[4]

But though Cinna was likely sympathetic to Marius, he was not among those twelve principal Marian leaders named by Sulla. It is highly unlikely Cinna took part in the fighting surrounding Sulla's first march on Rome. He might not have even been in Rome at the time, but rather out with one of Rome's various armies stomping out the last smoldering flames of the Social War. If Cinna did not return to Rome until after Sulla captured the city, he would be untainted by the entire affair and able to effectively tap those united by a common abhorrence of Sulla's march on Rome. It is possible he ran on a platform of bringing Sulla to trial for his conduct.[5]

But even with Cinna making noise about political prosecution, Sulla refused to take the bait. Disqualifying Cinna would prove that Sulla was exactly what his enemies said he was. There were multiple candidates in the race, but Sulla refused to help or hinder any of them. The other strongest candidate was Gnaeus Octavius. An old optimate conservative, Octavius was no friend of Marius and supported Sulla's reforms in theory—but the way Sulla had gone about it burned him to the edges of his toga. Octavius could not be counted on to stand in the way if Cinna decided to prosecute Sulla.[6]

When election day came, the Assembly elected Cinna and Octavius consuls. Sulla put a fine face on the election and said it was the ultimate proof that his enemies lied when they called him a tyrant. Would a tyrant let a man like Cinna be consul? The answer is no. Whatever Sulla's crimes, raw tyrannical power was never his object. Sulla was fundamentally a conservative republican; the power he would acquire during his career was always at the service of conservative republican morality. At least in his own mind.

But though he accepted the election of Cinna, Sulla was not without tricks. As the man who would administer the oath of office to the new consuls, Sulla forced them to swear an oath that they would not disturb his political reforms. In front of a large crowd, the incoming consuls swore the oath, and cast a stone on the ground to accept the punishment of exile if they broke their word.[7]

As he vacated the consulship, Sulla could rest easy knowing that as long as he held his military command he would be shielded from political prosecution. To offer the same protection for his friend and colleague Pompeius, Sulla arranged for Pompeius to take over Rome's army at Asculum. Pompey Strabo had been at his post for three years, and now that the siege was over, it was time for a change in command. At Sulla's insistence, the Senate directed Pompeius to take over Strabo's army. This would not only protect Pompeius personally, but it would give Sulla a reliable army stationed just over the Apennines if Rome should make trouble while Sulla was in the east. But neither Pompey Strabo nor his men appreciated the abrupt change in command. Within days of his arrival in camp, Pompeius was unceremoniously murdered. The assailants were never caught, but Strabo himself was naturally suspected of masterminding the assassination.[8]

The murder of Pompeius shocked Sulla, and Rome suddenly felt less safe. Sulla kept himself under a tight bodyguard as he wrapped up a few last pieces of business in Rome. Within a few days, he departed for the safety of his legions at Capua.[9]

It did not take long for Cinna to break his oath after assuming the consulship in January 87. At the first opportunity, Cinna dispatched a tribune to indict Sulla for the illegal murder of Roman citizens. Sulla could plead senatus consultum ultimum all he wanted, but unlike Opimius in 121, and Marius in 100, the Senate never issued the Final Decree to Sulla in 88. But since a tribune's authority only extended to the city limits of Rome, Sulla ignored the charges and instead continued mobilizing his legions to head east. He left one legion behind to maintain the siege of Nola and moved the other five down to the southeastern port of Brundisium (modern-day Brindisi). From there they would depart for Greece.[10]

Unable to prevent Sulla from leaving Italy, Cinna shredded the rest of the sacred oath he had sworn. Making a bid for widespread Italian support, he announced that he was going forward with Sulpicius's program to disperse the Italians evenly through the thirty-one rural tribes. His colleague Octavius was appalled at the broken oath and rallied both conservative opinion and armed gangs.[11]

With political debates now inevitably decided in the streets, both sides rallied large groups of menacing partisans. Cinna called in throngs of Italians while Octavius mustered the plebs urbana, who were acutely aware they would be buried forever if the Italians were distributed evenly throughout the tribes. Inside Rome, the plebs urbana outnumbered the Italians, so when the two sides clashed, Cinna was forced to flee the city. Octavius then induced the Assembly to strip Cinna not just of his consulship, but his citizenship. To replace Cinna, the Assembly elevated a nonentity named Merula. His selection was not an accident—Merula was a member of an obscure priesthood that forbid participation in almost any public business. Octavius would wield sole power in Rome.[12]

But despite being outnumbered in Rome, Cinna had the numerical advantage everywhere else. The Italians were now aware the fight for political equality had moved from civitas to suffragium. They all now held Roman citizenship thanks to the Lex Julia, but knew they would have to keep fighting for the right to participate equally in elections. With Cinna promising full and equal suffrage, the communities that had lately been fighting for "Italia" readily agreed to fight for Cinna. After leaving Rome, Cinna ran a circuit south through Tibur, Praeneste, and Nola that saw him raise more than ten legions.[13]

Cinna also had links to a large network of disaffected nobles he could call on to join him. Gnaeus Papirius Carbo—last seen in 89 passing a citizenship bill on behalf of the Italians—rallied forces of his own and joined Cinna. Also joining was Quintus Sertorius, a young officer who had shown loyal service to Marius while running supply networks out of Cisalpine Gaul during the Social War. Sertorius bore an implacable hatred of Sulla that would make him the last Marian general carrying on the Civil War, even after the rest were dead or defeated.[14]

As he raised Italian legions, Cinna also induced the defection of the single legion left behind by Sulla to maintain the siege of Nola. Addressing the legion, Cinna dramatically laid his symbols of office down on the ground and said, "From you, citizens, I received this authority. The people voted it to me; the Senate has taken it away from me without your consent. Although I am the sufferer by this wrong I grieve amid my own troubles equally for your sakes . . . Where will after this be your power in the Assemblies, in the elections, in the choice of consuls, if you fail to confirm what you bestow, and whenever you give your decision fail to secure it." Cinna then fell to the ground and lay there until the men picked him up, returned the symbols of office, and swore an oath to follow him.*[15]

While Cinna forged this huge army, his consular colleague Octavius could call on few forces beyond the plebs urbana. The armies of Pompey Strabo remained near Asculum, but Strabo's loyalties were unclear. Strabo was his own man and would not likely subordinate himself to Cinna, but he was also furious at Sulla for the attempt to strip him of his army. Cinna skillfully exploited Strabo's anger and vanity, and proposed an alliance sealed by a shared consulship in 86. If Cinna and Strabo joined forces they would be stronger than any other faction in Italy—and more than a match even for Sulla when their shared enemy returned from the east.[16]

The only other army Octavius could call on were the legions of Metellus Pius. But Pius was pinned down trying to subdue the last of the Samnites and could not break away. In desperation, the Senate ordered Pius to cut a deal with the Samnites to end the war so he could come back to Rome. Aware they were in a strong bargaining position, the Samnites demanded "citizenship be given not alone to themselves but also to those who had deserted to their side"; they also "refused to give up any of the booty which they had, and demanded back all the captives and deserters from their own ranks." But Pius refused to let the rebels retire on such generous terms. Cinna jumped at Pius's hesitation. He sent a hard-line

---

* They were also pretty mad Sulla had left them behind.

Marian partisan named Gaius Flavius Fimbria to present his own terms
to the Samnites: Cinna would accept their demands if they joined his
fight against Octavius. The Samnites agreed. Rome trembled.[17]

A FTER THE SLAUGHTER of the Italians, Mithridates ruled Asia
unchallenged in 87. Most of Asia had already accepted the king's
generous terms, but a few stubborn cities like Rhodes held out. With
his opening gambit such a success, Mithridates let his ambitions grow.
He now planned to cast himself as the liberator of Greece, expel the
Romans, and reign over an empire that stretched from the Black Sea to
the Adriatic.[18]

While the king himself stayed behind in Asia to integrate the new domains, he sent out a two-pronged invasion of Greece in early 87. On land,
an army of mercenary Thracians descended on Macedonia. By sea, the main
Pontic army sailed under the command of General Archelaus. Archelaus
had been one of Mithridates's longest-serving generals, and even tangled
directly with Sulla in Cappadocia over the installation of the puppet king
Ariobarzanes in 95. Archelaus sailed his massive fleet across the Aegean
Sea to Athens. There, with the help of a friendly political faction, he secured an Athenian declaration of allegiance to Mithridates. The Athenians
knew their declaration meant war with Rome, but with Archelaus's fleet
already bobbing in their harbor, Rome's vengeance was a distant threat.[19]

When Athens went over to Mithridates, most of Greece followed its
lead. With the entire region throwing off Roman authority, only the few
lonely legions under the command of a praetor named Sura remained
to hold the line. Guarding the Macedonian frontier, Sura fended off the
Thracian invasion, but unless he was reinforced, Rome would lose Greece
as quickly as they had lost Asia. Luckily for the beleaguered praetor, help
was on the way.[20]

Leaving his domestic troubles behind, Sulla sailed across the Adriatic in the spring of 87. As he marched his five legions east, every city he
passed declared their undying loyalty to Rome—because of course they
did, what would you do? But unexpectedly, Archelaus did not march his
own army out to halt Sulla's advance. This allowed Sulla to march all the

way to the walls of Athens. Upon arrival, he demanded the city surrender. When the Athenians refused, Sulla ordered siege lines built around the city. But there was a problem—Archelaus controlled the seas. As long as the Pontic navy occupied the harbor of Piraeus, the Romans could never break the siege. To deal with this problem, Sulla dispatched one of his most loyal officers, Lucius Licinius Lucullus,* to make a circuit of the various eastern kingdoms and demand they provide ships for Rome. While he waited for Lucullus to return, Sulla camped in front of Athens. While outside Athens, he received reports about the situation back in Italy. He did not like what he heard, but the most unsettling bit of news was that Gaius Marius had returned.[21]

M ARIUS MADE PREPARATIONS to leave his temporary safe haven on the island of Cercina as soon as he heard Cinna was raising an army of Italians, many of whom would have been Marian veterans. Within a few weeks he cobbled together a small army of loyalists drawn from the inhabitants of Africa, including an infamous band of three hundred Illyrian bodyguards. Dubbed the "Spiked Boots," these cold-blooded mercenaries would show little sympathy for spluttering Romans begging for their lives.[22]

When he sailed back to Italy, Marius swung north of Rome and landed in Etruria. The Third Founder of Rome was beloved here among the northern Italians. Marius had delivered them from the Cimbri, and then generously expanded the rights and privileges of those who served under him. These Etruscan communities were outraged that the great Marius had been chased out of Rome like a common criminal. When Marius landed, "his flight and exile had added a certain awe to his high reputation," and he raised new recruits everywhere he went. Marius soon commanded a personal legion six thousand strong. This force was not as large as the vast army controlled by Cinna, but it was enough to get Marius an audience. Far from the power hungry lunatic he is occasionally

---

* Son of the Lucullus who behaved so disgracefully during the Second Servile War. Also probably the unnamed quaestor who remained with Sulla for the march on Rome.

portrayed as being, Marius met Cinna and scrupulously placed himself under Cinna's command. Cinna was, after all, still consul. Cinna appreciated the gesture and invited Marius into his war council.[23]

This senior war council—now including Cinna, Carbo, Sertorius, and Marius—devised a strategy to surround and blockade Rome. Marius would capture the critical port of Ostia. Cinna would take Arminium and Placenta. Carbo's legions would stake out the upper Tiber River. When they were all in place Rome would be strangled. But even as he watched these enemy forces fan out, back inside Rome, Octavius refused to surrender.[24]

Octavius's stubborn resilience was soon rewarded. After considering all his options, Pompey Strabo decided to fight Cinna rather than join him. With Metellus Pius trapped in Samnium, and Sulla in Greece, Strabo knew the walls of Rome were being defended by an irregular militia of plebs urbana who would never stand against tens of thousands of veteran soldiers. Especially not after those Italians had cut off Rome's access to food and water. So Strabo decided there was an opportunity to play savior. If he swooped in to deliver Rome from the threat he would not only make himself a hero to the Senate and People of Rome, he would be left as the most powerful general in Italy.[25]

Having completed their envelopment of the surrounding countryside, Cinna's forces finally launched a direct assault on Rome in late 87. But reinforced by Strabo, the city withstood the attack. It appeared that Strabo really would be the hero of the hour—but then fate dealt one of its most famous blows. Over the winter of 87–86, plague swept through legionary camps, and more than ten thousand died, among them Pompey Strabo. He was disliked by all, so much so that a sensationalized story circulated that fate struck him dead with lightning. The sudden death of Strabo changed the entire political and military dynamic of the conflict. When Cinna and Marius returned to Rome next time, there would be no one standing in their way.[26]

A FTER THE SHOCKING death of Strabo, the Senate despaired at its chances of surviving the siege. To keep the war going, Octavius slipped out of the city and joined with his strongest supporters, Metel-

lus Pius and Marcus Crassus Dives.* Operating in the Alban Hills near
Rome, Octavius tried to raise levies from the Latin communities that had
stayed loyal through the Social War. But he could not raise troops fast
enough, and with Cinna's army preparing to march on Rome again, the
Senate ordered Metellus Pius to go negotiate a peace. Cinna's first demand
was that Pius treat him as consul. He said, "I left Rome as consul, and I
will not return there as a private man." After a few rounds of negotiations,
the Senate agreed to Cinna's terms. The recently elevated priest-consul
Merula formally resigned. In exchange, Cinna said he would not pur-
posefully kill anyone when he reentered the city. But no one could miss
Marius standing behind Cinna glowering ominously. As soon as these
negotiations were complete, Metellus Pius prudently withdrew himself
to Africa.[27]

Settlement in hand, the Senate ordered the gates of Rome opened. The
restored consul Cinna entered the city at the head of an army. But for the
moment, Marius did not follow. The old man refused to enter until his
status as an enemy of the state was formally repealed. So as soon as he
entered the city, Cinna arranged for the Assembly to lift the ban on the
twelve Marian exiles and restore their civil dignity. He then induced the
Assembly to turn the tables on the man who had engineered the expulsion of the Marians. Under Cinna's close watch the Assembly declared
Sulla an enemy of the state.[28]

With his dignity restored, Marius entered Rome. For a few hours everything was calm. Then the killing began. Though Cinna had pledged
not to go on a punitive murder spree, Marius had made no such promise,
and the soldiers were eager to be let off the leash. Whether they were
Italian veterans of the Social War or foreign mercenaries, the chance to
sack Rome was an opportunity they did not want to miss. So for five
days, the people of Rome cowered under a bloody terror in which "neither reverence for the gods, nor the indignation of men, nor the fear of
odium for their acts existed any longer among them . . . They killed re-
morselessly and severed the necks of men already dead, and they paraded
these horrors before the public eye, either to inspire fear and terror, or

---

* The father of THE Marcus Crassus.

for a godless spectacle." But the killings were not indiscriminate. The marauding troops concentrated on the wealthier quarters of the city and ignored the lower-class plebs. This discriminating eye helped form a perverse bond between the soldiers and the poor Romans; indeed, after dreading contact for so long it might have surprised both sides to learn they had a common enemy in the rich nobles on the Palatine Hill.[29]

No man had a bigger target on his back than Cinna's colleague Octavius, who was furious the Senate had surrendered. Though he commanded no troops, Octavius refused to hide. But while Cinna had promised not to *knowingly* put anyone to death, what his men did of their own accord was beyond his control. It did not take long for a Cinnan soldier to track Octavius down, unceremoniously murder him, and deliver the head to Cinna. Far from condemning the murder, Cinna ordered Octavius's head posted in the Forum for all to see. This was only the beginning.[30]

With the Cinnans running amok, the great optimate orator Marcus Antonius found himself targeted by Carbo, the son of the man Antonius had driven to suicide twenty-five years earlier. After tracking Antonius to an inn, a tribune loyal to Carbo sent some soldiers upstairs. But Antonius was "a speaker of much charm," who had lost none of his persuasive talents. He "tried to soften [them] with a long discourse, appealing to their pity by recalling many and various subjects, until the tribune, who was at a loss to know what had happened, rushed into the house." Furious to find Antonius nearly talking his way out of danger, the tribune "killed him while he was still declaiming." Antonius's head was posted in the Forum.[31]

But not all the killings were carried out in the street. The unfortunate priest-consul Merula was offered the dignity of a formal trial, but he elected to commit suicide rather than accept a sentence of death. He "opened his veins and, as his blood drenched the altars, he implored the gods to whom, as priest of Jupiter, he had formerly prayed for safety of the state, to visit their wrath upon Cinna and his party." Marius's old colleague Catulus—the man who always tried to take credit for the Battle of the Raudian Plain—was also offered the courtesy of a show trial. Aware that he was in mortal danger, he approached Marius and begged for his life. Marius merely replied, "You must die." Catulus returned home and suffocated himself.[32]

Over the course of these bloody five days we know of fourteen named victims, including a shocking six former consuls. Lucius Caesar and his brother Gaius perished, as did Crassus Dives, who committed suicide along with his eldest son as they were on the verge of capture. One poor soul named Ancharius died because he greeted Marius in the street and Marius did not acknowledge him. The Spiked Boots chopped him down right there on the spot. Watching as heads mounted on the rostra, the people of Rome were mortified that "what their ancestors had graced with the ships' beaks of the enemy was now being disgraced by the heads of citizens."[33]

At this point, Marius himself is often portrayed as crazed with blood-lust, a man "whose anger increased day by day." Painted as an old man driven mad with senile vengeance, he "thirsted for blood, kept on killing all whom he held in any suspicion whatsoever." But if we stand back from the bloody chaos, Marius appears no better and no worse than any of the others; he settled personal vendettas and let his men run wild, but so did they all. That said, it does appear Marius was willing to carry on the terror longer than his colleagues, and he certainly did nothing to rein in his infamously brutal Spiked Boots. It was left to Cinna and Sertorius to finally restore order with one last brutal slaughter. In the middle of the night, they surrounded the Spiked Boots and massacred every last one of them. The slaughter of the Spiked Boots marks the end of the five-day terror.[34]

With the killing concluded, anyone who wished to depart Rome was now free to do so. This led to an exodus of families who may have survived the terror but still wanted no part of Cinna's Rome. Sulla's wife Metella and her children were among the refugees and they headed straight for Athens to bring Sulla the news that Marius had captured Rome, their friends were dead, and Sulla was an enemy of the state.[35]

MUCH TO SULLA'S great consternation, the siege of Athens was still ongoing over the winter of 87–86. The city should have fallen by now, but Lucullus had still not returned from his quest to gather a navy. It was while Sulla sat unhappily outside of Athens that his wife and children showed up. He was shocked to see them, and even more shocked by the news they bore: Rome had fallen to his enemies, all his property had been razed to the ground, and the Assembly had declared him an enemy of the state. Worst of all, Marius would almost certainly be voted commander of the war against Mithridates.[36]

Now cut off from cash and supplies from Italy, Sulla started pumping the local Greeks for money to fund his war not just against Mithridates, but also what looked like a looming civil war with Marius. Sulla's brilliant expedient was to target well-endowed shrines like the Oracle at Delphi. The stiff tribute he imposed on these religious treasuries caused great moral agonizing, even for Sulla's own agents, who were "loath to touch the sacred objects, and shed many tears . . . over the necessity of it." But that didn't stop them from taking the money and running.[37]

After a winter of bad news, Sulla vented his frustrations on Athens in March 86. As the winter drew to a close the city fathers came out to beg for mercy, but were so long-winded in their defense of Athens, the shining beacon of light and reason, that Sulla snapped, "I was not sent to Athens by the Romans to learn its history, but to subdue its rebels." Out of patience Sulla ordered a daring gambit to capture the city. One night, a few cohorts of Roman soldiers used tall ladders to climb into Athens at an ill-attended corner of the wall. These advance cohorts successfully threw open the gates and let their comrades in. What followed was like a scene from the terror in Rome, only worse. Sulla did not restrain his men, giving them rein to rob, kill, and rape at their pleasure. A witness later said that "the blood that was shed in the market-place covered all the Cerameicus inside the Dipylon gate; nay, many say that it flowed through the gate and deluged the suburb." Only after the desperate pleading from both Greek and Roman friends did Sulla allow himself to be persuaded to end the sack.[38]

After capturing Athens, Sulla turned his full attention to its port of Piraeus. The legions overwhelmed the defenses and forced Archelaus's fleet to retreat out to sea. Sulla then ordered the famous docks of Piraeus burned and its walls destroyed. Consolidating his victory, Sulla made plans to conquer the rest of Greece before turning to face the armies of Marius.[39]

BACK IN ROME, Cinna spent the last few days of 87 arranging his own reelection to the consulship. To preserve the veneer of constitutional government, Cinna allowed elections to proceed but likely used his own powers as consul to disallow any other candidates. As had been arranged in advance, the only other man allowed to run was Gaius Marius. In January 86 Marius finally entered the seventh consulship he claimed was his destiny.[40]

The division of labor in the Cinna-Marius regime is clear. Marius would assume command of the war against Mithridates. He would raise an army, march to Greece, and depose Sulla. Cinna meanwhile would remain in Rome and see to the political and economic settlement of Italy. If all went well, Sulla could be pushed aside, Marius would win the war, and then return to a friendly regime that would divide up the spoils and make them the permanent masters of Rome.[41]

Unfortunately, it didn't go like that. Though he had long denied it, Marius was an old man in bad health. He had recently undergone an operation for varicose veins, and just a few weeks after taking office, he contracted pneumonia. Before anyone realized how serious his condition was, Gaius Marius died. Just seventeen days after inaugurating his seventh consulship, with maps of Greece spread out on his desk and plans for a final showdown with Sulla in the works, Gaius Marius died one of the all-time anticlimactic deaths in history.[42]

Gaius Marius was a pivotal figure in Roman history. When he first embarked on his public career he was merely a novus homo Italian. But through steady persistence, he had climbed his way up the cursus honorum. As he climbed, he helped unlock the populare forces that challenged senatorial supremacy. He was connected to publicani merchants, a friend of the Italians, and patron to legions of poor veteran soldiers. He had fought and won wars against Jugurtha and the Cimbri, and at the peak of his power was hailed as the Third Founder of Rome. His spectacular career set an example for ambitious men of future generations, though this example was not uniformly positive. At the end of his life Marius came to embody the dark side of relentless ambition: "It can therefore be said that as much as he saved the state as a soldier, so much he damaged it as a citizen, first by his tricks, later by his revolutionary actions." Above all Marius was a man whose ambitions could never be satisfied, for though he was the "first man to be elected consul for the seventh time, and was possessed of a house and wealth which would have sufficed for many kingdoms at once, he lamented his fortune, in that he was dying before he had satisfied and completed his desires."[43]

CINNA NOW RULED alone. The presence of Marius in his coalition had always been uncomfortable, and the death of the old man was a welcome relief. Cinna was now able to claim the Marian standard without having to worry about Marius himself. The Marian partisans were an important pillar of Cinna's coalition, which now included publicani merchants and moderate senators looking to keep the peace. But the most important pillar was the Italians, to whom Cinna owed his power. The army that captured Rome was mostly Italian, and led by a man who promised them full political equality. In a very real sense, Cinna's regime represented the triumph of the Italians in the Social War.

While he consolidated his domestic regime, Cinna also reassessed his foreign policy. Marius's death meant he needed new leadership for the war in the east. So Cinna took what would have been a single unified army under Marius and divided it between two men: Lucius Cornelius Scipio Asiaticus and Lucius Valerius Flaccus. Cinna induced the Senate to assign Asiaticus to the province of Macedonia, and induced the Assembly to elect Flaccus consul and assign him to the province of Asia.[44]

But Cinna was not as concerned about the war in the east as he was about the situation in Italy. The Italian economy was in shambles and things had only gotten worse since the murder of Asellio three years earlier. There were still no taxes from the east to augment the money supply, and estates across Italy were still ruined. So before he left for the east, Flaccus carried a measure through the Assembly that canceled three-fourths of all outstanding debts. The act was necessary medicine. Until Asia was retaken and money circulated in Italy again, there was nothing else to be done. But the law did have key points that kept the creditors from total ruin: First, the act guaranteed the publicani bankers would at least get *something* when it appeared possible they would get *nothing*. Second, most of them were themselves debtors; their own pressing burdens were canceled along with everyone else's.[45]

After Flaccus and Asiaticus departed for the east in the summer of 86, Cinna inaugurated another measure to help stabilize the economy. During the Social War, debasement of coinage and massive counterfeiting had destroyed everyone's faith in the money supply. Families took to hording their sound money, which further decreased the amount of good money in circulation. To restore faith in the coinage, a commission met to establish uniform metal ratios, exchange rates, and methods for testing suspect coins. We know all of this because one of the commissioners was another nephew of Gaius Marius, named Marcus Marius Gratidianus. Before the commission could announce the results jointly, Gratidianus snatched the plan, ran down to the rostra, and presented the whole thing as his own initiative. Everyone was crazy about the new system. The city fell in love with Gratidianus while the other commissioners were left sputtering inaudible protests.[46]

B Y THE SPRING of 86, Sulla had heard of the death of his old rival Marius, and with some relief turned his attention to Archelaus. After departing Athens, the Pontic army finally put back to shore in northeastern Greece. Archelaus disembarked with an army of 120,000 men and marched into the interior. Racing up to meet them, Sulla maneuvered Archelaus toward Chaeronea, where the two armies finally ran into each other. Despite being outnumbered, Sulla's legions destroyed the Pontic army without breaking a sweat. To give you a flavor of the typical exaggeration of the ancient sources, Sulla reported that at the Battle of Chaeronea over one hundred thousand Pontic soldiers died, while he himself lost only fourteen men. This is a bald-faced lie, but it does not mean Sulla did not win a stunning victory. Archelaus himself managed to escape, but with no army to command, it looked like the brief Pontic occupation of Greece was over.[47]

In the aftermath of his victory, Sulla turned his attention west. Flaccus had by now crossed two legions to Greece, though his intentions were not clear. Prior to his departure the new consul had sent advanced units across the Adriatic, but as soon as these units made contact with Sulla's legions, they defected. Now in Greece himself, Flaccus was wary of letting the rest of his men anywhere near Sulla's magnetic pull. So rather than confront Sulla directly, Flaccus kept marching straight to the Hellespont. While he marched, Asiaticus crossed with his own two legions and planted himself on the Macedonian frontier. With Sulla bogged down fighting Archelaus, Flaccus and Asiaticus might just be able to steal Sulla's thunder by racing into Asia and capturing Mithridates.[48]

Despite the losses at Chaeronea, Mithridates's Black Sea empire still had manpower left to draw on. Sulla was forced back on campaign when Archelaus sailed back over to Greece at the head of *another* army 120,000 strong. The two armies met at Orchomenus, and this time Sulla's troops wavered in the early stages of the fight. But Sulla confronted a cohort in retreat and yelled, "For me, O Romans, an honorable death here; but you, when men ask you where you betrayed your commander, remember to tell them, at Orchomenus." Shamed into action, the men turned and fought. The Pontic army was once again smashed. Even Mithridates did not have the resources to come back with a *third* army of 120,000 men. The Battle of Orchomenus marked the end of the war in Greece.[49]

Flaccus meanwhile was nearly to the Hellespont when he fell victim to an unnatural death at the hands of his legate, Gaius Flavius Fimbria. Why the two men began quarreling is a mystery, but as the legions approached the Hellespont, Fimbria was already deep into plotting a mutiny. To curry favor with the men he allowed them to plunder the countryside as they marched and was lax with camp discipline. With his preparations complete, Fimbria staged his mutiny. Flaccus tried to run, but he was hunted down and killed. Fimbria took control of the army.[50]

Now in command, Fimbria led the two legions into Asia on a campaign of punitive plundering. Far from entering as an army of liberation, Fimbria meant to punish the Asian cities for turning against Rome. With Fimbria's army on the rampage and almost all his troops now lost in Greece, Mithridates was forced to flee Pergamum for Pitane, and even then Fimbria nearly captured him. At that moment, the long-lost Lucullus finally came sailing into the Aegean at the head of a fleet. Lucullus could have easily blockaded the harbor at Pitane and prevented Mithridates from escaping by sea, but ever the loyal legate, Lucullus was not about to let any enemy of Sulla get credit for capturing Mithridates. So Lucullus kept sailing and Mithridates got away.[51]

M ITHRIDATES MAY HAVE gotten away but he could see the walls closing in. Calculating that he would get better terms from Sulla than Fimbria, Mithridates opened a channel through General Archelaus. Archelaus approached Sulla with an enticing offer: Sulla would get the full backing of Mithridates for his domestic wars if Sulla agreed to leave Asia in Pontic hands. But Sulla laughed this off and delivered his own terms: Asia would return to Roman provincial status; Cappadocia and Bithynia would be ruled by Roman client kings; and Mithridates would return to Pontus. But beyond simply restoring *status quo ante bellum*, Sulla did demand something for all the trouble Mithridates had caused: seventy warships and a heaping load of silver that Sulla would presumably use to subdue his enemies in Italy. Given the enormity of the crime that was the massacre of the Italians, this was an incredibly good deal for Mithridates.[52]

In early 85, Sulla and Mithridates finally met in person on an island in the northern Aegean. The meeting began with a battle of wills over who would speak first. Sulla finally broke the silence to say, "It is the part of suppliants to speak first, while victors need only to be silent." Mithridates then went into a long and not entirely incorrect account of how he had been provoked into war by the machinations of Aquillius and the other Romans. Sulla interrupted this story to tick off the list of Mithridates's own crimes, up to and including the murder of eighty thousand Italians. Unable to deny these crimes, and without an army to hide behind, Mithridates agreed to all of Sulla's terms. With the treaty complete, Sulla allowed the king to return to Pontus where Mithridates rebuilt his power and planned his next move, "just as fire not wholly extinguished bursts forth again into greater flames."[53]

Sulla's own forces could not believe the terms of the peace when they found out. Jugurtha had bribed a few old senators, and as punishment was paraded through the streets of Rome in chains and deposited naked in a dank cell to starve to death. Mithridates had been guilty of unconscionable aggression and mass murder. How was Mithridates *not* going to be at the head of Sulla's own triumphal parade? Why was Mithridates allowed to return home? Why was he still a king? It was outrageous.[54]

The explanation for Sulla's lenient terms are simple. They left him free to turn his attention to his domestic enemies. As soon as he left the meeting with Mithridates, Sulla moved against Fimbria's legion in Asia. Leading his own army across the Hellespont, Sulla located Fimbria's army and set up a camp nearby. Outnumbered by superior forces, Fimbria's two legions had no intention of putting up a fight. Sulla was a great conquering warlord; Fimbria was a murderous renegade legate. When his officers told him they would not fight, Fimbria agreed to vacate his command and leave the country. Fimbria departed for Pergamum, where he killed himself.[55]

The war now over, Sulla reorganized Asia. The former arrangement of the province still traced its roots back to the original will of King Attalus III, which stipulated that many cities would be free of taxation. Sulla swept all that aside. As punishment for collaborating with Mithridates, there were no free cities anymore—they were now *all* taxpaying cities. What's more, to cover lost property and emotional distress, Sulla imposed an indemnity equivalent to five years' back taxes. This was to be paid immediately, and with the old publicani networks destroyed, Roman soldiers spent the winter of 85–84 gathering up everything that wasn't nailed down to pay for whatever lay ahead in Italy.[56]

B ACK IN ROME, the city lay quiet under an uneasy calm. Just a few years earlier it had been a war zone; the Forum had been consumed by violent street clashes. Now everything was calm and quiet. After completing his service in the legions under the command of Pompey Strabo, young Marcus Tullius Cicero settled in Rome to study rhetoric and oratory during the years of Cinna's government. He later reported that in "the three following years, the city was free from the tumult of arms."[57]

For the moment there was not much to fight about. The Italians now had everything they ever wanted. Though there is a great deal of ambiguity in the sources, it is almost certain Cinna fulfilled his promise to disperse the Italians among the thirty-one rural tribes. Though it would not be until after the Civil War that the Italians were *fully* counted, the years of the Cinnan regime mark the permanent entrance of the Italians onto the citizen rolls. With the grateful Italians squarely behind him, Cinna could expect their staunch support if and when Sulla returned from the east. For the Italians, Sulla was the guy who had marched an army into Rome specifically to *stop* the spread of Italian equality. Though Italy was quiet for now, the old battle lines of the Social War would be reignited when Sulla came home.[58]

But by the end of 85, the anxious fog that hung over Italy began to clear, as the regime made first contact with the victorious Sulla. Pretending that he had not been outlawed, Sulla sent back to Rome a huge official accounting of his campaign, diplomacy, and ledgers. This put the Senate in an awkward position. They sent an embassy to meet with Sulla and sound out his intentions. While they waited, Cinna and Carbo won another controlled election for the consulship of 84 and mobilized the Italians for war.[59]

Sulla's response to the senatorial envoys was furious but exact. Sulla denounced the foul treatment he had received from his enemies. He recounted his victories. Listed his credentials. He had just won back Asia! And his thanks? To be declared an outlawed. To have his property seized and burned. His wife and children forced in exile. But with a magnanimous heart Sulla offered simple terms: the Senate and People of Rome must restore his dignity and his property. That was all. He did also say that when he returned he might not spare his enemies—but if the Senate cared to spare them, he would respect their decree.[60]

WHILE THESE ENVOYS went to Asia and back, Cinna and Carbo continued to raise forces. The Senate ordered them to cease preparing for war until the envoys to Sulla returned, but the consuls merely nodded and went back to recruiting. It would be folly to sit back in Italy and wait patiently for their blood enemy to return at the head of five veteran legions. In fact, they now hoped to stop him before he reached Italy at all.[61]

With the peninsula only just putting itself back together after the devastation of the Social War, Cinna's plan was to ferry an army across the Adriatic and confront Sulla in Greece. He already had two legions in Macedonia under Asiaticus. If all went according to plan, by the time Sulla finally made his way home from Asia, he would find his path blocked in Greece by a huge army of implacably hostile Italians ready to fight to the death to protect civitas and suffragium. But the consuls' impatience to put men into position had fatal consequences. In what remains something of a historical mystery, Cinna refused to wait until spring to ship his new levies across the Adriatic, instead putting them on boats in the early winter months of 84.[62]

The first troop transports crossed the water fine, but a second convoy was caught in a terrible storm. The resulting shipwrecks drowned half the men. When the survivors washed up on the beach they promptly mutinied. This incident sent shivers through the rest of Cinna's army, and a detachment in the city of Ancona refused to make the crossing. Cinna was forced to come in person to confront the men and remind them that the only thing he required of them was obedience. But the new recruits were angry, scared, and hostile.[63]

When Cinna arrived, he called for a general meeting to address the troops. But when he entered the throng of assembled soldiers, one man refused to give way and was struck by one of Cinna's guards. The man fought back, so Cinna ordered him arrested. This order only inflamed the rest of the men. They pelted Cinna with furious insults and then pelted him with stones. Dodging this sudden onslaught, Cinna tried to extract himself from the mob, but he was grabbed by an angry centurion. The apprehended consul allegedly offered the man a ring to let him go, but the centurion growled, "I am not come to seal a surety, but to punish a lawless and wicked tyrant." Without further debate the centurion pulled out his sword and cut Cinna down where he stood. Having only just appeared from historical thin air three years earlier, Cinna vanished as abruptly as he arrived.[64]

While on the public stage, Cinna was the dominant leader of a tense coalition that ruled Rome for three years. And while Cinna obviously had a dismissive attitude toward republican norms, so did everyone else. Despite repeated attacks from men like Cicero who called him a "monster of cruelty," Cinna was no more a lawless and wicked tyrant than any of the other men who played the deadly new game of violent politics. Cinna was certainly not an unimaginative dictator who used brutality only to secure petty whims and pleasures. The regime Cinna led tried to address the economic devastation of Italy, begin the process of fully integrating the Italians, and lay the groundwork for a return to peace. It was not inevitable that Sulla would win the looming confrontation, and there was a real possibility that it would be the Cinnans, not the Sullans, who would define the future of the Republic. But Cinna would not be there to lead the defense of his regime. Instead, he was murdered by a random soldier in the heat of an argument. The historian Velleius Paterculus concluded, "He was a man who deserved to die by the sentence of his victorious enemies rather than at the hands of his angry soldiers. Of him one can truly say that he formed daring plans, such as no good citizen would have conceived, and that he accomplished what none but a most resolute man could have accomplished, and that he was foolhardy enough in the formulation of his plans, but in their execution, a man."[65]

CHAPTER 12

CIVIL WAR

Thus the seditions proceeded from strife and
contention to murder, and from murder to open
war . . . Henceforth there was no restraint upon
violence either from the sense of shame, or regard for law, institutions, or country.

APPIAN[1]

I N THE WAKE OF CINNA'S SUDDEN DEATH, CARBO CANCELED THE
plan to fight in Greece. If war came, it would be fought in Italy. Returning to Rome, Carbo faced pressure from the Senate to ensure
that it did not come to that. Though he never stopped mobilizing, Carbo
did try to outflank his enemies by proposing that *both* sides demobilize
their legions, making it look like he was the one seeking a peaceful solution while Sulla was the aggressor.* While in Rome, Carbo also faced
pressure to hold an election to replace Cinna. But Carbo successfully
delayed the issue until the regular elections for the following year came
around. Cinna's vacant chair was never filled.[2]

Now sole consul, Carbo spent all of 84 BC raising an army. Despite
the mutiny in Ancona, it was not hard to raise soldiers. Under Cinna's
guidance the Senate already passed a decree recognizing both citizenship

---

* Pompey would attempt the same trick with Julius Caesar in 49.

and voting equality for the Italians. Recruiters made the obvious case that when Sulla came back all these advances would be canceled. Even if they cared little for the dynamics of high Roman politics, every Italian could agree that civitas and suffragium were worth fighting for. As long as Sulla remained hostile to the idea of Italian equality, he could expect endless waves of resistance upon his return to the peninsula.[3]

Waves of Italians weren't the only thing Sulla would face upon his return—also on board with the growing anti-Sullan coalition were the plebs urbana of Rome. The plebs urbana had been staunchly opposed to Italian citizenship and were thus unhappy additions to the Cinnan fold. But they did not have much of a choice. If Sulla returned to Rome, he was not likely to be as benevolent as he was after the first march. The murder of his friends and destruction of his property guaranteed that there would be a vicious punitive response. Tales of the sack of Athens had already filtered back to Italy. Fearing the same treatment, the plebs urbana lined up behind Carbo as he orchestrated a pan-Italian defense. By the time Sulla sailed for Italy, Carbo could call on as many as 150,000 men and the wealth and resources of the entire western empire.[4]

Their years of power in Rome had allowed the Cinnan regime to place loyal men in key positions across the empire. Scipio Asiaticus was still out on the Macedonian frontier with two legions. A loyal Cinnan partisan named Hadrianus had secured control of Africa and was raising men and supplies. Sertorius had strong connections in Cisalpine Gaul that could be turned to the cause. The island of Sicily, meanwhile, had long ago fallen into the hands of longtime populare stalwart Gaius Norbanus. As a tribune in 103, Norbanus had worked with Saturninus to stir up the riots that exiled Caepio and Mallius. He had survived the bloody purge of 100 and resumed a regular career, eventually being elected praetor and assigned to Sicily. But shortly after he arrived on the island the Social War broke out and the Senate extended all provincial commands. Norbanus remained in place through the Social War, and when the Cinnan regime captured Rome, Norbanus gladly pledged his loyalty. By the spring of 84, Norbanus had been governing Sicily for at least seven years; its all-important grain and manpower were in his safe hands.[5]

A wild card in all of this was Gnaeus Pompeius, the twenty-one-year-old son of the late Pompey Strabo. The man known to history as Pompey the Great was still too young to hold a magistracy, but had become the head of the Pompeius household when his father died over the winter of 87–86. This assumption of authority gave Pompey control over the impressive client network his father had built up in northern Italy. Far more popular than his father, Pompey consolidated personal control over the family network thanks to his ambitious charisma. Cicero says Pompey was "a man who was born to excel in every thing, would have acquired a more distinguished reputation for his eloquence, if he had not been diverted from the pursuit of it by the more dazzling charms of military fame." Though he had barely emerged into adulthood, Pompey already commanded attention—and securing his loyalty would be a key objective of both sides in the coming civil war.[6]

After a year of careful preparation made possible by Sulla's lingering in Asia, Carbo finally presided over new consular elections. Rather than stay in office himself, Carbo orchestrated the election of two close allies of the regime for the consulship of 83: Scipio Asiaticus and Gaius Norbanus. Though sometimes portrayed as moderate members of the Cinnan party, Asiaticus and Norbanus were amongst Sulla's most implacable opponents and were elevated specifically because they were men capable of prosecuting a civil war without craving reconciliation like the tired old men in the Senate. Carbo himself meanwhile set down the consulship to become proconsul of Cisalpine Gaul, a country full of resources and men that sat poised atop the peninsula. Carbo's path from consul of Rome to proconsul of Cisalpine Gaul blazed a trail that would be followed by both Julius Caesar and Mark Antony.[7]

The elections complete, Carbo settled a matter of pro forma business: he induced the Senate to decree the senatus consultum ultimum. This gave the new consuls the absolute power to do what was necessary to protect the state, which the Cinnans had just as much claim to as Sulla did: "For the sympathies of the people were much in favor of the consuls, because the action of Sulla, who was marching against his country, seemed to be that of an enemy, while that of the consuls, even if they were working for themselves, was ostensibly the cause of the republic." The decree in hand, Asiaticus and Norbanus received Italy as their consular province. With the entire western empire at their backs, they entered 83 feeling good about their odds of burying Sulla and his vaunted legions.[8]

O N THE OTHER side of the Adriatic, Sulla was also preparing. The settlement of Asia was not just about restoring Roman domination: it was about putting the wealth of the province at his disposal. With his coffers stocked from a winter of tax collection, Sulla could afford whatever came next. He also built a fleet of over a thousand ships to ferry his men to Italy and keep them supplied indefinitely from Greece and Asia. As the Cinnans claimed the resources of the west, Sulla claimed the east.

But while the Cinnans could call upon waves of recruits, Sulla could count on the strength of his five veteran legions that had now been following him since the Social War. In the spring of 83, these five legions were the best-trained and most experienced army anywhere in the Mediterranean. But that did not mean Sulla could trust them completely. The length of their service, and the hardships they had endured, meant there was a strong possibility they would demand to be demobilized upon return to Italy. Sulla had pointed them at Rome once before and they followed. But their obedience had been partly because they sought riches and glory in the east. Now that they had both, would they follow Sulla to Rome a second time? So as he prepared his men to sail for home, Sulla administered an oath that they faithfully fight for him until he released them from service—but how many would hold to that oath Sulla did not know.[9]

Sulla finally crossed the Adriatic and landed in Italy in the spring of 83. Arriving in the port of Brundisium, he got his first omen that things might work out. In his talks with the Senate, Sulla hinted that when he returned, he would accept both Italian civitas and suffragium without further argument. When he arrived in Brundisium, he followed through and declared the Italians had nothing to fear. He was as committed to their new place in the Republic as his enemies. The inhabitants of Brundisium were thrilled by this news, and any rising opposition to his arrival evaporated. Rather than fighting the first battle of a long hard slog to Rome, Sulla set out on the Via Appia without yet pulling sword from scabbard.[10]

But aside from the immediate impact on the course of the Civil War, Sulla's arrival in Brundisium also marks the end of the long Social War between Romans and Italians. The question of Italian citizenship had been the third rail of Roman politics for fifty years. The conflict stretched as far back as Tiberius Gracchus's *Lex Agraria*, then moved through the legislation of Fulvius Flaccus and Gaius Gracchus, then through the rise of Marius, the revolution of Saturninus, the expulsion bill of Crassus and Scaevola, and the assassination of Drusus. Fifty years of tension and hostility had exploded into the bitter and destructive Social War, which climaxed with Cinna capturing Rome with the help of an Italian army. The looming civil war with Sulla looked like it was going to be an extension of that long-running conflict. Had Sulla maintained hostility to Italian citizenship, it is entirely likely an ocean of Italian resistance would have swallowed his well-trained legions. But Sulla was an astute politician and unwilling to stake his life to the imagined purity of Roman citizenship. By announcing in the spring of 83 that he would maintain Italian civitas and suffragium, Sulla ended the Social War. No matter who won the coming war, the Italians would be integrated equally into the Republic.

As Sulla advanced up the Via Appia, he continued to demonstrate his benevolent intentions. His troops were not allowed to plunder or terrorize the countryside. And he further trumpeted his respect for the Italian citizenship to undermine whatever resistance might have been brewing the past few years. Wherever he passed, cities and towns welcomed him openly—even as he walked through Apulia and Samnium, two of the most implacably anti-Roman regions during the Social War.[11]

Sulla's promulgations and peaceful approach melted armed resistance, but his own civil status remained in doubt. Technically his command of the legions since 87 had been illegal. By law, he should have given up his command to Flaccus and gone into exile. Inside the Senate, men who might be willing to compromise with Sulla were troubled that he was operating an illegal command while the executive magistrates, the Senate, and the Assembly still considered him an outlaw.[12]

But the hand wringing of these nervous fence sitters was greatly reduced when powerful, but thus far neutral, parties started to join Sulla's slow moving procession up the Via Appia. Of these the most important was Metellus Pius. After departing Italy, Pius had fled south to Africa to stay out of the way of both Cinna and Sulla. But after carefully considering the situation, Pius decided that Sulla represented the more legitimate side of the conflict—even if the returning proconsul was technically an enemy of the state. So as Sulla moved up the Via Appia, he was delighted when Metellus Pius arrived to join the march. Sulla was aware what a boon this was to his fortunes and grandly welcomed Pius into camp, affording him every honor and all but naming Pius co-commander of the army.[13]

But where Pius was a political weight almost as great as Sulla, Sulla also accepted the allegiance of two young men on the rise. Like Metellus Pius, neither were strictly partisans of Sulla, but circumstances conspired to convince both to join. In time, both of these young men would become central figures in the final collapse of the Republic: Pompey the Great and Marcus Licinius Crassus.[14]

Still in his early twenties, Pompey was a man operating well above his station. He had never held a magistracy and currently held no official position in the army—but his family's extensive client network made him a powerful force in Italy. During the years of Sulla's absence, the Cinnans attempted to secure an alliance with young Pompey, but much to their horror, Pompey raised a personal army and led them to rendezvous not with Asiaticus and Norbanus, but with Sulla. Pompey was brash and cocky, but, eager to cement Pompey's loyalty, Sulla indulged the boy like he was already a great man, going so far as to stand when Pompey entered a room. The defection of Pompey to the Sullans was a blow to Carbo and the other old Cinnans: not only were they denied the forces at Pompey's disposal, but northeast Italy went from being a secure base of operations to a hostile front line.[15]

Also joining Sulla's slow-moving army was a man who would become Pompey's great rival in the years to come. Now over thirty, Marcus Licinius Crassus was the younger cousin of Crassus the Orator, but more importantly, the son of one of the proscribed victims in the Marian terror. While his father and older brother had been forced to commit suicide, Crassus himself had gotten away. After fleeing Rome, Crassus went to

Spain, where his father had built an extensive network of clients. Taken in by a loyal friend of the family, Crassus lived in cave near the sea for eight months, his food, supplies, and even two slave girls provided by his benefactors. When Cinna died, Crassus emerged from hiding and, like Pompey, went round raising a personal legion to contribute to Sulla's inevitable war effort. With a small army under his command, Crassus sailed to Italy and presented himself to Sulla. It was while in Sulla's camp that Crassus opened his legendary rivalry with Pompey. Sulla treated young Pompey like a near equal while Crassus was treated as a junior officer—and Crassus sulked over the perceived slight. When Sulla dispatched Crassus north to recruit more men and Crassus asked for a military escort, Sulla shot back: "I give you as an escort your father, your brother, your friends, and your kinsmen, who were illegally and unjustly put to death, and whose murderers I am pursuing."[16]

In addition to winning over neutral leaders, Sulla also attracted former enemies now looking to secure a spot on the winning side. Though Sulla knew how to nurse a grudge, he was also eager to make ostentatious displays of forgiveness. The consummate survivor Marcius Philippus—last seen in 91 railing against the optimates during the tribunate of Drusus the Younger—abandoned Rome and presented himself to Sulla. Far from being punished for collaborating with the Cinnans, the ex-consul was given a high command in Sulla's army. Sulla's broad clemency at this late stage even applied to core members of Marius's inner circle. Publius Cornelius Cethegus had been among the twelve proscribed men specifically named by Sulla after his first march on Rome. Cethegus had managed to dodge Sulla's patrols but now delivered himself into the hands of his former pursuer in the hope of surviving this latest crisis. Sulla welcomed these supplications as a chance to show clemency and forgiveness. And it was not just an empty show. Cethegus was given important responsibilities during the war. But the time was fast approaching for Sulla's benevolence to give way to sterner treatment for his more incorrigible enemies.[17]

N OT EVERYONE WAS flocking to Sulla's banner, though, and the consuls Norbanus and Asiaticus still commanded large armies. With Sulla marching up from the south, both consuls deployed their forces in Campania, blocking the two principal roads to Rome. With the south already falling under Sulla's control, the goal now was to make a stand in Campania and block the final approach to Rome.[18]

Sulla's legions first made contact with Norbanus's army at Tifata on the Via Appia. Even on the eve of battle, Sulla was not sure how his men would respond to the order to fight. But the next morning they more than proved their loyalty. Fighting as tenaciously as they had against the armies of Mithridates, Sulla's legions broke Norbanus's army and sent it back to the safety of Capua. Sulla later said it was after the Battle of Tifata that he knew he was going to win the war—his men would follow him anywhere.[19]

With Norbanus now cooped up behind the walls of Capua, Asiaticus approached Sulla from the north. But where Sulla's men had just proved their invincible loyalty, Asiaticus's men were getting mighty ambivalent about following the consul into battle. Sulla's promise to respect Italian citizenship had already made the rounds, and this, combined with word of Sulla's victory at Tifata, made fighting seem as pointless as it was dangerous. Asiaticus was aware that the commitment of his men was wavering, so after camping a short distance from Sulla's army, Asiaticus proposed negotiations. Sulla naturally agreed, and the two leaders declared a cease-fire and exchanged hostages. Then each designated three men to carry the negotiation: Asiaticus was almost certainly accompanied by his chief legate Sertorius, while Metellus Pius accompanied Sulla.[20]

Ostensibly the talks were supposed to settle the political dispute and avoid open war. But Sulla's negotiators entered talks "not because they hoped or desired to come to an agreement, but because they expected to create dissensions in Asiaticus's army, which was in a state of dejection." While he stalled in the negotiating tent, Sulla sent his men to mingle with the soldiers in Asiaticus's camp to spread the word that Sulla was great, his promises would be kept, that this was really only about settling business with a few personal enemies. Sulla was the enemy of neither Rome nor Italy. Sulla's troops also recalled that Norbanus's army had just been trounced. Not without cause, Asiaticus's men fell under the seductive influence of Sulla's veterans.[21]

Sertortius disapproved of letting the men anywhere near each other and likely divined Sulla's real intentions. So when Asiaticus dispatched Sertortius to inform Norbanus of the developing talks and solicit his colleague's opinion, Sertorius made a calculated detour on the way to Capua. The town of Suessa had recently declared loyalty to Sulla, but Sertorius entered the town and occupied it by force—a clear violation of the cease-fire. When Sulla found out about the breach of peace, he declared an end to negotiations. Both sides returned their hostages and prepared for battle—just as Sertorius likely intended.[22]

But by then it was too late. After the breakdown of negotiations, Asiaticus ordered his men to prepare for war, but instead they prepared to surrender. When Sulla's army marched on Asiaticus's position, Asiaticus's men dutifully suited up to meet them. But as the two sides lined up on the plains, Sulla gave the signal and Asiaticus's troops crossed over to the welcome embrace of their new commander. Unable to do anything about this mass defection, Asiaticus was found in his command tent and taken prisoner. Trying to display benevolence with every step, Sulla interviewed Asiaticus and then let the consul go free. When Carbo received word that Sulla had successfully induced the defection of an entire consular army, he said "that in making war upon the fox and the lion in Sulla, he was more annoyed by the fox."[23]

Sulla's newly combined force then turned its attention to Norbanus in Capua. Sulla sent envoys to the other consul requesting talks, but Norbanus was well informed of what had befallen his colleague and sent the envoys away without a response. Norbanus then extracted himself from Capua before Sulla's legions arrived, and spent the rest of the war trying to avoid contact so his men would not defect.[24]

The confrontations with Norbanus and Asiaticus marked a turning point in Sulla's conduct toward his enemies. Until now, he had welcomed all former enemies into his camp and avoided punitive sacking of the countryside. The limits of his magnanimity were now reached with the grand defection of Asiaticus's army, which clearly demonstrated the gods favored Sulla. Anyone left on the other side was now beyond hope and would be treated as enemies to be exterminated rather than potential allies to be won over.

B ELIEVING TIME WAS on his side, Sulla was in no hurry to force a cli-
mactic battle. Instead he recruited and politicked his way through
communities throughout southern Italy to bring everyone over to his
side. To combat these efforts, Carbo returned to Rome in July 83 and
had the Senate declare everyone who joined Sulla an enemy of the state.
Over the summer both sides fanned out to towns and cities across Italy
to make their pitches. Sulla's agents were able to point to their recent
victories, defections of troops, and the allegiance of eminent statesmen.
But most importantly they made the devastating promise that citizenship for the Italians would be respected. Carbo's agents said that Sulla
was known for his cruelty and duplicity. His brutal campaigns against
the Hirpini and Samnites during the Social War were well known. Plus
the sequence of events that had led to Sulla's first illegal march on Rome
had been kicked off by Sulla's opposition to Italian citizenship. Most
of Italy did not know whom to believe: "They were therefore obliged
to shift their pretended allegiance from one side to the other, and to
appease whoever was present."[25]

The battle for control of Picenum was particularly fierce as Carbo's
agents tried to blunt the damage of Pompey's defection. But with most
of the leading men in the region already siding with the young general,
Pompey was able to raise two more legions on Sulla's behalf. Carbo sent
in a detachment of legates to disrupt Pompey's efforts, but instead they
were driven out of the region, which now fell decisively into Pompey's
hands. Sertorius had better luck recruiting in the old Marian stronghold
of Etruria, and when Asiaticus arrived after being released by Sulla, Sertorius was able to present the consul with four fresh legions.[26]

Asiaticus led these four legions into Picenum to confront Pompey directly, but was forced to endure the same shame he had endured at Sulla's
hands. After planting his legions near Pompey's army, the soldiers began
mingling, and Asiaticus's men were again amenable to the promises made
by the other side. When Asiaticus woke up in the morning, he once again
found his men had all deserted to the other side to the enemy. In an age
where conflicts were led by men who commanded unprecedented personal loyalty—Marius, Sulla, Pompey, Pius, Sertorius—Scipio Asiaticus

was a singularly uninspiring leader who watched two full armies abandon him on the eve of battle. He fled into Gaul, never to return. Sulla,
meanwhile, was now even more impressed that Pompey, "who was still
extremely young, had snatched such a large army away from the enemy,
but those who were far superior to him in age and reputation could hardly
keep even their own servants in a dependable alliance."[27]

Asiaticus's loss of the legions he had just raised also convinced Sertorius that the time had come to move along. Disillusioned with the leadership of the anti-Sullan forces, Sertorius decided that Italy was likely
lost—and if the cause was to survive, a prudent withdrawal was in order.
Having been elected praetor for the year and given Spain as his province,
Sertorius abandoned Italy and made his way overland toward Spain to
raise new armies. After Sulla won the Civil War and liquidated all his
enemies in Italy, Sertorius's Spanish legions would be the only force left
in the world opposing him. Sertorius would emerge as principal leader of
the opposition to the coming Sullan regime. Many refugees fled Rome for
the safety of Sertorius's army and he managed to avoid defeat for nearly a
decade, embarrassing the authorities in Rome who were trying to pretend
like everything was settled and life had returned to normal.[28]

D ESPITE SULLA'S MOMENTUM, however, the war was far from over.
Most of north and central Italy remained in opposition and skep-
tical of his ultimate intentions. It is telling that Sulla was still not willing
to risk all in battle, because it was a battle he might lose. In the fall of 83,
Rome still remained in the hands of his enemies.

With Norbanus and Asiaticus having proven themselves unequal to
the task of defeating Sulla, Carbo returned to Rome for the consular elections for 82. The Assembly returned Carbo to his third consulship and
for a colleague elected Marius's son, Gaius Marius the Younger. Still in his
late twenties, Marius the Younger had never served a magistracy and was
not eligible to stand for the consulship. But Carbo engineered the young
man's election because, as a matter of family honor and personal predilec-
tion, Marius the Younger was a relentless—even cruel—enemy of Sulla.

Besides, he was not being elected for any special military leadership or political skill. Even by Carbo's own admission, Marius was elected because the name Marius still meant something.[29]

Both sides suspended war operations over the particularly harsh winter of 83–82. When the spring of 82 arrived it brought with it the first anniversary of the Civil War. It is important to remember that despite what Sulla might tell you, he did not just land in Brundisium, march on Rome, and take it. There was a prolonged fight for the hearts, minds, and swords of Italy. Even now, after a year of conflict, the end result was still in doubt.[30]

With the dawn of the campaign of 82, the old Cinnan strategy to control armies and supplies in Gaul, Africa, Sicily, Italy, and Macedonia had come to naught, and the remaining anti-Sullan partisans were now hunkered in a final defensive crouch in northwest Italy. Carbo returned to the north to defend Etruria, Umbria, and Cisalpine Gaul from encroachment by Pompey. Meanwhile, Marius the Younger led eight legions down to Campania to face off against Sulla—proof enough against later Sullan propaganda that Italy simply melted into his hands the minute he arrived.[31]

With Marius on the way, Sulla advanced, forcing Marius to withdraw to an unknown site identified only as "Sacriportus." Sulla ordered his men to pursue Marius, but after a chase lasting all day, Sulla's legates convinced their general to order a halt and break camp for the night. Sulla reluctantly agreed. But just as his men were setting themselves to the task, Marius the Younger showed a little initiative: rather than sitting back on his heels waiting to be cornered, he ordered his men to attack Sulla's legions as they pitched camp. It wasn't a bad plan necessarily, but Sulla's tired soldiers were enraged they were being forced to drop their shovel and pick up their swords. Carried by this rage, they rallied and sent Marius's legions careening backward toward the city Praeneste (modern Palestrina).[32]

The citizens of Praeneste hated Sulla and were prepared to receive Marius, but not at fatal risk to themselves. With Sulla's army on the way, the Praenestians refused to dismantle their fortifications and open the gates. Marius and a small group of officers were hoisted into the city by a rope and sling, but the vast majority of his men were left behind in the dusty plain at the base of the wall. When Sulla's legions appeared, they commenced a bloody slaughter. As Marius the Younger watched from the ramparts, his men were pinned against the wall and attacked mercilessly. Only after a suitable venting of blood to satisfy their rage did Sulla's troops allow the survivors to surrender.[33]

When Sulla himself arrived, he displayed calculated cruelty. He ordered the survivors rounded up and all captured Samnites herded off to one side. Once disarmed and surrounded, the Samnites were slaughtered upon Sulla's orders. He then ordered his troops to begin a siege of Praeneste. By trapping Marius, Sulla could now survey all of southern Italy; he spied no enemy army standing between him and Rome. He decided it was finally time to go home.[34]

B ACK IN ROME, the defeat of Marius the Younger cloaked the city in dread. Most of the Sullan partisans had long since departed the city, leaving behind only Sulla's enemies or neutral leaders who still hoped to broker a peace. In this latter group were a small collection of prominent senators who had never been "Marian" or "Cinnan," but who had remained in Rome for the duration of their regime. With Rome all but indefensible, Marius the Younger sent instructions for all remaining anti-Sullan partisans to vacate the city and join Carbo for a last stand in Etruria. But he also sent a list of men to be dealt with before the evacuation.[35]

With this list in hand one of the praetors convened the Senate under false pretenses and, as soon as everyone was inside, let loose a pack of assassins. Two senators were killed immediately, including Carbo's cousin, who was now suspected of being in league with the Sullans. Another senator tried to run but was tackled at the door of the Senate house and stabbed to death. The big name on the list, though, nearly got away. Publius Mucius Scaevola was among the last of the old generation of optimates. A friend of Scaurus, Crassus, and Antonius, Scaevola had been present at Crassus's house for the fateful discussion of the orators on the eve of the Social War.

Scaevola had remained in Rome after Cinna captured the city, and was given a wide latitude as a potential ally to be cultivated. Now marked for death, Scaevola escaped the killing in the Senate house and sought shelter inside the Temple of Vesta. The temple was a sacred sanctuary, but the assassins barged in, located Scaevola, and murdered him. The bodies of the dead, as usual, were dumped in the Tiber.[36]

The murders complete, the remaining anti-Sullan partisans evacuated Rome for the north. When they decamped they left only the frightened plebs urbana behind. The inhabitants of Rome had only recently joined the anti-Sullan coalition, and they had only joined out of fear of what Sulla might do when he came back. Now they would find out what their punishment would be. Sulla's legions appeared on the road and methodically surrounded Rome. Eventually, the entourage of Sulla himself appeared, swinging around the city and arriving at the Campus Martius. Determining that death by starvation was worse than a quick death by the sword, the citizens of Rome opened the gates.[37]

But the plebs urbana were in for a pleasant surprise. After bracing for a bloody purge, they instead got word that Sulla had called a mass meeting to address the people of Rome and make his objectives clear. When the people assembled on the Campus Martius, Sulla announced that he planned to be a surgeon, not a butcher. While he would of course reclaim his own property and punish a few select enemies, the rest of the population had nothing to fear. Then, leaving behind a few trusted officers with a small garrison, Sulla departed for the north as quickly as he had come.[38]

Sulla's first swing through Rome was calculated to soothe fears and induce men to lie down rather than stand up. And so far nothing in his career led anyone to believe it was not sincere. As Plutarch says, "Sulla had used his good fortune moderately, at first, and like a statesman, and had led men to expect in him a leader who was attached to the aristocracy, and at the same time helpful to the common people." But the next time Sulla came to Rome—when the war was finished and there was no one left to challenge him—it would be quite a different story: "His conduct fixed a stigma upon offices of great power, which were thought to work a change in men's previous characters, and render them capricious, vain, and cruel."[39]

U P IN THE north, the war continued to go badly for Carbo and his remaining forces. While Sulla led the drive up the Via Latina, Metellus Pius and Pompey charged up the Adriatic coast to secure Pompey's home territory of Picenum. After inducing the defection of Asiaticus's legions, the Sullan generals sent an army north into Cisalpine Gaul and another west into Etruria to attack Carbo's last strongholds.[40]

But though darkness was closing in, Carbo still led enough legions to hold his own. He made a base on the Adriatic coast and tried to block Pius's attempt to take Ravenna, but without a proper navy, there was nothing he could do. So he headed back into the interior and soon ran into Sulla himself, who was advancing north after the swing through Rome. Since almost all of the most hard-core anti-Sullan partisans were in Carbo's army, there would be no defections this time. So instead of another bloodless victory, Sulla had to fight. Far from caving, Carbo's legions held their own all day, and nightfall ruled the battle a draw. The war was still far from over.[41]

But now the dynamic of the war had changed. The original plan laid out by Cinna was to harness the full resources of Italy to overwhelm Sulla and his five legions, to make their position untenable in the long run by limiting access to reinforcements. Now the situation was reversed. But by the summer of 82, it was Sulla who could draw on manpower reserves and Carbo who was isolated. When Crassus and Pompey invaded Umbria, Carbo was forced to send detachments to reinforce his bases there. But the reinforcements were ambushed by a detachment of Sulla's army, costing Carbo some five thousand men—men he could not afford to lose.[42]

The real downfall of the anti-Sullan forces, though, was the loss of Marius the Younger's legions in the south. Instead of Sulla feeling pressure from two fronts, his armies could now surround Carbo. Recognizing that the siege of Praeneste had to be lifted, Carbo withdrew back to the

Adriatic coast and peeled off vital forces to relieve the city. If they were successful, the balance of the war would shift again. But the first relief army never even made it to Praeneste. They were jumped and destroyed by Pompey en route. The defeated soldiers ran off in every direction. Most never came back.[43]

With resistance to Sulla collapsing, the Samnites and Lucanians got together and raised one last great army. Having never been defeated in the Social War, these men bore a particular hostility to Sulla. Mostly on their own initiative, they raised tens of thousands of men to relieve the siege of Praeneste. Sulla knew as well as Carbo that everything hinged on relieving the siege, so he positioned his own army near the city. Despite a strong push by the Samnite and Lucanian army, Sulla's legions beat back the attempt. The siege of Praeneste held.[44]

Carbo's legions in the north still numbered as many as forty thousand men, but with a string of failures mounting, one of Carbo's lieutenants opened secret communications with Sulla. The lieutenant secured a promise of leniency if he could "accomplish anything important." To accomplish this "anything important," the lieutenant invited a group of Carbo's officers to dinner—including the ex-consul Norbanus. Suspecting treachery, Norbanus himself stayed away, but the others accepted the invitation. When they arrived they were all arrested and executed. The traitorous lieutenant then fled to Sulla's camp while Norbanus himself despaired of victory and boarded a ship that sailed for the Greek city of Rhodes.[45]

Carbo, meanwhile, continued to send detachments to Praeneste, but they repeatedly failed to reach the city. With Carbo focused on the south, Metellus Pius, Pompey, and Crassus enveloped all of Cisalpine Gaul behind his back. Carbo's old province was supposed to be a stronghold of last resort—now it was in enemy hands. The war in Italy lost, Carbo determined his only hope was to escape to the provinces and somehow keep the war going from the periphery of the empire. Sertorius was already in Spain, and Norbanus had just fled to Greece. Carbo decided that if he headed to Africa, by way of Sicily, the war might yet be won. Leaving a joint command of officers in charge of the northern army, Carbo fled Italy. Despite all his military justifications for departing, Carbo was now as much concerned about his head as he was winning the war.[46]

After getting whipped in battle by Pompey, the joint command
Carbo left behind determined the only thing to be done was abandon the north completely. They would instead swarm on Praeneste and
keep the war going in Samnium, a region known for its deep hostility to
Sulla. The northern army came down and combined with the independent Samnite and Lucanian forces now led by the Samnite general Telesinus. All these forces joined together and tried one last time to relieve
Praeneste in early November 82. But the fortifications blocking all the
roads were simply too strong and they were forced to retreat.[47]

With all reasonable strategies having come up empty, the only thing
left to do was launch one last dramatic attempt to salvage the war. Despite
the fact that Italy was swarming with Sullan armies, Telesinus noticed
there was, at that moment, no army standing between them and Rome.
With winter descending, and the armies of Sulla closing in on their position, Telesinus proposed pulling up stakes in the middle of the night and
racing to Rome to recapture it before Sulla could stop them. The other
officers agreed.[48]

When dawn broke the next morning, the people of Rome found an
army forty thousand strong camped outside the Colline Gate. Newly
inspired Sullan partisans raised a force and sallied out in the hope of
scattering the enemy in case it was just a bluff to intimidate the city. But
it was no bluff. The force that rode out the gates didn't come back. This
triggered a panic inside Rome. With Telesinus's army mostly composed
of Samnites and Lucanians, they would not be merciful if they breached
the walls. Indeed, as they stood before the Colline Gate, Telesinus gave
his men a fiery speech: "The last day is at hand for the Romans . . . These
wolves that made such ravages upon Italian liberty will never vanish
until we have cut down the forest that harbors them."[49]

Sulla was not far behind. After discovering the enemy had decamped
for Rome the night before, he spent the morning racing to catch up. At
about noon, the first of his men arrived at Rome, and once they were
all assembled, the battle trumpets sounded. Despite all his success over
the past eighteen months, Sulla spent the rest of the day convinced that
all was lost. He personally commanded the left wing of his army, which
buckled under the weight of the Samnites. In the confusion of battle,

Sulla believed Fortuna had finally abandoned him. Scattered messengers even raced back to Praeneste to tell the men there to break off the siege and reinforce Sulla's battered legions. But what Sulla did not know was that on the other side of the battle, Crassus had smashed the enemy and captured their camps. It was not until hours later that Sulla realized he had actually won the battle—and only then after Crassus sent Sulla a request for more food to feed his victorious troops. When all the dust cleared, the Battle of the Colline Gate was in fact not just a victory, but an utter route: fifty thousand enemies killed and eight thousand taken prisoner. Telesinus was himself found wounded in the field. He was killed and his head hoisted on a spear.[50]

When Sulla's legions returned to Praeneste bearing the heads of the Samnite generals, the inhabitants of the city gave up and opened the gates. Marius the Younger tried to escape through an underground tunnel, but when he found all exits guarded he committed suicide rather than accept capture. When Sulla himself arrived at the defeated city, he ordered the inhabitants divided up into three groups: Romans, Samnites, and Praenestians. He said the Romans deserved to die but that he would be merciful in victory and pardon them. The Samnites and Praenestians, on the other hand, were surrounded and massacred. Sulla then allowed the forces that had been prosecuting the siege to brutally sack Praeneste. The head of Marius the Younger was carried back to Rome. After his head was posted in the Forum, it became an object lesson in the folly of youth. The laughing Romans quoted Aristophanes: "First learn to row, before you try to steer."[51]

WITH ALL HIS enemies now defeated, Sulla himself returned to Rome. When he arrived the inhabitants of the city found him a very different man than the one who had addressed them a few months earlier. As the historian Cassius Dio later wrote:

> Sulla up to the day that he conquered the Samnites . . . was believed to be a very superior man both in humaneness and piety . . . But after this

event he changed so much that one would not say his earlier and his later deeds were those of the same person. Thus it would appear that he could not endure good fortune. For he now committed acts which he had censured in other persons while he was still weak, and a great many others still more outrageous. Thus Sulla, as soon as he had conquered the Samnites and thought he had put an end to the war ... changed his course, and leaving behind his former self, as it were, outside the wall on the field of battle, proceeded to outdo Cinna and Marius and all their successors combined.[52]

CHAPTER 13

DICTATOR FOR LIFE

The republic is nothing, a mere name
without body or form.

JULIUS CAESAR[1]

I N THE AFTERMATH OF HIS DECISIVE VICTORY AT THE COLLINE
Gate, Sulla set up a headquarters on the Campus Martius. Though
he was the master of Rome, at the moment he held no official magistracy. He was not a consul, or a praetor, or a legate, or even a quaestor.
His only claim to constitutional sovereignty came from his proconsular
assignment to the Mithridatic War. That appointment was now five years
old and concerned a war that had already been won, but it was all Sulla
had. By law, a provincial governor's sovereignty expired when he crossed
the sacred Pomerium and reentered Rome. In the routine course of empire this was a mere formality as men entered and exited office, but for
Sulla, it trapped him outside of Rome. If he crossed the city limits, he
would lose all his sovereign authority.

Despite ignoring the Pomerium so brazenly during his first march on
Rome, Sulla now elected to maintain this strange façade of constitutional
scruples. So he called the Senate to assemble at the Temple of Bellona
outside the walls rather than cross the sacred boundary. When the Senate
assembled, Sulla did not discuss the Civil War, but instead presented an

account of his actions in the Mithridatic War. After he listed his accomplishments in the east, he requested the right to enter the city in triumph. It was as if the last two years hadn't happened.[2]

But there was a dark backdrop to this charade. Before addressing the Senate, Sulla ordered six thousand Samnite prisoners herded into the adjacent Circus Flaminius. The Samnites had been told they were going to be counted and processed as prisoners of war, but they soon learned the truth. As Sulla began reading his report on the Mithridatic War to the Senate, his men surrounded the six thousand prisoners in the Circus Flaminius and methodically massacred them. Their screams were impossible to ignore inside the Temple of Bellona, and the dumbfounded senators were horrified. But Sulla bade them to please continue to listen to his remarks and "not concern themselves with what was going on outside, for it was only that some criminals were being admonished."[3]

When the killing was done, and the disturbed senators departed, Sulla called an open meeting to address the people of Rome. He reiterated that only his enemies need fear his wrath. For the first time, Sulla specifically said the defection of Asiaticus's army was the dividing line. Those who had exercised wisdom and joined him before that point could expect peace and friendship. Those who had remained under arms after that point were to be liquidated as enemies of the state. But he also pointedly said that the plebs urbana and common soldiers had nothing to fear from him. Sulla scrupulously allowed that these men had merely followed wicked leaders—and it was the leaders, not the followers, who should pay.[4]

With anxiety running high in the richer quarters of the city, a small deputation of senators approached Sulla and asked for some relief. They said, "We do not ask you to free from punishment those whom you have determined to slay, but to free from suspense those whom you have determined to save." When Sulla replied that he did not know whom he would save, one senator said, "Let us know whom you intend to punish." If everyone knew whom Sulla considered his mortal enemy, it would resolve a lot of anxiety on the Palatine Hill. Sulla took their words to heart and spent the night with his closest advisers talking it through. Obviously men who had served magistracies or senior commands in the

Cinnan regime would be marked for death, as would any noncombatant senator who had actively collaborated with the regime. The next morning, Sulla posted an inscribed tablet containing eighty names. These named men could be killed on sight and their property confiscated. The Sullan proscriptions had begun.[5]

THE LIST OF proscribed enemies started as way to free the innocent from fear. When the original list of eighty names went up, it seemed that the surgeon Sulla was going back to work. Yes, it was a seven-fold increase of the twelve men named after the first march on Rome, but a lot had happened since then. Sulla's enemies had declared him an enemy of the state, seized his property, exiled his family, killed his friends, and forced him to fight a civil war. Eighty seemed a bargain to atone for all that. But though a few of these eighty men scrambled to extract themselves from Rome, most already knew they could expect no mercy. Carbo, Norbanus, and Sertorius were all on the list. They had fled already. Since Marius had escaped Sulla's wrath by dying, Sulla settled for demolishing Marius's monuments and digging up the body of his late nemesis and scattering the bones.[6]

But the next day, the people of Rome awoke to a frightening revision. Overnight Sulla posted in the Forum a new list with 220 additional names. Men who had breathed a sigh of relief the day before now faced death. The following morning *another* new list went up. It now contained more than five hundred names. Now everyone lived in fear that at any moment they would be proscribed. A man who had been spared from the original lists arrived in the Forum one day to discover his name was now posted. When he discovered he was marked for death, he tried to cover his face and withdraw, but he was spotted, attacked, and killed on the spot. Another man reveled in the early days of the killing and mocked those who faced grim death. His name appeared on the list the next day; he was killed and his property confiscated. In addition to the proscribed themselves, anyone caught harboring a fugitive was also subject to immediate execution. Far from relieving tension, the proscription blanketed Italy under a reign of terror.[7]

As the proscriptions continued, the promise to limit victims to Sulla's personal enemies went up in smoke. Sulla not only paid a bounty for every head delivered, but he allowed the murderers a share of the victim's property. This led to an odious mingling of political proscription and personal profit as men with hard hearts and empty wallets fanned out across the peninsula to get rich killing Sulla's enemies. With the official proscription list ever changing, a man's name could be added to the list simply because he was rich and held valuable property. An apolitical Equestrian named Quintus Aurelius found his name posted on the list and lamented that he was, "done for because of my Alban Farm."[8]

Out in the countryside of Italy, the list itself acted as a basic guideline with improvisation left to the discretion of senior officers. Among those sent forth was Marcus Licinius Crassus, the hero of the Battle of the Colline Gate. Accompanied by a greedy and brutal young officer named Gaius Verres, Crassus traveled a circuit across Italy taking testimony from locals about anti-Sullans in their midst. The guidelines of the proscription now included any family that had rendered material aid to Sulla's enemies, so local merchants, bankers, and magistrates were seized and executed. But, as often as not, local pro-Sullan leaders took the opportunity to eliminate personal rivals, naming men who were not enemies of Sulla, but enemies of themselves. Little care or notice was taken why a man was named, but the punishment was always the same: execution and confiscation of property. Crassus and Verres both became experts at this swift and profitable justice. Beginning his infamously sadistic career in real estate, Crassus had a man executed in Bruttium just to seize an attractive estate.[9]

Aside from Sulla's formal representatives like Crassus, unofficial murder gangs also now roamed the streets. Professional proscription became a lucrative business to get into. Joining these gangs was another ambitious youth with a cruel streak named Lucius Sergius Catilina, more commonly known as Catiline. In twenty years, Catiline would stand at the center of another cycle of revolutionary upheaval, but for the moment he was simply a young Sullan partisan on the make. Coveting the property of his brother-in-law, Catiline killed the man to get title to the land. Then he made a run through the Equestrian merchant class, murdering his way to an impressive portfolio. He rounded this out by targeting his other brother-in-law—who just so happened to be Marcus Marius Gratidianus, the nephew of Marius who had introduced the measure to guarantee coins during the Cinnan regime. Falsely accusing Gratidianus of murdering Catulus during the Marian terror, Catiline dragged his brother-in-law to Catulus's tomb and brutally murdered him.[10]

With the rules collapsing, the proscription became self-perpetuating as new victims could always be named. One man was killed for lamenting the death of his friend. One of Sulla's freedmen killed another man to settle a personal score, then conspired to add the victim's name to the list after the fact. Another freedman was dragged to face Sulla after he was discovered hiding one of the proscribed. To his astonishment, Sulla discovered the man was his old upstairs neighbor from when he lived in the rented apartment before his public career began. Sulla ordered his old neighbor tossed from the Tarpeian Rock.[11]

The proscriptions soon reached beyond Italy as many of Sulla's principal enemies had fled the peninsula. Norbanus was located in Rhodes. Agents of Sulla demanded the city hand him over or face grave consequences. As the Rhodians debated what to do, Norbanus did them all a favor by going down to the marketplace and committing suicide. Sulla also dispatched Pompey to personally hunt down Carbo. Following intelligence that Carbo was on an island off the coast of Sicily, Pompey sailed for Sicily. Upon arrival Pompey convened summary tribunals to identify and execute known anti-Sullan partisans. When the people of Messana protested that the tribunals were illegal, Pompey snapped, "Cease quoting laws to us that have swords." Carbo was soon tracked down and dragged before the tribunal. Though Carbo was still technically consul of Rome, Pompey paid the sanctity of the office no mind. He ordered Gnaeus Papirius Carbo, three-time consul of Rome, executed on the spot.[12]

In the final stage of the proscriptions, the killing became indiscriminate. Because this was ancient Rome and not the digital age, no one *really* knew what a proscribed man actually looked like. When a proscription gang had trouble tracking down the real victim, they seized random people off the street. These anonymous heads were then presented to Sulla as if they were real men from the list. Sulla asked few questions and always paid the bounty. The idea that there was any rationality or morality to the proscriptions became a cruel joke: "The whole state was now plunging headlong into ruin . . . avarice furnished a motive for ruthlessness; the magnitude of one's crime was determined by the magnitude of his property; he who possessed riches became a malefactor and was in each case the prize set up for his own murder. In short nothing was regarded as dishonorable that brought profit."[13]

As the weeks passed and the killing continued, some effort was finally made to end the terror. Sulla announced that no more names would be proscribed after June 1, 82. In the meantime, men already on the list might use friends influential with Sulla to get their names *off* the list, the most famous case of this sort being nineteen-year-old Gaius Julius Caesar—*the* Gaius Julius Caesar. In addition to the crime of being Marius's nephew, Caesar had also married Cinna's daughter. Sulla ordered Caesar to divorce his wife, but Caesar refused. So Caesar's name went on the proscription list and he was forced into hiding. But the young man had friends deep in Sulla's inner circle, and after a few weeks they secured him a pardon. Sulla did not grant the pardon without reservation, however, and said, "Have your way and take him; only bear in mind that the man you are so eager to save will one day deal the death blow to the cause of the aristocracy, which you have joined with me in upholding; for in this Caesar there is more than one Marius."[14]

The sweeping orgy of terror finally wound itself down after the June 1 deadline came and went. Guilty men could still be tracked down and killed, but the worst was now over. A final accounting will never be possible, but at a minimum about a hundred senators and over one thousand Equestrians were killed in the Sullan proscriptions—with the total death toll possibly as high as three thousand. But good to his word, Sulla and his assassins mostly left the lower classes of Italy alone; not only were they spared for noble reasons, but also because they had no property that was liable to make them "guilty." As the killing wound down, it was time for Sulla to embark on the rejuvenation of the Republic made possible by his purge of his enemies.[15]

WHILE HIS AGENTS prowled the streets, Sulla himself had not yet found a way to enter Rome without losing his constitutional authority. The best option would be to secure election as consul, but technically the consuls for the year were still Carbo and Marius the Younger. With Carbo dead in Sicily and Marius the Younger's head rotting in the Forum, they were not available to convene elections. So Sulla had to get more creative.

While Sulla fretted over his sovereignty, the remaining rump of the Senate took steps to legitimize his actions. They accepted his report on the Mithridatic War and confirmed all the settlements he had made in Asia. They repealed the decree making him an enemy of the state. They even ordered a large statue of Sulla be erected in the Forum bearing an inscription of Sulla's own devising: LUCIUS CORNELIUS SULLA FELIX. The title "Felix" now entered his official propaganda; it meant Sulla the Fortunate. But all of those decrees still left Sulla on the other side of the walls. So Sulla offered a radical suggestion: revive the ancient Dictatorship.[16]

It had been 120 years since Rome gave itself over to the hands of a dictator. Once a ubiquitous office in the early days of the Republic, the Dictatorship had been abandoned in the triumphant era of the Republican Empire. Even recent existential emergencies like the Cimbrian Wars and the Social War had not triggered a revival of the office, nor had the violent unrest of the Gracchi and Saturninus. From his headquarters on the Campus Martius, Sulla composed a long letter to the Senate proposing they make him dictator. He said that Italy was devastated, the Republic gutted by the fire of a brutal civil war. There was no aspect of social, political, or economic life that had not been upended by the events of the last decade. If Sulla was to fulfill his destiny and restore the Republic to its former glory, he needed more than consular authority. He need absolute and unquestioned authority.[17]

Sulla's suggestion was a shocking deviation from all accepted custom, but what was the Senate to do? Say no? It was like asking the legions surrounded in Numantia in 137 if they wanted to be slaughtered. So they complied with Sulla's request. To bridge the constitutional gap now that both sitting consuls were dead, the Senate revived the ancient office of *interrex*. The Republic had occasionally used an interrex to oversee consular elections if the consuls were dead or so indisposed that they could not return to Rome. Since this was obviously the case, the interrex convened the Assembly and presented a bill to make Sulla *dictator legibus faciendis et reipublicae constitienae*: "Dictator for the making of laws and settling of the constitution." The Assembly passed the bill unanimously.[18]

With plenty of legal advisers on hand, and with a decent grasp of constitutional law himself, Sulla ensured his new title came with all requisite powers to act without constraint. As dictator, Sulla now had the power of life and death over all Romans. He had sole discretion over declarations of war and peace. He could appoint or remove senators. He could confiscate property at will. He could found new cities and colonies. He could punish and destroy existing cities. He had the final say in all matters in the provinces, the treasury, and the courts. Most importantly the dictator's every decree automatically became law. The enormous constitutional force of the Assembly now existed at Sulla's mere word.[19]

Despite the irregular way Sulla entered the Dictatorship, this was all mostly in keeping with the ancient powers of the office. He even appointed a Master of the Horse, the traditional partner of the dictator who answered to no one *but* the dictator. But there was a large and unprecedented omission from the law naming him dictator: an expiration date. Old Roman dictators never served terms longer than six months, a limit literally written into the law that created their dictatorship. But Sulla conveniently left that part out. After hinting to the Senate that six months might not be enough to restore the Republic, Sulla implied his dictatorship was to be held in perpetuity. With no legal obligation to ever set his vast array of powers aside, Lucius Cornelius Sulla was now Dictator for Life.[20]

Despite all the constitutional reforms he was about to unveil to restore the proper order of the Old Republic in the next generation, the mundane rules of republican order paled in comparison to the example of a single man holding unlimited power indefinitely. And it would be the Dictatorship of Sulla, not the Republic of Sulla, that would be his lasting legacy.

S ULLA HAD ALREADY revealed much of what he planned for the Republic after his first march on Rome. Before leaving to take command of the Mithridatic War, he carried laws to expand the power of the Senate, including moving all voting to the less democratic Centuriate Assembly, expanding the rolls of the Senate, and requiring the Senate's consent before a bill could be presented to the Assembly. After Cinna took over Rome these reforms were canceled, but now they returned as a part of Sulla's final constitutional settlement. To his original kernel of reforms, the dictator Sulla introduced a package of new laws to place the Senate back at the center of the Republic.[21]

With the tribunate so often used to lob antisenatorial bombs, Sulla severely curtailed their power. Originally designed to protect the individual rights of plebeians, the office had morphed into a dangerous instrument of demagogues and tyrants. So in addition to requiring a tribune to seek permission from the Senate before introducing a bill, Sulla also abolished the all-purpose, all-powerful veto. A tribune could now only levy a veto in matters pertaining to individual requests for clemency. But more important than these procedural restrictions, Sulla decreed that men elected tribune were barred from all other magistracies. This prohibition ensured that ambitious young leaders would never seek the office again. What once had been a springboard into politics was now a dead end.[22]

The tribunes contained, Sulla then formalized the rest of the republican list of magistracies. Until now, rules of progression up the cursus honorum from quaestor to consul had always been vague and unspoken. Sulla formalized the path. He also expanded the ranks of offices, doubling the number of quaestors to twenty and adding two more praetors. Rome was long overdue to add more official administrative posts to match their expanded empire. Sulla also decreed that two years had to elapse in between offices no matter what, and ten years had to pass before a man could run for the same office. There would not be repeat consulships in Sulla's republic.[23]

Sulla did not want repeated governorships either. With eight praetors and two consuls now serving annually, there would be no need to keep men in provinces for more than a year or two. But this was not about improving provincial administration. Provincial assignments gave men access to wealth, connections, and power. Keeping a high rate of turnover in the provinces did nothing to help Roman provincials, but it helped maintain the balance of power back in the Senate. It went without saying that all provincial assignments would be also controlled by the Senate. The Assembly would have nothing to do with it.[24]

To match the expanded cursus honorum, Sulla also doubled the rolls of the Senate from three hundred to six hundred. As dictator, Sulla naturally took the liberty to assign all the new senators. The course of the civil wars had dwindled the number of living senators below two hundred anyway, so over the course of his dictatorship he regularly elevated loyal officers and virtuous friends into the Senate. But even Sulla did not personally know four hundred worthy candidates; he took suggestions from various parties and created a whole cohort of grateful senators, loyal not just to Sulla, but to the reformed Republic he created.[25]

With an expanded Senate now filling up, Sulla could also restore control of the courts. The fight that had been ongoing back to the days of the Gracchi would now be settled once and for all. The jury pool for permanent courts would be the Senate. The decree enlarging the Senate was partly meant to give the Senate sufficient manpower to dispense justice in the array of permanent courts Sulla now established.[26]

The first permanent court the Romans established was the Extortion Court way back in 149. Over the years, other courts had been created to serve various needs: almost certainly a court to try cases of electoral fraud, and most famously Saturninus's treason court that had been established in 103. Sulla now proposed to clean up and systematize the hodgepodge of tribunals and courts with seven new permanent courts for murder, counterfeiting and forgery, electoral fraud, embezzlement, treason, personal injury, and provincial extortion. Some of these already existed, some were new, and others were altered from previous iterations. Saturninus's treason court, which originally resembled a revolutionary tribunal, was now limited to a few explicit crimes. There would be no revolutionary tribunals in Sulla's republic.[27]

Sulla also used his dictatorial power to address the always-vital question of land distribution. The chaos of the civil wars—and Sulla's ultimate victory—opened up wide new swaths of land in Italy for settlement for the first time in thirty years. Tons of Italian land already lay vacant thanks to the upheavals of the past few years, and Sulla also doled out heavy punishment to regions that had opposed him. Etruria, Umbria, and Samnium—deep wells of anti-Sullan resistance—were targeted for mass seizure of property and redistribution to Sulla's own veterans.[28]

Sulla's run of reforms was designed to roll the Republic back to its roots as a senatorial aristocracy. Almost all authority now emanated from the Senate. The tribunes were stripped of their power, the autonomy of the Assembly curtailed. Equestrians and publicani returned to a state of political and economic subservience. He even made an attempt at passing sumptuary laws to limit expenses on games, banquets, and personal finery, but as usual these came to nothing—Sulla himself ignored his own limits routinely. But it would be unfair to say that Sulla's head was stuck in the past: he believed he was building a regime to address specific problems of the present that had plagued the Republic, and with his reforms they might not plague the Republic in the future.[29]

One of the biggest problems that could not be solved by looking to the past was the fate of the Italians. Looking to the past would have meant going back to the old confederal hierarchy of citizenship, but Sulla never considered breaking his word to honor civitas and suffragium. When the next census arrived, the number of citizens on the rolls doubled, and from that point on the Italian question was never heard again. Just as they had always feared, the old Romans lost influence and Italians gained a larger voice. But so what? There was no longer any reason to treat a man born in Latium any different than a man born in Picenum; the voice of the Roman citizen was not lost, it simply changed pitch with the addition of new voices. Rome now belonged to everyone.[30]

DESPITE HIS DICTATORIAL power being held in perpetuity, Sulla never intended to stay in the Dictatorship indefinitely. He considered himself a unique and special lawgiver, but he was at heart a republican, not a king. He meant exactly what he said when he assumed the Dictatorship: he was going to make laws and settle the constitution. Not being a petty tyrant, Sulla had no intention of infinitely delaying when the constitution would be declared "settled." He was there to do the job he believed the gods wanted him to do, and then resign.

Sulla began the process of shedding power about a year after he assumed office. In mid-81, he announced that he would be a candidate for consul alongside Metellus Pius. Still scrupulously treated as a near-equal, Sulla considered Pius's continued partnership with his regime one of the last great examples of Fortuna's favor. Pius could have made a great deal of trouble for the dictator, but instead accepted the transformation Sulla promised to inaugurate. Their shared consulship would be a sign not only of continued friendship, but also Sulla's intention to *not* remain dictator for life.[31]

But though this was all going great for Sulla, and he was ready to start playing the part of a republican again, one of his subordinates stepped forward to make a nuisance of himself. The election for 80 was supposed to be a stage-managed affair, but instead one of Sulla's praetors got it into his head to take a crack at the consulship. Sulla had sent word round forbidding such distractions, but out of inexplicable bravado the man entered his name anyway. Even after he was explicitly told to stand down, the oblivious praetor returned to the Forum to canvass for votes. Sulla had no choice but to order the man killed where he stood.[32]

This unpleasant business concluded, Sulla called for a mass meeting to address all the citizens of Rome. As he had done so many times before, Sulla was ready to share his plans to create an honest bond of trust between them all. He planted himself in the Forum and announced he was resigning the Dictatorship; he now stood before them as a citizen of Rome and was ready to answer all questions or challenges. Then he dismissed his official bodyguards and walked out into the streets. He was no longer dictator of Rome. He was simply citizen Sulla. But in an amusing coda to his voluntary renunciation of power, when Sulla departed the Forum he was followed by a boy who heckled him mercilessly. Entering his house and leaving the obnoxious jeers behind, Sulla wryly quipped, "This young man will prevent any future holder of such power from laying it down."[33]

But Sulla was himself serious about shedding power. He and Pius were elected consuls for 80, but after this further year governing Rome not as dictator but as consul, Sulla was ready to move on. When the Assembly returned Sulla as consul for 79, he declined to serve. He accepted an almost honorary proconsulship in Cisalpine Gaul but never visited the province. Instead, he moved down to a country villa in Campania. There he lived at the center of a country court that signaled a freewheeling embrace of his old carefree ways. He hosted his old friends in the theater community, intellectuals from across the Mediterranean, and the political elite from across the known world. Sulla never stopped paying close attention to Roman politics—and Roman politics never stopped paying attention to Sulla—but the Sullan era was truly over.[34]

Back in Rome, the Sullan faction was for the most part united around Sulla's constitutional reforms, but that did not mean they were united in purpose. Their allegiance to one another had come from a shared allegiance to Sulla. Now that he was withdrawing, everyone was free to pursue their own factional backbiting. Metellus Pius was too imperious. Pompey too arrogant. Crassus too greedy. Sulla's republic may have tried to confine these disputes to a healthy give-and-take in the political arena, but that did not mean there would be harmony.

In between drinking sessions, Sulla spent much of his time composing an enormous memoir that would explain and justify everything he had ever said or done. He filled it with detailed accounts of every campaign he fought in, every office he held, every piece of public business he had transacted, why his friends were his friends and why his enemies were his enemies. This memoir was meant to paint a clear picture of Sulla as the chosen son of Fortuna who was guilty only of courage, fidelity, patriotism. Sulla's final plan to control events was a masterful success, as later historians relied heavily on the memoir as a primary source. Our own understanding of Sulla some two thousand years later is still very often *his* version of events.[35]

W HEN HE RETIRED, Sulla was still only about sixty years old—not young by any means, but also nowhere near death. As Sulla completed his memoirs, he no doubt looked forward to at least another decade of honorable retirement. His wife Metella had recently died, but he had taken a new bride and had another new baby on the way. But he also had premonitions of his imminent demise. He described a dream where his dead son "appeared to him . . . and besought his father to pursue an end to anxious thoughts, and come with him to his mother Metella, there to live in peace and quietness with her." But even these unsettling dreams did not deter him from working on his memoir or transacting business that presented itself.[36]

But while conducting a piece of public business in 78, Sulla was suddenly stricken. A local magistrate had been caught embezzling money from the city treasury, and while Sulla yelled at the thief, something ruptured inside his body and he spurted blood out of his mouth. Almost certainly caused by liver failure or a huge ulcer, Sulla collapsed in a heap of blood and bile and was carried back home, where he spent "a night of wretchedness." By morning, Lucius Cornelius Sulla was dead.[37]

When word of the dictator's death reached Rome, a debate erupted over how to respond. Some believed that it was already time to mark his career infamous and deny funeral rights. Sulla had murdered his fellow citizens and made himself tyrant. But Pompey stepped forward and retorted that he believed that a great man like Sulla deserved an elaborate public funeral, and he couldn't believe it was even a question. The elaborate funeral was duly staged. But the debate over Sulla's legacy was only beginning. In later years, what one thought of Sulla spoke volumes about one's character.[38]

Sulla's ashes were laid in his ancestral tomb, and a monument to him was erected in the Campus Martius. His enduring credo was emblazoned on the monument for all time: "No friend ever surpassed him in kindness, and no enemy in wickedness."[39]

THE SULLAN CONSTITUTION did not survive. In the first years of the new regime, the senior Sullan leaders who took over Rome—Metellus Pius, Pompey, and Crassus chief among them—scrupulously followed Sulla's constitution. But as the memory of Sulla faded and new political rivalries emerged, these leaders abandoned the Sullan decrees whenever expedient. In the end, it turned out Sulla's "final" settlement was just another milestone on the Republic's road to ruin.

One of the reasons Sulla's constitution fared so poorly was that those who supported it did so mildly, and those who hated it did so passionately. Sulla's proscriptions had left a mob of enemies in their wake. After the killing was over, the dictator Sulla barred their sons and grandsons from running for office. These families were among the most prominent in Rome, and cutting off their access to public office sowed permanent resentment. Many of them joined an aborted revolt against Sulla's constitution, led by the consul Lepidus in 78. The revolt was quickly suppressed, but it showed how tenuous the peace really was. Even when the ban on the proscribed families was lifted and they were allowed to return to public life, it was certainly not with the same veneration for republican morality—and certainly with no respect for Sulla's constitution.[40]

The law curtailing the power of the tribunes lasted barely a decade. Despite Sulla's efforts, the populare path to power was still a viable option, and leaders curried favor with the people throughout the 70s by promising to restore the tribunes to their full dignity. The men who finally capitalized on this popular promise were Pompey and Crassus, who restored the ancient power of the tribunes during their shared consulship in 70. In that same year, the praetor Lucius Aurelius Cotta passed a law undoing Sulla's judicial laws and opening the jury pool to both the Senate and Equestrians. Sulla's attempt at Italian land redistribution fared no better. Just as had happened with the Gracchan program, within a generation Sulla's veterans had mostly sold their land to rich magnates, and the end result was the Italian peninsula being dominated by large estates like never before. The provincial reorganization was similarly inadequate. Even with Sulla's expanded roster of magistracies, the Roman Empire was still only run by perhaps a hundred men. It was not until the Augustan settlements that something resembling a permanent bureaucracy stabilized the corrupt and inadequate provisional administration.[41]

No one was more to blame for the failure of the Sullan constitution than Sulla himself. The facts of Sulla's career spoke louder than his constitutional musings. As a young man he had flouted traditional rules of loyalty and deference to spread his own fame. When insulted, he marched legions on Rome. While abroad, he ran his own military campaigns and conducted his own diplomacy. When challenged back in Rome, he launched a civil war, declared himself dictator, killed his enemies, and then retired to get drunk in splendid luxury. The biography of Sulla drowned out the constitution of Sulla, and the men who followed him paid attention to what *could* be done rather than what *should* be done.

In the final analysis, Sulla's attempt to restore the Republic was doomed because he misdiagnosed the problem. In Sulla's estimation the political upheavals that wracked Rome from the time of his birth in 138 until his death in 78 were the result of the Senate losing their dominant position. But what he did not realize is that the senatorial domination he had grown up with was a recent development. In fact, that domination was a leading *cause* of the problem, not a solution. Sulla thought he was resetting the constitutional balance to its natural state. Instead he was just winding back the clock on a ticking time bomb.

As would be predicted by Polybius's constitutional theory, the restored domination of the senatorial oligarchy provoked populare demagogues, leading to an even more ferocious series of civil wars in the 40s and 30s. But Polybian theory did not hold for long. The fall of the senatorial oligarchy was precipitated by rhetorical populists, but their aim was never democracy, nor did democracy follow. Instead, weary of a generation of civil war, the Romans moved directly to the stable hand of an enlightened monarch. Unlike Sulla, however, when Augustus ascended to sole power he did not retire. So in the end, Sulla's constitution did not lead to the permanent triumph of the aristocratic element, but rather the permanent triumph of the monarchical element. Though there never would be another king of Rome, there would be emperors. And they would rule Rome for a very long time.

THE CORE OF the future Caesarian coalition that would reduce the Senate to a tiresome social club was rooted in the old Gracchan coalition of rural peasants, plebs urbana, publicani merchants, and renegade nobles. Mixing popular rhetoric with direct appeals to self-interest, the Caesars would be able to harness these powers to finally destroy the senatorial aristocracy. But that did not mean every member shared equally in the spoils.

The original demographic tapped by the Gracchans was the rural poor. The small farmers had been the focus of reform efforts going back to Tiberius Gracchus's original *Lex Agraria*. The Gracchi had tried to rebuild the population of small farmers by redistributing ager publicus to poor citizens. But within a generation the rich had bought back all the plots. Gaius Marius addressed the problem by recruiting landless plebs into the armies and then discharging them with land in the province in which they had fought. Marian colonies now existed in Africa, Sicily, and Gaul. Sulla then attempted one last redistribution of Italian land, but as we just saw this redistribution also failed. The economic momentum toward sprawling *latifundia* was by then inexorable. The solution to the problem of the small farmer in Italy was only solved when they were all dead.[42]

The plebs urbana, meanwhile, grew in numbers and strength. As the dislocations in rural Italy continued, migration to the cities began in earnest. By the age of Augustus, the population of Rome had ballooned to 750,000. During the imperial Golden Age in the 100s AD, it went over a million. The growth of Rome is partly attributable to expansion of the grain dole. The subsidized grain supply introduced by Gaius Gracchus became a permanent feature of Roman municipal policy. But it is important to remember that the grain dole only applied to male citizens, and only entitled those citizens to a subsistence ration. So though the idleness of the plebs urbana was a frequent complaint, true idleness would have been fatal. For the rest of the Republic, and the entirety of the imperial age, feeding the plebs urbana a stable supply of cheap grain was a routine part of municipal administration. The grain dole helped create stability— as welcome to the rulers as to the ruled.[43]

Benefiting most from the triumph of the Caesars were the Equestrians. After the death of Sulla, Rome only continued to expand and open up new opportunities for business. As the principal merchants of the most dominant power in the Mediterranean, the Equestrians controlled huge quantities of wealth. When Augustus imposed his imperial settlement in the 20s, he used men of Equestrian rank to fill his growing provincial bureaucracy. In Egypt, Augustus would not even let a man of senatorial rank enter. Under Augustus's regime, the governor of Egypt *had* to be a man of Equestrian rank. The Equestrians would go on to manage the empire for the next five hundred years.[44]

One pillar of the original Gracchan coalition that had triumphed already was the Italians. The Italian question had been answered when Sulla accepted unqualified civitas and suffragium in the spring of 83. Now full and equal citizens, every Italian was legally indistinguishable from a Roman. Prosperous Italian Equestrians became prosperous Roman Equestrians. Powerful Italian leaders became powerful Roman leaders. There was, of course, always lingering social elitism. To the snobs on the Palatine Hill a man like Cicero would always be a novus homo Italian. This snobbery would persist for a thousand years but was legally meaningless. Rome was Italy, and Italy was Rome.

Supplanting the Italians as Rome's second-class citizens would be the foreign provincials. Republican governors continued to pump the provinces for money, much of which went to fund factional politics back in Rome. This problem was not solved until the Augustan settlements of the 20s BC. With Augustus claiming supreme proconsular authority outside Italy, his provinces were run by stable groups of Equestrian administrators operating under Augustus's personal sovereignty. Recognizing that the provincials were just as deserving of good government as the Italians, Augustus dialed back the haphazard exploitation and created a self-perpetuating balance between power and mercy. The emperor Tiberius would chide an overzealous governor: "It was the part of a good shepherd to shear his flock, not skin it."[45]

Oddly enough, the issue of provincial citizenship never became a major object of conflict. After the unification of Italy, the other provincial centers in Spain, Greece, and Africa remained merely subjects of Rome. This was a pattern that continued as Rome expanded into Gaul and Syria. But individuals could be awarded citizenship (the legions in particular became a frequently trod path), and soon there were Roman citizens of Spanish, Gallic, African, Greek, and Syrian origin. But mass provincial citizenship was never considered until the third century AD, and even then was imposed from the top down. With many noncitizens exempt from certain taxes, the emperor Caracalla decreed universal citizenship in 211. As the historian Cassius Dio says, "nominally he was honoring them, but his real purpose was to increase his revenues." So mass provincial citizenship was only extended once it became a burden rather than a privilege.[46]

THESE GROUPS REENTERED the historical stream after the death of Sulla and proceeded to get back to the business of jockeying for power. The brief revolt led by the populare consul Lepidus in 78 reminded everyone how volatile the situation remained. The provinces of Spain also remained an open wound. Having escaped Italy, Quintus Sertorius established a base in Iberia and kept up the war against the Sullans even after the heads of all his former compatriots rotted in the Forum. Joined by other Marian exiles fleeing the proscriptions, Sertorius spent ten years keeping the war alive. Both Metellus Pius and Pompey failed to subdue him. When Pompey got sick of being stuck in the Spanish quagmire, he extracted himself by orchestrating the assassination of Sertorius in 72. This was the last fire of a conflagration that had begun with the Social War nearly twenty years earlier.[47]

Meanwhile, the victorious Sullans fractured. Metellus Pius, Pompey, and Crassus withdrew to their respective corners and pursued their own agendas. Crassus and Pompey, in particular, detested each other. When Spartacus raised the final great slave revolt that consumed Italy in 73–72, Crassus was the one who finally ended the uprising. But to Crassus's fury, Pompey managed to swing back from Spain, defeat the last remaining cohort of renegade slaves, and take credit for *truly* ending the conflict. The bitter rivalry of Crassus and Pompey helped define the next twenty years of Roman politics.[48]

But between Crassus and Pompey rose an ambitious young noble who would outshine them both: Gaius Julius Caesar. Having survived the proscription, Caesar emerged in the 70s as an ambitious young political talent. In 69, he took the provocative step of openly mourning the death of his aunt Julia—the wife of Gaius Marius. During her funeral procession, Caesar displayed images of Marius for the first time since Sulla's dictatorship. It annoyed the optimates in the Senate, but it ginned up a wave of popular sympathy for Marius, whom they had once called the Third

Founder of Rome. This helped pave the way for the ban on proscribed families being lifted, but those who had felt the indignity of the proscription formed an unspoken bond, and an affinity for populare politics. Caesar skillfully exploited their lingering resentment.[49]

While the nobles fought, Rome continued to expand. The war with Mithridates had never really ended. Undeterred by his earlier defeat, Mithridates launched a series of major wars against Rome that lasted all the way until his death, at the hands of Pompey the Great, in 63. With Mithridates finally defeated, Pompey took the legions on a grand tour of the eastern Mediterranean, organizing the east into a network of allied client kingdoms. When Pompey returned to Rome, Caesar successfully reconciled Pompey and Crassus and together they formed a secret alliance called the First Triumvirate that would dominate Rome for the next decade. The Triumvirate awarded land to Pompey's veterans, approved a war in Syria for Crassus, and made Caesar proconsul of Gaul. While Pompey remained in Rome, Caesar successfully conquered all of modern France. Crassus meanwhile was led into an ambush in Syria and died a gruesome death in 53.[50]

The death of Crassus broke the alliance between Caesar and Pompey, and the political factions realigned again for a final showdown in the 40s. Pompey lined up with the optimates in the Senate. Caesar lined up with his own network of populare partisans and loyal veterans. After crossing the Rubicon in 49, Caesar defeated all his enemies and had himself declared dictator for life. Mocking Sulla by saying that "Sulla did not know his ABCs when he laid down his dictatorship," Caesar clearly did not plan to relinquish the Dictatorship, so a gang of senators led by Brutus and Cassius murdered him in 44. After the Ides of March, Caesar's heirs Octavian and Mark Antony* combined to defeat the remnants of the Senate, and then waged a civil war against each other for control of the empire. Victorious over all his enemies, Octavian transformed himself into Augustus in 27, and the Roman Republic transformed into the Roman Empire.[51]

Augustus's imperial settlement was premised on the accumulation of all sovereign authority in the hands of one man. The Centuriate Assem-

---

* Grandson of the late Marcus Antonius.

bly elected Augustus consul, so he held consular authority. The Plebeian Assembly simultaneously elected him tribune, so he held tribunician authority. With that authority, Augustus could veto any bill and was immune from physical attack. The Senate also granted him proconsular power in all the provinces, making him commander in chief of almost all of Rome's armed forces. In time, he also became pontifex maximus and controlled the priesthoods and temples. Augustus maintained the charade of republican government throughout his reign. Annual elections proceeded as before, as did meetings of the Assembly. Augustus also met regularly with a senior council of senators to give them the appearance of equal participation. Augustus never created a new office of "emperor"— that is simply the label later Romans gave to the bound-together *fascist* of individual sovereign powers now collectively vested in the hands of one man. Augustus himself preferred to be called simply *princeps*—the first citizen among equals.[52]

But underneath the charade of republican ritual, the monarchical element of the Polybian constitution had permanently triumphed. Still, contrary to Polybius's theory, the triumph of the Caesars did not inevitably lead to an aristocratic response. The imperial administration created by Augustus entered a mode of permanent self-perpetuation. Provincials and Equestrians thrived under the new order, and if a few senators lost power, so what? Inside the Senate there was hope the Old Republic would be revived, but the Republic was never coming back. Sulla died in 78 believing he had breathed new life into the Republic. But what looked like the dawning of a new age was really the last moments of light before the Roman Republic disappeared over the horizon.

ACKNOWLEDGMENTS

A NY LIST OF acknowledgments must begin with my wife, Brandi, to whom this book is already dedicated. She has been with me every step of the way and been an unfailing source of strength, support, and love. I would also like to thank my children, Elliott and Olive, who have been wonderful through the entire process and who I hope like the book once they learn how to read. My parents, Doug and Liz Duncan, have also provided incredible support not just while the book was being written, but throughout my entire life. Without them this book would not exist. My success is their success.

This book would also not exist without my literary agent, Rachel Vogel, who sent me an e-mail one day asking if I had ever considered writing a book. She then nursed a half-baked idea from infancy to maturity and guided me through the long and convoluted process of selling, writing, and promotion. I could not have asked for a better shepherd through the often baffling world of publishing.

I was also lucky enough to have landed with my editor, Colleen Lawrie, at PublicAffairs. She not only said yes to the project in the first place, but provided expert advice and guidance as we took the manuscript from a blank piece of paper to a completed manuscript. The rest of the team at PublicAffairs has also been fantastic—especially for a first-time author. Managing editor Katie Haigler, publicist Kristina Fazzalaro, copy editor Bill Warhop, designer Linda Mark, marketing coordinator Miguel Cervantes, and marketing director Lindsay Fradkoff were all a pleasure to work with. The book is better for all of their hard work.

For research, I am incredibly grateful to the University of Wisconsin, which is a bastion of enlightened civic engagement. UW offers residents of the state of Wisconsin full run of their libraries and unlimited access to otherwise impossible-to-find academic journals. Without these resources I would have been lost. The Wisconsin Idea of fostering a collaborative educational network linking academics, public servants, and citizens is among the most noble endeavors in the history of western civilization. In 1905, UW president Charles Van Hise said, "I shall never be content until the beneficent influence of the University reaches every family of the state." I cannot speak for everyone, but the beneficent influence of the university has certainly reached me.

I am also eternally indebted to the community of classical academics and enthusiasts who maintain online databases of ancient literary sources—fully searchable and instantly available. In particular, I relied on the work of the Perseus Digital Library at Tufts University, Jona Lendering and Livius.org, Bill Thayer and his LacusCurtius archives, and Andrew Smith at Attalus.org. This book would have been a poor effort were it not for their efforts.

Finally, I would like to thank every single listener of the *History of Rome* and *Revolutions* podcasts, who truly made all this possible. I will remain forever grateful that you have allowed me to turn a passion for history into a career in history. I hope you liked the book.

NOTES

ALL MODERN BOOKS about ancient Rome derive from the corpus of surviving ancient literary texts (with crucial gaps filled in by archaeology, numismatics, and epigraphy). Writing about Rome is akin to creating a mosaic from fragments of tile left in disorganized chaos after two thousand years of admirable, but still inadequate, storage and maintenance. The mosaic of the period 146 to 78 BC is built around four principal authors: Appian, Plutarch, Sallust, and Cicero. But surrounding those four principal sources, critical details are filled in by other Greek and Roman historians, scholars, and commentators. To give the reader a clear sense of how our knowledge of the ancient world is pieced together, the endnotes focus on the ancient literary sources. A reference table and explanation for how to read the notes is included. Hopefully the reader will be encouraged to discover the joy of studying the ancient masters for themselves.

PROLOGUE

1. Polyb. i.1.
2. Polyb. xxxviii.21–22; App. *Pun.* xix.132; Diod. xxxii.24.
3. Paus. vii.16.7–10; Strabo viii.6.23; Cic. *Leg. Agr.* ii.87, *Off.* i.35; Flor. i.32.16; Livy 52.
4. Polyb. vi.57; Sall. *Cat.* 10, *Jug.* 41; Vell. Pat. ii.1; Flor. i.1; Oros. v.3.
5. Livy i.4–7; Plut. *Rom.* 3–12; Diony. i.75–88; Diod. viii.3–6; Dio i.5; Flor. i.1.6–8; Oros. ii.4; Vell. Pat. i.8; App. *Reg* i.2; Strabo v.3.2.

6. CAH VII.2 ch. 2.

7. Livy i.8, 19–20, 42–44, 58–60; Diony. ii.4–16, 63–74, iv.13–23, 64–85; Plut. *Rom.* 13, *Num.* 8–13, *Pub.* 1; Flor. i.1–2, 6.

8. Quote: Appian *BC* i.1. See also: Livy ii-iii; Flor. i.4.

9. Livy ii.31–33, 56–57, iii.6, 55; Plut. *Cor.* 6–7; Diony. vi.45–90; Dio iv.14–15.

10. See Hölkeskamp, *Reconstructing the Roman Republic*, ch. 2.

11. Livy viii-x; Diony. xv-xvii; Diod. xix.76, 101; Dio viii; App. *Samn.*; Flor. i.11.16–12.17; Strabo vi.4.2; Oros. iii.15, 21–22.

12. Diod. xix.103–110, xx.10, 17–18, 38, 40, 43, 59, 61–62, 64, 67, 69.

13. Polyb. ii-iii, xii-xii, xv; Livy xxi-xxx; App. *Han.* i-ix, *Pun.* i-vii, *Iber.* i-ii; Plut. *Fab. Max.* 2–16, *Marc.*; Diod. xxiii-xxvii; Strabo iii.6, vi.4.2; Dio ix- xvii; Flor. i.13.18, 22.6.33–34; Vell. Pat. i.6; Oros. iv.6–19.

14. Polyb. xv.17–18; Livy xxx.16, 37–38, 43–44; App. *Pun.* viii-ix; Diod. xxxii.4.4; Dio xvii.

15. Quote: Livy xxxiii.32. Second Macedonian War: Polyb. xv.20–25, xvi.1–12, 22, 24–35, 38, xviii.1–12, 18–27, 34–48; Livy xxxi.1–47, xxxii.3–25, 32–40, xxxiii.2–21, 27–35; Plut. *Flam.*; App. *Mac.* i.2–4; Diod. xxviii, xxxi.8; Dio xviii; Flor. i.23.7; Oros. iv.20; Strabo vi.4.2.

16. Livy xxx-xli; App. *Iber.*vii.38–43; Plut. *Cato Maj.* 10; Diod. xxix.26; Strabo iii.13, vi.4.2; Dio xviii; Flor. i.33.17.

17. Aemilianus's birthdate is deduced from Livy xliv.44; Diod. xxx.22; Cic. *Rep.* vi.12.

18. The Third Macedonian War: Polyb. xxii.18, xxv.3, xxvii.1–11, 14–16, xviii.3–17, xxix.3–11, 14–19; Livy xli.19, 22–26, xlii.5–6, 10–19, 24–26, 29–32, 36–67, xliii.18–23, xliv.1–42; App. *Mac.*; Paus. 7.10; Diod. xxix.27–34, xxx.1–12, 19–21; Dio xx; Flor. i.28.12; Oros. iv.20; Vell. Pat. i.9.

19. Livy xix-xxxviii, xli-xlv; Polyb. xv-xvi, xviii, xxii, xxv, xxvii-xxx; App. *Mac.* i.2–5; Plut. *Flam.*, *Cato Maj.*; Diod. xxviii-xxxi; Dio xx, xvii-xix, xxx-xxxi; Vell. Pat. i.9; Flor. i.23.7, 24.8, 28.12; Oros. iv.20; Strabo vi.4.2, viii.7.3; Paus. 7.10.

20. Polyb. xxviii.6, 12, xxxi.23.

21. Polyb. xxxi.23–25; Diod. xxxi.26.

22. Polyb. vi.1.

23. Polyb. vi.5–9.

24. Polyb. vi.12, 15; Livy ii.1; Strabo v.7; CAH IX ch. 2.

25. Livy ii.18, iii.29, xxiii.22, xxxiii.2; Diony. v.70–7; Cic. *Rep.* i.63, ii.56, *Leg.* iii.9; App. *BC* i.3; Dio iv.13; Flor. i.5.11, i.26; CAH IX ch. 2.

26. Polyb. vi.13, 16; CAH IX ch. 2.

27. Polyb. vi.14, 17; Livy i.36, 43; CAH IX ch. 2.

28. See all of Polyb. vi.

29. Livy vi.36–42, vii.1; Flor. i.17.22–26.

30. Livy iv.43, vii.1 xxiii.41, xxxiii.42, xxxix.7, lxii.6, lxiv.7, lxv.13; Polyb. vi.12–13, 31; Tac. *Ann.* xi.22; Ulp. *Dig.* i.13.pr; Cic. *Verr.* ii.1.37, *Flacc.* 30, *Att.* ii.6.2, *Phil.* ix.16.

31. Cic. *Leg.* iii.7, *Verr.* v.14, *Fam.* viii.6, *Phil.* ix.17, *Har. Resp.* 27; Livy iii.6, 55, vii.1, xxxvi.50, 56, xl.44; Diony. vi.90, vii.26, xxxv.3–4; Fest. 258–9; Plut. *Caes.* 5.

32. Cic. *Leg.* iii.8; Livy vi.42, vii.1. Mummius elected praetor: Diod. xxxi.42; App. *Iber.* x.56.

33. Diod. xxxi.39–40; Livy *Per.* 47; Flor. i.33.17–18.

34. App. *Iber.* x.56–57. See also: Livy i.35.

35. Polyb. xxxv.5, xxxvi.8; App. *Iber.* 53–54, *Pun.* 102–104; Diod. xxxii.8; Livy *Per.* 48–49; Vell. Pat. i.12; Flor. i.33.17.

36. Quote: Plut. *Cato Maj.* 27. See also: App. *Pun.* x.69; Plut. *Cato Maj.* 26; Vell. Pat. i.13; Flor. i.31.15.

37. App. *Pun.* x.74-xiii.94, xvi.112; Polyb. xxxvi.3–7; Diod. xxxii.1–3, 6–9; Dio xxi; Vell. Pat. i.12; Flor. i.31.15; Oros. vi.22; Livy *Per.* 49–51.

38. Paus. vii.15.1. Last novus homo was M. Acilius Glabrio (cos. 191): Livy xxxvii.57.

39. Quote: Paus. vii.14.6. See also: Paus. vii.11–16; Diod. xxxii.9, 15; Vell. Pat. i.11; Flor. i.32.16; Dio xxi; Oros. vi.22; Livy *Per.* 48–51.

40. Paus. vii.13–16; Diod. xxxii.9, 15; Livy *Per.* 48–50; Dio xxi; Flor. i.32.16; Oros. vi.22; Vell. Pat. i.11.

41. Plut. *Mar.* 1; Flor. i.32.16; Paus. vii.16; Oros. v.3; Livy *Per.* 52.

42. Diod. xxxii.26–27; Vell. Pat. i.11–13; Strabo viii.23; Dio xxi; Flor. i.32.16; Oros. v.3; Livy *Per.* 52.

43. App. *Pun.* xvi.113-xix.132; Polyb. xxxviii.19–22; Diod. xxx.ii.22–25; Livy *Per.* 51; Dio xxi; Flor. i.31.15; Oros. vi.22; Strabo vi.4.2; Vell. Pat. i.12.

44. Quotes: Polyb. xxxviii.21, App. *Pun.* xix.132; Diod. xxxii.24.

CHAPTER 1: THE BEASTS OF ITALY

1. Cato, *ORF,* 2nd ed., p. 91.

2. Quote: Livy xxxvii.7. See also: Plut. *TG* 1; Sall. *Jug.* 42; Diod. xxxiv/xxxv.6; Vell. Pat. ii.2; Dio xxiv.83.

3. Quote: Val. Max. iv.4.pr. See also: Plut. *TG* 1; Cic. *Brut.* 104; Diod. xxxiv/xxxv.6; Vell. Pat. ii.2. More on Cornelia: Plut. *TG* 1, 4, 8; Cic. *Brut.* 104, 211, *Div.* ii.62; Tac. *Orat.* 28.

4. Quotes: Vell. Pat. ii.2. See also: Flor. ii.2.14; Cic. *Har. Resp.* 19.41; Plut. *TG* 2.

5. Plut. *TG* 8.

6. Plut. *TG* 4.

7. Quote: Cic. *Har. Resp.* 19.41. For more on Claudius: Plut. *TG* 4; Livy *Per.* 53; Cic. *Cael.* 34, *Brut.* 108, *Rep.* i.31, *Scaur.* 32; Val. Max 5.4.6; Oros. 5.4; Dio 74; "Plut." *Apoph.* Sm.9.

8. Livy xxxiv.52, xxxvii.59, xli.7.

9. Quotes: Livy xxxiv.4; Pliny 33.53. Sumptuary Laws: Livy xxxiv.1, 8, xl.44; Val. Max. ix.1.3; Pliny *NH* x.71; Gell. ii.24; Tac. *Ann.* ii.33–34; Macr. xvii.3–6.

10. Quote: Sall. *Jug.* 41. See also: App. *BC* i.10; Plut. *TG* 8.

11. App. *BC* i.7; Sall. *Jug.* 41; Hor. *Odes* ii.18; Juv. xiv.140. On agriculture: Cato *RR* Preface; Cic. *Off.* 1.151.

12. Quote: App. *BC* i.7.

13. Quote: Plut. *TG* 8.

14. Cato *RR* 136; Pliny xviii.7; Cic. *Off.* 2.73.

15. For the Spanish Wars: App. *Iber.* ix-xii; Diod. xxxiii; Flor. xxxiv.

16. Livy *Per.* 48, 55; Cic. *Leg.* iii.20; Polyb. xxxv.4.

17. Quote: App. *Iber.* xiii.78. See also: Livy *Per.* 47, 57; Sall. *Jug.* 69; Plut. CG 9; Cic. *Leg.* iii.20.

18. Cic. *Leg* iii.35, *Amic.* 41, *Brut.* 97, *Sest.* 103; Pliny Min. *Lett.* 3.20.

19. For lowering property requirements: Livy i.43; Polyb. vi.19; Cic. *Har. Resp.* ii.40.

20. Plut. *TG* 5; Vell. Pat. ii.1–2; Flor. i.34.18; Oros. v.4; Eutr. iv.17; Livy *Per.* 55.

21. Plut. *TG* 5–6; Vell. Pat. ii.2. For the treaty of Gracchus the Elder: Polyb. xxxii.2; App. *Iber.* 43–44; Livy *Per.* 41.

22. Quote: Vell. Pat. ii.1. See also: Plut. *TG* 7; Dio xxiii.79; Flor. i.34.18; Oros. v.4; Eutr. iv.17; Livy *Per.* 55.

23. Plut. *TG* 7; Vell. Pat. ii.2; Dio xxiv.83; Flor. ii.2.14; Oros. v.8.

24. App. *BC* i.7–9; Plut. *TG* 8–9; Polyb. vi.17; Diony. xi.63; Gell. 4.12; Cic. *Leg.* iii.7.

25. App. *BC* i.9–10; Plut. *TG* 8; Livy xxxiv.48, vi.35, 42; Pliny *NH* xviii.17; Varro *RR* i.2.9; Cato *ORF*, 3rd ed., p. 65.

26. Plut *TG* 9. For Scaevola: Cic. *Leg.* ii.47–57, *Verr.* i.52, *Brut.* 108, 239, *Orat.* i.212, *Off.* 2.47, *Rep.* i.31, *Fin.* i.12. Mucianus: Cic. *Orat.* i.170, 239–40, *Brut.* 98, 127; Gell. i.13.19.

27. Quote: App. *BC* i.9. See also: App. *BC* i.7–9, 19–21. Plutarch does not mention the Italians at all.

28. See discussion in Bernstein, *Tiberius Gracchus*, ch. 4.
29. App. *Iber.* 84; Cic. *Rep.* vi.11; Vell. Pat. ii.4; Oros. v.7; Livy *Per.* 56.
30. App. *Iber.* 84; Plut. *Mar.* 36.
31. App. *BC* i.9–10; Plut. *TG* 9; Cic. *Sest.* 103, *Leg. Agr.* ii.81.
32. App. *BC* i.9; Plut. *TG* 9; Vell. Pat. ii.2; Oros. v.8; Livy *Per.* 55.
33. Quote: Diod. xxxiv/xxxv.6. See also: App. *BC* i.10.
34. Quote: Diod. xxxiv/xxxv.6. See also: App. *BC* i.11; Plut. *TG* 10; Dio xxiv.83.
35. Quotes: Plut. *TG* 9. See also: Flor. ii.2.14.
36. App. *BC* i.11–12; Plut. *TG* 10.
37. Quote: Plut. *TG* 10.
38. Plut. *TG* 10; Dio xxiv.83.
39. Quote: Dio xxiv.83. See also: Plut. *TG* 10; Gell. ii.13.
40. App. *BC* i.12; Plut. *TG* 11; Livy xxxiv.38; Polyb. vi.16.
41. Quote: App. *BC* i.12. See also: Plut. *TG* 11.
42. App. *BC* i.12; Plut. *TG* 11–12; Vell. Pat. ii.2; Flor. ii.2.14; Livy *Per.* 58.
43. See Taylor, *Roman Voting Assemblies*, ch. 3–4.
44. App. *BC* i.12; Plut. *TG* 12; Cic. *Brut.* 95, 222, *Milo.* 72, *Leg.* iii.24; Diod. xxxiv/xxxv.7.1; Vell. Pat. ii.2; Flor. ii.2.14; Oros. v.8; Livy *Per.* 58.
45. App. *BC* i.12; Livy *Per.* 58.
46. App. *BC* i.9, 13; Plut. *TG* 13; Cic. *Leg.* iii.24, *Milo* 72, *Brut.* 95; Vell. Pat. ii.2; Flor. ii.2.14; Livy *Per.* 58.
47. Cic. *Leg. Agr.* ii.32; Plut. *TG* 13.
48. Quote: Plut. *TG* 13. See also: Gell. ii.13.
49. Plut. *TG* 14; Vell. Pat. ii.4; Strabo 13; Flor. i.35.20; Oros. v.8; Eutr. iv.18; Just. xxxvi.4; Livy *Per.* 58.
50. Quote: Flor. i.35.20. See also: Plut. *TG* 14; Pliny xxxiii.53; Oros. v.8; Livy *Per.* 58.
51. Quotes: Polyb. vi.13. See also: Plut. *TG* 14, Livy *Per.* 58.
52. App. *BC* i.14; Dio xxiv.83; Flor. ii.2.14; Oros. v.8.
53. App. *BC* i.14; Plut. *TG* 16; Dio xxiv.83.
54. App. *BC* i.14; Plut. *TG* 16; Dio xxiv.83.
55. App. *BC* i.14–15; Plut. *TG* 16; Dio xxiv.83; Gell. ii.13.
56. App. *BC* i.15; Plut. *TG* 18–19; Oros. v.9.
57. Quote: Plut. *TG* 19. See also: App. *BC* i.16; Sall. *Jug.* 7, 31; Flor. ii.2.14; Livy *Per.* 58.
58. Quote: App. *BC* i.16. See also: Plut. *TG* 19; Cic. *Amic.* 41; Sall. *Jug.* 7, 31; Flor. ii.2.14; Livy *Per.* 58.
59. App. *BC* i.16; Plut. *TG* 19; Diod. xxxv/xxxvi.7.3; Vell. Pat. ii.3; Flor. ii.2.14; Oros. v.9; Livy *Per.* 58.

60. Quote: App. *BC* i.17. See also: Plut. *TG* 19; Diod. xxxiv/xxxv.7.3; Vell. Pat. ii.3; Flor. ii.2.14; Oros. v.9; Livy *Per.* 58.
61. Quote: Plut. *TG* 20.
62. Plut. *TG* 20; Oros. v.9.
63. Quote: Vell. Pat. ii.3.

CHAPTER 2: THE STEPCHILDREN OF ROME

1. Diod. xxxiv/xxxv.2.33.
2. Quote: XII.11. See also: Polyb. vi.14, 16; Cic. *Amic.* 41, *Leg* iii.11, 44, *Rep.* ii.61; Varro *LL* vi.90–92.
3. Plut. *TG* 20; Sall. *Jug.* 31; Vell. Pat. ii.7.
4. Quote: Val. Max. v.3.2. See also: Plut *TG* 21; Cic. *Dom.* 91, *Planc.* xxxvi.88, *Flacc.* 75, *Orat.* ii.285; Pliny vii.34; Strabo xiv.1.38.
5. Plut *TG* 21; *CIL* I^2.719.
6. Quote: Flor. i.34.18; See also: App. *Iber.* xiv-xv; Vell. Pat. ii.4; Front. vi.1, 8; Strabo iii.4.13; Val. Max. ii.7.1–2; Oros. v.7; Eutr. iv.17; "Plut." *Apoph.* Sm.15–16; Livy *Per.* 57, 59.
7. Quote: Diod. xxxiv/xxxv.7.
8. Plut. *TG* 21, *Mor.* 201.e.
9. App. *Iber.* xv.98; Cic. *Phil.* xi.18; Pliny xxxiii.50; Flor. i.34.18; Oros. v.7; Eutr. iv.19; Livy *Per.* 59.
10. Cic. *Leg.* iii.35, *Orat.* ii.170; Livy *Per.* 59.
11. Quotes: Vell. Pat. ii.4. See also: Plut *TG* 21, *Mor.* 201e-f; Cic. *Amic.* 96, *Orat.* ii.106, 170, *Milo* 8; Val. Max. vi.2.3; Livy *Per.* 59.
12. CAH IX ch. 17.
13. Ibid.
14. Ibid.
15. Ibid.
16. Ibid.
17. Quotes: Diod. xxxiv/xxxv.2.1–3, Athen. xii.542. Acquisition of Sicily: Polyb. i.62; App. *Isl.* i.2; Oros. iv.11.
18. Diod. xxxiv/xxxv.2.4–16, 38–42; Flor. ii.7.19; Livy *Per.* 56.
19. Diod. xxxiv/xxxv.2.17–18, 24–25, 43; Flor. ii.7.19; Livy *Per.* 56.
20. Diod. xxxiv/xxxv.2.8–9; Flor. ii.7.19; Val. Max. ii.7; Oros. v.9; Livy *Per.* 56, 58.
21. Diod. xxxiv/xxxv.2.20; Flor. ii.7.19; Front. vi.1; Oros. v.9; Livy *Per.* 59.
22. Quote: Diod. xxxiv/xxxv.2.22. See also: Diod. xxxiv/xxxv 44–48; Cic. *Verr.* ii.4.112; Strabo xi.2.6; Val Max. ii.7.3; Flor. ii.7.19; Oros. v.9; Livy *Per.* 59.

23. CAH IX ch. 15.
24. Ibid.
25. Ibid.
26. Cic. *Verr.* ii.3.195, 4.56, *Mur.* 46, *Brut.* 106, *Off.* 2.75.
27. Plut *TG* 20, *Flam.* 21; Vell. Pat. ii.4; Strabo xiv.1.38; Just. xxxvi.4; Flor. i.35.20; Eutr. iv.20; Livy *Per.* 59.
28. Quote: Flor. i.35.20. See also: Vell. Pat. ii.4; Strabo xiv.1.38; Val. Max. iii.2.12; Just. xxxvi.4; Oros. v.10; Livy *Per.* 59.
29. Vell. Pat. ii.4; Strabo xiv.1.38; Just. xxxvi.4; Flor. i.35.20; Oros. v.10; Livy *Per.* 59.
30. Quote: Flor. i.35.20. See also: Strabo xiv.1.38; Just. xxxvi.4.
31. App. *Mith.* 57; Sall. *Hist.* iv.67; Vell. Pat. ii.38; Strabo xiv.1.38.
32. Livy xxi.63; Cic. *Verr.* ii.3.130, 140. For a full discussion see Badian, *Publicans and Sinners.*
33. Livy i.36, 43, v.7, xxxix.19, 44; Polyb. vi.17.
34. Ulp. *Dig.* xxxix.4.1.1; Livy v.47, xliii.16, xliv.16, xlviii.5; Polyb. vi.17; Cic. *Pro. Cons.* 12, *Fam.* xiv.12, 20, *Planc.* 32; Pliny *NH* x.51.
35. Quote: Diod. v.38. See also: Livy xxxiv.21; Strabo iii.59.7.
36. Livy xxxii.7, xxxiv.45, xl.51, xlv.18; Polyb. vi.17; Cic. *Off.* ii.76, *Tusc.* iii.48, *Verr.* ii.3.18, 167; Vell. Pat. ii.6; Pliny xxxiii.56.
37. Cic. *Leg. Man.* 14, Livy xliii.1, xlv.18; Plut. *Pomp.* 45, *Aem. Paul.* 38.
38. White, *The Roman Citizenship,* ch. 1.
39. Ibid., ch. 2.
40. Ibid., ch. 3.
41. Ibid., ch. 4.
42. App. *BC* i.18; Cic. *Rep.* i.31; Livy *Per.* 59.
43. App. *BC* i.18. Cic. *Rep.* i.31, iii.41; Livy *Per.* 59.
44. App. *BC* i.19; Cic. *Rep.* i.31; Livy *Per.* 59.
45. App. *BC* i.19.
46. App. *BC* i.19; Oros. v.10; Dio xxiv. 84.
47. Quotes: App. *BC* i.19. See also: Plut. *CG* 10; Cic. *Amic.* 12, *Rep.* vi.12; Vell. Pat. ii.4; "Plut." *Apoph.* Sm.23; Oros. v.10.
48. App. *BC* i.20; Plut. *CG* 10, *Rom.* 27; Cic. *Milo* 16; Vell. Pat. ii.4; Oros. v.10; Livy *Per.* 59.
49. Quote: Vell. Pat. ii.4; For Cornelia and/or Sempronia: App. *BC* i.20; Livy *Per.* 59; Oros. v.10. Gaius and Flaccus: Plut. *CG* 10. Carbo: Cic. *Quint.* ii.3.3, *Fam.* ix.21.3. Suicide: App. *BC* i.20; Plut. *Rom.* 27.
50. Pliny vii.59.
51. Quote: Plut. *Mor.* 2.

CHAPTER 3: DAGGERS IN THE FORUM

1. Sall *Hist*. i.12.
2. Quotes: Cic. *Div*. i.56; Plut. CG 1. See also: Val. Max. i.7.6.
3. Quotes: Plut. *TG* 2. See also: Dio xxv.85.
4. Plut. CG 2.
5. Quotes: Cic. *Har. Resp.* 41; Plut. CG 1. See also: Plut. CG 5; Cic. *Brut.* 125–6; Dio xxv.85.
6. Plut. *TG* 21, CG 1.
7. App. *BC* i.21, 34.
8. Quote: App. *BC* i.21.
9. Quotes: App. *BC* i.21, Cic. *Off*. iii.47. See also: Cic. *Brut.* 109; App. *BC* i.34; Pliny *NH* xxix.8; Festus in *ORF*, 2nd ed. pp. 179–80.
10. App. *BC* i.34; Flor. i.37.2; Tac. *Hist.* iv.73; Livy *Per.* 60.
11. Quote: Livy xxvii.10. See also: Livy xiii.22, xxvi.9.
12. Quote: "Cic." *Rhet.* iv.22, 37. See also: Vell. Pat ii.7; "Cic." *Rhet.* vi.13; Cic. *Planc.* 70; Val. Max. ii.8.4; Ascon. 17; Amm. xv.9.10; Livy *Per.* 60.
13. Vell. Pat ii.7; Cic. *Planc.* 70.
14. Plut. CG 1–2; Livy *Per.* 60.
15. Plut. CG 2; Livy *Per.* 60.
16. Plut. CG 2; Diod. xxxiv/xxxv.7.24.
17. Gell. xv.12. See also: Plut. CG 2.
18. App. *BC* i.21; Plut. CG 2; Diod. xxxiv/xxxv.7.24.
19. Plut. CG 3.
20. App. *BC* i.22, *Mith.* 57; Cic. *Orat.* ii.188, 194–6, *Div. Caec.* 69, *Font.* 38; Sall. *Hist.* iv.67; Vell. Pat. ii.4.
21. Gell. xi.10.
22. Quote: Plut. CG 3. See also: Cic. *Orat.* iii.214, *Brut.* 126, *Har. Resp.* 43.
23. Quote: Plut. CG 3. See also: App. *BC* i.21; Diod. xxxiv/xxxv.724.
24. Quote: Vell. Pat. ii.6. See also: Diod. xxxiv/xxxv.7.25.1.
25. Plut. CG 4; Diod. xxxiv/xxxv.7.25.2. See also: Stockton, *The Gracchi*, ch. 6.
26. Plut. CG 4; Diod. xxxiv/xxxv.7.27; Cic. *Rab. Perd.* 12, *Cat.* iv.10, *Brut.* 128, *Leg.* iii.26, *Red. Sen.* 37, *Dom.* 82, 87, *Rep.* i.6, *Clu.* xxxv.95; Vell. Pat. ii.7.
27. App. *BC* i.34; Plut. CG 5; Vell. Pat. ii.6; Oros. v.11; Livy *Per.* 60.
28. App. *BC* i.23; Plut. CG 5; Vell. Pat. ii.6; Livy *Per.* 60.
29. Plut. CG 7; App. *BC* i.23.
30. Quote: Cic. *Sest.* 103. See also: App. *BC* i.22; Plut. CG 5; Cic. *Off*. ii.72; Diod. xxxiv/xxxv.7.25.1; Vell. Pat. ii.6; Flor. ii.3; Oros. v.11; Livy *Per.* 60.
31. Plut. CG 5; Diod. xxxiv/xxxv.7.25; Oros. v.11.
32. App. *BC* i.21; Cic. *Verr.* ii.3.12; Diod. xxxiv/xxxv.7.25.1.

33. App. *BC* i.22; Plut. *CG* 5; Diod. xxxiv/xxxv.7.25.1; Vell. Pat. ii.6; Livy *Per.* 60.
34. App. *BC* i.21; Plut. *CG* 8, 11.
35. Plut. *CG* 8.
36. Quote: Plut. *CG* 6.
37. App. *BC* i.23; Plut. *CG* 8–9; Cic. *Brut.* 109, *Fin.* iv.66; Tac. *Ann.* iii.27.
38. App. *BC* i.23, 34; Plut. *CG* 8; Vell. Pat. ii.6.
39. Quote: App. *BC* i.23.
40. App. *BC* i.24; Plut. *CG* 10–11; Vell. Pat. i.15, ii.6; Oros. v.12; Eutr. iv.21; Livy *Per.* 60.
41. App. *BC* i.24; Plut. *CG* 11; Oros. v.12; Livy *Per.* 60.
42. App. *BC* i.24; Plut. *CG* 10–11; Cic. *Orat.* iii.213–14.
43. Plut. *CG* 11–12.
44. Plut. *CG* 12.
45. App. *BC* i.24; Plut. *CG* 13; Flor. ii.3.15; Oros. v.12.
46. App. *BC* i.25; Plut. *CG* 13; Diod. xxxiv/xxxv.7.27; Oros. v.12.
47. Quote: Cic. *Orat.* iii.213. See also: App. *BC* i.25; Plut. *CG* 13; Diod. xxxiv/xxxv.7.27; Oros. v.12.
48. App. *BC* i.25; Plut. *CG* 14.
49. Quote: Cic. *Phil.* viii.14. See also: Caes. *BC* i.5; App. *BC* i.25; Plut. *CG* 14; Cic. *Cat.* i.4. *Dom.* 102; *Phil.* viii.14; Sall. *Jug.* 16; Livy *Per.* 60.
50. Quote: Cic. *Div.* i.56. See also: Plut. *CG* 14.
51. Quotes: Plut. *CG* 15.
52. App. *BC* i.26; Plut. *CG* 16; Cic. *Phil.* viii.14; Flor. ii.3.15; Livy *Per.* 61.
53. App. *BC* i.26; Plut. *CG* 16; Cic. *Phil.* viii.14; Vell. Pat ii.6; Oros. v.12.
54. App. *BC* i.26; Plut. *CG* 16; Cic. *Cat.* i.4, *Dom.* 102, *Phil.* viii.14; Sall. *Jug.* 16, 31; Vell. Pat ii.6; Oros. v.12; Livy *Per.* 61.
55. App. *BC* i.26; Plut. *CG* 17; Vell. Pat ii.6; Val. Max. iv.7.2; Oros. v.12.
56. App. *BC* i.26; Plut. *CG* 17; Cic. *Cat.* i.4; Diod. xxxiv/xxxv.29; Vell. Pat ii.6; Val. Max. iv.7.2, vi.8.3; Oros. v.12; Livy *Per.* 61.
57. App. *BC* i.26; Diod. xxxiv/xxxv.7.27–29; Vell. Pat ii.6; Val. Max. ix.4.3; Flor. ii.3.15.
58. Plut. *CG* 17; Vell. Pat ii.7; Val. Max. vi.3.1; Pliny xxxiii.14; Flor. ii.4.16; Oros. v.12.
59. Quote: Cic. *Orat.* ii.170. See also: Cic. *Brut.* 103, *Sest.* 140, *Fam.* ix.21.3, *Orat.* ii.106, 132, *Verr.* ii.3.3; Val. Max. iii.7.6, vi.5.6; Livy *Per.* 61.
60. App. *BC* i.27.
61. Quotes: Plut. *CG* 19. See also: Plut. *CG* 4; Pliny xxxvi.14.
62. Quote: Sall. *Jug.* 41.
63. Quote: Sall. *Jug.* 42.
64. Quotes: Cic. *Leg.* iii.20, Plut. *CG* 17. See also: App *BC* i.26.

CHAPTER 4: A CITY FOR SALE

1. Cic. *Verr.* ii.5.126.
2. Quotes: Vell. Pat. ii.11; Sall. *Jug.* 63. See also: Plut. *Mar.* 2.
3. Quote: Plut. *Mar.* 3. See also: Cic. *Balb.* 47.
4. Quotes: Plut. *Mar.* 6.
5. See Prologue. For more on the career of Macedonicus: Diod. xxxii.9, 15; Polyb. xxxviii.17–18; App. *Iber.* 76; Front. i.1.12, iii.7.3, iv.1.11, 1.23, 7.42; Paus. vii.13–15; Dio xxiii.82; Vell. Pat. i.11, ii.5; Flor. i.30.14, 32.16, 33.17; Oros. v.3; Livy *Per.* 50, 52–53.
6. Cic. *Fin.* v.82, *Orat.* 264, *Scaur.* 46 *Clu.* 119; Flor. i.43.8; App. *Ill.* 10–11; Vell. Pat. ii.8; Ascon. 28; Strabo iii.5.1; Val. Max. ii.9.9; Oros. v.13; Livy *Per.* 60, 62. See also: FC and FT.
7. Quotes: Cic. *Orat.* ii.283; Sall. *Jug.* 15. See also: Cic. *Orat.* i.214; Plut. *Mor.* 318.e; Val. Max. iv.4.11; "Vict." *Vir. Ill.* 72.
8. Quote: Cic. *Orat.* ii.365. See also: Chapter 3.
9. Quotes: Cic. *Orat.* i.364, *Clu.* 140. See also: Cic. *Phil.* 134, *Brut.* 165, *Orat.* i.24.
10. Sall. *Jug.* 63; Diod. xxxiv/xxxv.38; Strabo iii.5.1; Flor. i.43.8; Oros. v.13; Livy *Per.* 60.
11. Flor. xxxix.4.
12. Diod. xxxiv/xxxv.23; Vell. Pat. i.15; Strabo iv.1.5; Flor. i.37.2; Tac. *Hist.* iv.73; Amm. xv.12.5; Eutr. iv.22; Livy *Per.* 61.
13. Diod. xxxiv/xxxv.7.36; Vell. Pat. i.15, ii.10; Strabo iv.1.11, 2.3; Flor. i.37.2; Amm. xv.12.5; Oros. v.13; Livy *Per.* 61.
14. Cic. *Orat.* ii.223, *Brut.* 160; Diod. v.38.5; Vell. Pat. ii.7, 10; Val. Max. vi.9.14.
15. Plut. *Mar.* 4.
16. Plut. *Mar.* 4; Cic. *Leg.* iii.38.
17. Plut. *Mar.* 4; Cic. *Brut.* 222, *Off.* ii.72.
18. Plut. *Mar.* 5.
19. Plut. *Mar.* 5; Cic. *Planc.* 51; Val. Max. vi.9.14; Plut. *Mor.* 202.b.
20. Sall. *Jug.* 5; Eutr. iv.11.
21. Quote: Sall. *Jug.* 6. See also: Diod. xxxiv/xxxv.7.35.
22. Quotes: Sall. *Jug.* 7–8.
23. Quote: Sall. *Jug.* 9.
24. Sall. *Jug.* 9–13; Flor. i.36.1; Oros. v.15; Eutr. iv.26; Livy *Per.* 61.
25. Quotes: Sall. *Jug.* 14–15. See also: Flor. i.36.1.
26. Sall. *Jug.* 16; Plut. *CG* 18; Flor. i.36.1.
27. Quotes: Sall. *Jug.* 13, 15. See also: Flor. i.36.1.

28. Plut. *Mar.* 5; Val. Max. vi.9.14.
29. Plut. *Mar.* 5.
30. Plut. *Mar.* 5, *Mor.* 318.e; Cic. *Clu.* 119; Vell. Pat. ii.8; Val. Max. ii.9.9; Livy *Per.* 61.
31. Plut. *Mar.* 6.
32. Plut. *Mar.* 6, *Caes.* 1.
33. Sall. *Jug.* 20; Diod. xxxiv/xxxv.7.31; Livy *Per.* 64.
34. Sall. *Jug.* 21; Diod. xxxiv/xxxv.7.31; Livy *Per.* 64.
35. Sall. *Jug.* 21–22; Diod. xxxiv/xxxv.7.31; Livy *Per.* 64.
36. Sall. *Jug.* 25; Diod. xxxiv/xxxv.7.31; Flor. i.36.1.
37. Sall. *Jug.* 26; Diod. xxxiv/xxxv.7.31; Eutr. iv.26; Livy *Per.* 64.
38. Quote: Sall. *Jug.* 26. See also: Diod. xxxiv/xxxv.7.31.
39. Sall. *Jug.* 27; Livy *Per.* 64.
40. Sall. *Jug.* 27–28; Oros. v.15; Eutr. iv.26; Livy *Per.* 64.
41. Sall. *Jug.* 28.
42. Quote: Sall. *Jug.* 29. See also: Oros. v.15; Eutr. iv.26.
43. Quote: Sall. *Jug.* 28. See also: Flor. i.36.1; Oros. v.15; Eutr. iv.26.
44. Quotes: Sall. *Jug.* 31.
45. Quotes: Sall. *Jug.* 31.
46. Sall. *Jug.* 32; Flor. i.36.1; Livy *Per.* 64.
47. Sall. *Jug.* 33–34; Flor. i.36.1; Oros. v.15.
48. Sall. *Jug.* 33–34.
49. Sall. *Jug.* 35; Diod. xxxiv/xxxv.7.35a; Flor. i.36.1; Livy *Per.* 64.
50. Quote: Sall. *Jug.* 35. See also: Diod. xxxiv/xxxv.7.35a; Flor. i.36.1; Livy *Per.* 64.
51. Quote: Sall. *Jug.* 35. See also: Diod. xxxiv/xxxv.7.35a; Oros. v.15; Livy *Per.* 64.

CHAPTER 5: THE SPOILS OF VICTORY

1. Sall. *Jug.* 5.
2. App. *Gall.* 13; Plut. *Mar* 11; Tac. *Germ.* xxxvii.2; Flor. i.38.3.
3. Quote: Diod. xxxvii.1. See also: App. *Gall.* 13; Plut. *Mar.* 11; Strabo vii.2.2; Tac. *Germ.* xxxvii.2; Flor. i.38.3.
4. Quote: Strabo ii.3.6. See also: App. *Gall.* 13; Flor. i.38.3.
5. App. *Gall.* 13; Diod. xxxvii.1.
6. App. *Gall.* 13.
7. App. *Gall.* 13; Diod. xxxiv/xxxv.37; Vell. Pat. ii.12; Strabo v.1.8; Livy *Per.* 63.
8. Quote: Flor. i.39.4. See also: Diod. xxxiv/xxxv.30; Front. iii.10.7; Dio xxvi.88; Eutr. iv.24; Amm. xxvii.4.4; Livy *Per.* 63.
9. Dio xxvi.88; Front. ii.4.3; Flor. i.39.4; Amm. xxvii.4.10; Livy *Per.* 63, 65.

10. Cic. *Verr.* ii.3.184, 4.22, *Balb.* 28, *Fam.* ix.21.3; Vell. Pat. ii.8.

11. Sall. *Jug.* 36–39; Flor. i.36.1; Oros. v.15; Eutr. iv.26.

12. Sall. *Jug.* 43; Vell. Pat. ii.11.

13. Sall. *Jug.* 43; Cic. *Orat.* ii.275–276; Ascon. 68.

14. Plut. *Mar.* 7.

15. Sall. *Jug.* 43–46; Front. i.8.8.

16. Sall. *Jug.* 46–53; Plut. *Mar.* 7; Front. iv.2; Flor. i.36.1; Val. Max. ii.7.2; Oros. v.15; Eutr. iv.27; Livy *Per.* 65.

17. Sall. *Jug.* 54.

18. Quote: Sall. *Jug.* 40. See also: Cic. *Brut.* 127–128.

19. Quote: Plut. CG 18. See also: Cic. *Pis.* 95, *Brut.* 127–128, *Planc.* 69–70, *Sest.* 140; Vell. Pat. ii.7; Ascon. 17.

20. Cic. *Brut.* 127–128; Sall. *Jug.* 40.

21. Cic. *Brut.* 127–128.

22. Sall. *Jug.* 65; Cic. *Brut.* 127–128, *Orat.* ii.284.

23. Ascon. 68.

24. Quote: Flor. i.38.3. See also: Diod. xxxiv/xxxv.37; Vell. Pat. ii.12; Ascon. 68, 80; Eutr. iv.27; Livy *Per.* 65.

25. Quote: Diod. xxxiv/xxxv.37. See also: Vell. Pat. ii.12; Ascon. 68, 80; Flor. xxxviii.3; Eutr. iv.27; Livy *Per.* 65.

26. Sall. *Jug.* 55; Ascon. 80.

27. Sall. *Jug.* 56–61; Flor. i.36.1; Oros. v.15; Eutr. iv.27.

28. Sall. *Jug.* 61–62; Front. i.8.8.

29. Quote: Sall. *Jug.* 62. See also: Dio xxvi.88; Oros. v.15.

30. Sall. *Jug.* 63.

31. Quote: Plut. *Mar.* 7. See also: Diod. xxxiv/xxxv.38.

32. Quotes: Sall. *Jug.* 63. See also: Plut. *Mar.* 8; Pliny xi.73.

33. Quotes: Sall. *Jug.* 64; Plut. *Mar.* 8; Dio xxvi.89.

34. Quote: Sall. *Jug.* 64. See also: Sall. *Jug.* 65; Plut. *Mar.* 7; Vell. Pat. ii.11.

35. Sall. *Jug.* 66–67; Plut. *Mar.* 8; Dio xxvi.89.

36. Sall. *Jug.* 68–69; Plut. *Mar.* 8.

37. Sall. *Jug.* 69; Plut. *Mar.* 8.

38. Quote: Sall. *Jug.* 72. See also: Front. i.8.8.

39. Sall. *Jug.* 73; Plut. *Mar.* 8; Cic. *Off.* iii.79.

40. Sall. *Jug.* 74–76.

41. Sall. *Jug.* 80.

42. Sall. *Jug.* 80; Diod. xxxiv/xxxv.38; Oros. v.15.

43. Sall. *Jug.* 81–83.

44. Quote: Sall. *Jug.* 82. See also: Eutr. iv.27.

45. Quote: Cic. *Off.* iii.79. See also: Sall. *Jug.* 73; Plut. *Mar.* 8.

46. Quotes: Sall. *Jug.* 85. See also: Plut. *Mar.* 8.
47. Sall. *Jug.* 73; Gell. xvi.10.
48. Quote: Sall. *Jug.* 86. See also: Plut. *Mar.* 8; Gell. xvi.10; Flor. i.36.1.
49. Sall. *Jug.* 86; Flor. i.36.1.

CHAPTER 6: THE GOLDEN EARRING

1. Eur. *Phoen.* 532.
2. Sall. *Jug.* 95; Plut. *Sulla* 1; Vell. Pat. ii.17.
3. Sall. *Jug.* 95; Plut. *Sulla* 1–2; Vell. Pat. ii.17; Val. Max. vi.9.6.
4. Quotes: Sall. *Jug.* 95; Plut. *Sulla* 2. See also: Plut. *Mor.* 318.c.
5. Quote: Plut. *Sulla* 1.
6. Plut. *Sulla* 3; Vell. Pat. ii.12; Livy *Per.* 66.
7. Sall. *Jug.* 86; Plut. *Mar.* 10.
8. Sall. *Jug.* 88; Cic. *Att.* i.16.4, *Balb.* 11; Vell. Pat. ii.11; Val. Max. ii.10.1.
9. Sall. *Jug.* 87–88; Flor. i.36.1; Oros. v.15.
10. Sall. *Jug.* 89–92; Front. iii.9.3; Strabo xvii.3.12.
11. Quote: Sall. *Jug.* 96. See also: Plut. *Sulla* 3.
12. Sall. *Jug.* 97–101; Front. ii.1.3, 4.10; Flor. i.36.1; Oros. v.15; Eutr. iv.27; Livy *Per.* 65.
13. See Chapter 5.
14. Caes. *BG* i.7, 12, 14; Oros. v.15; Livy *Per.* 65.
15. Oros. v.15; "Cic." *Rhet.* i.25; Livy *Per.* 65.
16. Quote: "Cic." *Rhet. Her.* iv.34. See also: "Cic." *Rhet. Her.* i.25; Oros. v.15.
17. Quote: Cic. *Orat.* i.225. See also: Cic. *Orat.* ii.199, *Brut.* 161, 164.
18. Quote: Gell. iii.9.7. See also: Strabo iv.1.13; Oros. v.15.
19. Quote: Just. xxxii.3. See also: Strabo iv.1.13; Gell. iii.9.7; Dio xxvii.90; Oros. v.15.
20. Sall. *Jug.* 102; Plut. *Sulla* 3; Diod. xxxiv/xxxv.39; Dio xxvi.89; Flor. i.36.1; Oros. v.15; Livy *Per.* 66.
21. Quotes: Sall. *Jug.* 102. See also: Plut. *Sulla* 3.
22. Sall. *Jug.* 103; Plut. *Sulla* 3.
23. Quote: Sall. *Jug.* 104. See also: Plut. *Sulla* 3; Diod. xxxiv/xxxv.39; Vell. Pat. ii.12.
24. Sall. *Jug.* 106–107.
25. Sall. *Jug.* 108–109; Plut. *Mar.* 10.
26. Sall. *Jug.* 109–111.
27. Sall. *Jug.* 112.
28. Sall. *Jug.* 113; Plut. *Mar.* 10, *Sulla* 3.
29. Sall. *Jug.* 133; Plut. *Mar.* 10, *Sulla* 3, *Mor.* 806.d; Diod. xxxiv/xxxv.39, xxxvi.1; Vell. Pat. ii.2; Val. Max. vi.9.6; viii.14.4; Oros. v.15; Livy *Per.* 66.

30. Flor. xxxviii.3.
31. Dio xxvii.90; Flor. xxxviii.3; Oros. v.16.
32. Cic. *Planc.* 12, *Mur.* 36; Flor. xxxviii.3.
33. Plut. *Mar.* 16; Gran. xxxiii.11; Dio xxvii.91; Oros. v.16.
34. Gran. xxxiii.12; Cic. *Luc.* 27; Plut. *Cam.* 19; Vell. Pat. ii.12; Dio xxvii.91; Oros. v.16; Livy *Per.* 67.
35. Diod. xxxvi.1; Cic. *Orat* ii.199–200; Tac. *Germ.* xxxvii.5; Vell. Pat. ii.12; Flor. xxxviii.3; Oros. v.16; Livy *Per.* 67.
36. Diod. xxxvi.1; Plut. *Sert.* 3; Cic. *Orat.* ii.199–200; Tac. *Germ.* xxxvii.5; Vell. Pat. ii.12; Flor. xxxviii.3; Gran. xxxiii.12; Oros. v.16; Eutr. v.1; Livy *Per.* 67.
37. Plut. *Mar.* 14; Livy *Per.* 67.
38. Plut. *Mar.* 11–12; Cic. *Prov.* 19; Ascon. 78; Eutr. v.1.
39. Quote: Sall. *Jug.* 114. See also: Plut. *Mar.* 12, *Sulla* 3; Vell. Pat. ii.12; Pliny xxxiii.4; Just. xxxviii.6; Livy *Per.* 67.
40. Quote: Flor. i.36.1. See also: Plut. *Mar.* 12; Vell. Pat. ii.12; "Cic." *Rhet. Her.* iv.23; Val. Max. vi.9.14; Oros. v.15; Eutr. iv.27; Livy *Per.* 67.
41. Quote: Plut. *Mar.* 10. See also: Plut. *Sulla* 3, *Mor.* 806.d.

CHAPTER 7: MARIUS'S MULES

1. Plut. *Sulla* 12.
2. Plut. *Mar.* 16; Flor. i.38.3; Oros. v.16.
3. Quotes: Plut. *Mar.* 16. See also: Flor. i.38.3; Oros. v.16.
4. Quote: Plut. *Mar.* 18. See also: Flor. i.38.3; Oros. v.16.
5. Val. Max. ii.3.2; Front. iv.1.2, 2.2; Gran. 14.
6. Plut. *Sulla* 4; Vell. Pat. ii.17.
7. Plut. *Mar.* 13–14.
8. Diod. xxxvi.3.
9. Diod. xxxvi.3.1–2.
10. Diod. xxxvi.3.3; Dio xxvii.93.
11. Diod. xxxvi.4; Dio xxvii.93.
12. Diod. xxxvi.5–7; Flor. ii.7.19.
13. Cic. *Brut.* 129, *Off.* iii.77; See also: FC.
14. Cic. *Verr.* ii.2.118, *Nat. Deo.* ii.74, *Div. Caec.* 67; Ascon. 78, 80; Oros. v.15.
15. Cic. *Nat. Deo.* ii.74; Ascon. 78; Oros. v.15.
16. Cic. *Leg. Agr.* ii.18, *Scaur.* 1.b, *Deiot.* 31; Plut. *Mor.* 91.d; Vell. Pat. ii.12; Val. Max. vi.5.5; Ascon. 21; Dio xxvii.37, 92; Livy *Per.* 67.
17. Quote: Cic. *Off.* ii.73.
18. Plut. *Mar.* 13–14.
19. Plut. *Mar.* 13–14; Front. iv.1.7; Pliny x.5.
20. Plut. *Mar.* 25.

21. See Sampson, *The Crisis of Rome*, ch. 11.

22. Cic. *Pro. Cons.* 19; Livy *Per.* 67.

23. Plut. *Mar.* 14, *Sulla* 4, *Sert.* 3.

24. Quote: Diod. xxxvi.12. See also: Cic. *Har. Resp.* 43, *Sest.* 39, *Brut.* 224; Diod. xxxvi.12.

25. Quote: Cic. *Brut.* 224. See also: Cic. *Har. Resp.* 43, *Sest.* 39; Diod. xxxvi.12.

26. Cic. *Orat.* ii.124, 197, 199–204. "Cic." *Rhet. Her.* i.24; Val. Max. iv.7.3, vi.9.13; Gran. xxxiii.13.

27. Cic. *Orat.* ii.125; Gran. xxxiii.13.

28. Cic. *Orat.* ii.107, 201.

29. "Vict." *Vir. Ill.* 73; "Caes." *BA* 56.

30. Plut. *Mar.* 14; Livy *Per.* 67.

31. Diod. xxxvi.8.

32. Quote: Diod. xxxvi.9.

33. Quote: Diod. xxxvi.9. See also: Plut. *Luc.* 1.

34. Plut. *Mar.* 15; Flor. xxxviii.3.

35. Plut. *Mar.* 15; Oros. v.15; Livy *Per.* 68.

36. Plut. *Mar.* 18. See also: Plut. *Mar.* 15–22; Vell. Pat. ii.12; Pliny iii.4; Strabo iv.1.8; Flor. xxxviii.3; Oros. v.16; Livy *Per.* 68.

37. Quote: Plut. *Mar.* 18. See also: Front. ii.4.6, 7.12; Oros. v.16.

38. Quotes: Oros. v.16; Plut. *Mar.* 21. See also: Vell. Pat. ii.12; Livy *Per.* 68.

39. Quotes: Cic. *Mur.* 36; Plut. *Sulla* 4.

40. Plut. *Mar.* 23, *Sulla* 4, *Mor.* 202.d-e; Front. i.5.3; Oros. v.16; Livy *Per.* 68.

41. Front. i.5.3; Dio xxvii.93.

42. Quotes: Plut. *Mar.* 23.

43. Front. iv.1.13; Val. Max. v.8.4; "Vict." *Vir. Ill.* 72.

44. Quote: Plut. *Mar.* 23.

45. Quote: Oros. v.16. See also: Plut. *Mar.* 23; Dio xxvii.94; Flor. xxxviii.3.

CHAPTER 8: THE THIRD FOUNDER OF ROME

1. App. *BC* i.33.

2. Quotes: Cic. *Brut.* 224, *Orat.* iii.164.

3. Cic. *Sest.* 101; Val. Max. iii.8.6, ix.7.2; Flor. ii.4.16.

4. Val. Max. iii.8.6.

5. App. *BC* i.28; Oros. v.17.

6. App. *BC* i.28; Cic. *Sest.* 101; Val. Max. ix.7.2; Dio xxxviii.95; Oros. v.17.

7. Diod. xxxvi.15.

8. Quote: Diod. xxxvi.15. See also: Plut. *Mar.* 24.

9. Plut. *Mar.* 24; Oros. v.16.

10. Quote: Plut. *Mar.* 24. See also: Flor. i.38.3.

11. Plut. *Mar.* 25–27; Vell. Pat. ii.12; Flor. i.38.3; Oros. v.16.
12. See Sampson, *The Crisis of Rome,* ch. 10.
13. Plut. *Mar.* 25–27; Vell. Pat. ii.12; Front. ii.2.8; Flor. i.38.3; Oros. v.16; Eutr. v.2; Strabo iv.3.3; Pliny viii.61; Livy *Per.* 68.
14. Quote: Livy *Per.* 68. See also: Plut. *Mar.* 27.
15. Diod. xxxvi.10; Livy *Per.* 69.
16. Quotes: Diod. xxxvi.11.
17. Diod. xxxvi.10; Livy *Per.* 69.
18. Diod. xxxvi.10; Livy *Per.* 69.
19. Plut. *Mar.* 27; Cic. *Pro. Cons.* 26; Diod. xxxviii.4; Val. Max. iii.6.6, ix.12.4; Livy *Per.* 69.
20. Plut. *Mar.* 28; Livy *Per.* 69.
21. Quote: Plut. *Mar.* 28. See also: Oros. v.17.
22. App. *BC* i.28; Val. Max. ix.7.3; Flor. ii.4.16; Oros. v.17; Livy *Per.* 69.
23. Cic. *Verr.* ii.1.26, *Rab. Post.* 9, *Brut.* 224; Ascon. 21.
24. "Cic." *Rhet. Her.* i.21, ii.17.
25. Cic. *Balb.* 48; Vell. Pat. i.15; Strabo iv.6.7; Livy *Per.* 69.
26. Quote: Plut. *Mar.* 28. See also: Cic. *Balb.* 46–48; Val. Max. v.2.8.
27. App. *BC* i.30.
28. Quote: Plut. *Mar.* 29. See also: App. *BC* i.29–31; Flor. ii.4.16; Oros. v.17; Livy *Per.* 69.
29. App. *BC* i.32.
30. App. *BC* i.32.
31. Cic. *Brut.* 224, *Har. Resp.* 51.
32. Quote: Oros. v.17. See also: App. *BC* i.32; Cic. *Cat.* iv.4; Flor. ii.4.16; Livy *Per.* 69.
33. App. *BC* i.32; Plut. *Mar.* 30; Cic. *Rab. Perd.* 18–31, *Cat.* i.4; Val. Max. iii.2.18.
34. App. *BC* i.32; Plut. *Mar.* 30.
35. App. *BC* i.32; Plut. *Mar.* 30; Cic. *Rab. Perd.* 18–31, *Phil.* viii.15; *Cat.* iii.15; Vell. Pat. ii.12; Val. Max. iii.2.18; Flor. ii.4.16; Oros. v.17; Livy *Per.* 69.
36. App. *BC* i.33; Plut. *Mar.* 30; Cic. *Planc.* 69, *Red. Sen.* 38, *Rab. Perd.* 24; Diod. xxxvi.16; Vell. Pat. ii.15; Dio xxviii.95; Oros. v.17; Livy *Per.* 69.
37. Quotes: Vell. Pat. ii.11, Plut. *Mar.* 2. See also: Plut. *Mar.* 31–32.

CHAPTER 9: ITALIA

1. Flor. ii.6.18.
2. App. *BC* i.46; Diod. xxxvii.1.
3. Plut. *Cato Min.* 2.

4. Quote: Diod. xxxvii.10.
5. Livy ix.9–12, xiii.10, xxxix.3, xli.8.
6. Quotes: Gell. x.2.5, 2.9.
7. App. *BC* i.21.
8. See Dart, *The Social War*, ch. 3.
9. Diod. xxxvi.3; Plut. *Mar.* 28; Cic. *Balb.* 46–48; Val. Max. v.2.8.
10. See Dart, *The Social War*, ch. 3.
11. Cic. *Balb.* 48–49, 54, *Orat.* ii.257, *Brut.* 63, *Off.* iii.47; Sall. *Hist.* i.17–18;
    Ascon. 67–68.
12. Ascon. 67–68.
13. Quote: Cic. *Leg. Man.* 14.
14. Diod. xxxvii.5; Cic. *Planc.* 33, *Att.* vi.1.15; Dio xxviii.97; Val. Max. viii.15.6;
    Ascon. 15; Livy *Per.* 70.
15. Quote: Diod. xxxvii.5. See also: Dio xxviii.97; Livy *Per.* 70.
16. Cic. *Orat.* i.229–23; *Brut.* 115; *Pis.* 95, *Font.* 38; Vell. Pat. ii.13; Dio
    xxviii.97; Flor. ii.17; Val. Max. ii.10.5, vi.4.4; Livy *Per.* 70.
17. Vell. Pat. ii.13; Livy *Per.* 70.
18. Quote: Vell. Pat. ii.14. See also: Cic. *Dom.* 120; Diod. xxxvii.10; Dio
    xxviii.96.
19. App. *BC* i.35; Cic. *Orat.* i.24–25, *Brut.* 181, *Rab. Post.* 16; Diod. xxxvii.10;
    Vell. Pat. ii.13; Flor. ii.5.17; Livy *Per.* 70.
20. App. *BC* i.35; Flor. ii.5.17; Vell. Pat. ii.13; Ascon. 21; Livy *Per.* 71.
21. App. *BC* i.35; Flor. ii.5.17; Vell. Pat. ii.13; Livy *Per.* 71.
22. Quote: Flor. ii.5.17. See also: App. *BC* i.35; Vell. Pat. ii.13; Livy *Per.* 71.
23. Quote: Flor. ii.5.17. See also: Cic. *Orat.* i.24; Val. Max. ix.5.2.
24. App. *BC* i.38; Flor. ii.5.17; Oros. v.18; Livy *Per.* 71.
25. App. *BC* i.36; Vell. Pat. ii.14; Flor. ii.5.17, 6.18; Oros. v.18; Livy *Per.* 71.
26. Quote Cic. *Orat.* i.213.
27. Cic. *Orat.* i.24–27.
28. Quote Cic. *Orat.* iii.8. See also: Cic. *Quint.* xi.1.37.
29. Quote: Diod. xxxvii.10. See also: Cic. *Dom.* 41, 50, *Leg.* ii.14, 31; Ascon.
    68–69.
30. Quotes: Diod. xxxvii.13. See also: Oros. v.18; Livy *Per.* 71.
31. Quote: Vell. Pat. ii.14. See also: App. *BC* i.36; Cic. *Nat. Deo.* iii.80–81,
    Milo. 16; *Rhet. Her.* iv.31; Flor. ii.5.17; Oros. v.18; Livy *Per.* 71.
32. App. *BC* i.38; Vell. Pat. ii.15; Oros. v.18.
33. App. *BC* i.38; Cic. *Font.* 41; Diod. xxxvii.12; Vell. Pat. ii.15; Flor. ii.5.17;
    Oros. v.18; Livy *Per.* 72.
34. App. *BC* i.39; Diod. xxxvii.1–2; Flor. ii.5.17; Oros. v.18; Eutr. v.3; Livy
    Per. 72.

35. App. *BC* i.38, 40; Diod. xxxvii.1–2; Vell. Pat. ii.16; Flor. ii.5.17; Stabo v.241; Oros. v.18; Eutr. v.3; Livy *Per.* 72.

36. "Cic." *Rhet. Her.* ii.28, iv.9; Plut. *Cato. Min.* 1–2; Diod. xxxii.19; Livy *Per.* 72.

37. App. *BC* i.40; Cic. *Font.* 43.

38. App. *BC* i.37.

39. App. *BC* i.37; Val. Max. viii.6.4; Ascon. 22.

40. Cic. *Orat.* iii.11, *Brut.* 304–305, *Sest.* 101, *Scaur.* 3; App. *BC* i.37; Ascon. 22, 73.

41. Quote: Vell. Pat. ii.11. See also: App. *BC* i.37.

42. App. *BC* i.40; Plut. *Sulla* 6, *Sert.* 3.

43. Plut. *Sulla* 5; Val. Max. vii.5.

44. Plut. *Sulla* 5; App. *BC* i.77, *Mith.* 10; Front. i.5.18; Strabo xii.2.11; Livy *Per.* 70.

45. Plut. *Sulla* 5; Vell. Pat. ii.24; Fest. 15; Livy *Per.* 70.

46. Plut. *Mar.* 32, *Sulla* 6, *Mor.* 806.c-d.

47. Quote: Diod. xxxvii.18. See also: App. *BC* i.41–42, 45; Flor. ii.6.18; Oros. v.18; Livy *Per.* 73.

48. App. *BC* i.43; Vell. Pat. ii.16; Dio xxix.98; Flor. ii.6.18; Oros. v.18; Eutr. v.3; Livy *Per.* 73.

49. App. *BC* i.44; Livy *Per.* 73.

50. App. *BC* i.44, 46; Diod. xxxvii.15; Flor. ii.6.18; Oros. v.18; Eutr. v.3l; Livy *Per.* 73.

51. Quotes: Plut. *Mar.* 33.

52. App. *BC* i.47–48; Flor. ii.6.18; Oros. v.18; Livy *Per.* 73.

53. Quote: Diod. xxxvii.2.3.

54. App. *BC* i.49; Cic. *Balb.* 21; Vell. Pat. ii.16; Gell. iv.4.

55. Pliny *NH* iii.24; Ascon. 3.

56. Quote: Cic. *Arch.* 7. See also: "Cic." *Rhet. Her.* iii.2; Vell. Pat. ii.17.

57. App. *BC* i.50; Vell. Pat. ii.16; Flor. ii.6.18; Eutr. v.3; Livy *Per.* 73, 75.

58. App. *BC* i.48, 50, 52; Vell. Pat. ii.21; Oros. v.18; Livy *Per.* 75.

59. Quote: Oros. v.18. See also: App. *BC* i.48, 50; Diod. xxxvii.2; Flor. ii.6.18; Livy *Per.* 73, 76.

60. Diod. xxxvii.2.

61. App. *BC* i.50–51; Plut. *Sulla* 6; Diod. xxxvii.2; Vell. Pat. ii.16; Flor. ii.6.18; Oros. v.18; Eutr. v.3; Livy *Per.* 74.

62. Diod. xxxvii.1; Pliny *NH* ii.85; Flor. ii.6.18.

63. Quote: Oros. v.18. See also: Diod. xxxvii.24; Vell. Pat. ii.15; Flor. ii.6.18.

64. Oros. v.18.

65. Quote: App. *BC* i.54. See also: Livy *Per.* 73.

66. Cic. *Arch.* 11.

67. Obseq. 56.

68. App. *BC* i.53; Diod. xxxvii.2; Oros. v.8; Eutr. v.3.4; Livy *Per.* 76.

CHAPTER 10: THE RUINS OF CARTHAGE

1. App. *BC* i.57.

2. Plut. *Dem.* 4; Diod. xx.111; Strabo xii.3.11; Flor. i.40.5.

3. App. *Mith.* 112; Sall. *Hist.* ii.87–88, v.5; Just. xxxvii.1–2, xxxviii.1; Strabo x.4.10; Dio xxxvi.9.5; Eutr. vi.12.3; Oros. vi.5.

4. App. *Mith.* 112; Just. xxxvii.3; Strabo ii.1.1.6, vii.3.17–18, 4.3–4, 4.7, xi.2.18.

5. App. *Mith.* 62, 112, 118; Just. xxxviii.1; Diod. xxxvi.15; Flor. i.40.5; Fest. xi.3; Eutr. xi.12.3; Oros. vi.1.

6. Quote: Plut. *Mar.* 31–32.

7. Plut. *Sulla* 5; App. *BC* i.77, *Mith.* 10, 13, 57; Just. xxxviii.3; Flor. i.40.5; Front. i.5.18; Strabo xii.2.11; Livy *Per.* 70, 76.

8. App. *Mith.* 11, 56; Just. xxxviii.3; Livy *Per.* 74.

9. App. *Mith.* 11–12, 14, 57; Sall. *Hist.* vi.67; Dio xxx.99.

10. App. *Mith.* 11, 56; Sall. *Hist.* vi.67; Dio xxx.99.

11. App. *Mith.* 10, 15, 57, *BC* i.5; Flor. i.40.5; Dio xxx.99; Fest. xi.3; Eutr. v.4.

12. App. *Mith.* 17; Just. xxxviii.3; Livy *Per.* 77.

13. App. *Mith.* 17–19; Sall. *Hist.* iv.67; Diod. xxxvii.26; Just. xxxviii.3, 5; Flor. i.40.5; Strabo xii.3.40; Eutr. v.4; Oros. vi.2; Livy *Per.* 77.

14. App. *Mith.* 20; Diod. xxxvii.26–27; Plut. *Luc.* 4; Just. xxxviii.3; Vell. Pat. ii.18; Flor. i.40.5; Eutr. v.5; Oros. v.19, vi.1; Livy *Per.* 77.

15. Plut. *Mar.* 33, *Sulla* 6, *Luc.* 2; App. *BC* iv.25; Vell. Pat. ii.15–16; Diod. xxxvii.2.1.

16. Quote: Plut. *Mar.* 34. See also: App. *BC* i.55; Diod. xxxvii.29; Eutr. v.5.

17. Quote: Diod. xxxvii.2.12. See also: App. *BC* i.53; Cic. *Har. Resp.* 43, *Brut.* 226; Diod. xxxvii.25; Vell. Pat. ii.17; Ascon. 25; Livy *Per.* 75.

18. Quote: Vell. Pat. ii.18. See also: Cic. *Orat.* i.24–27, *Har. Resp.* 43, *Brut.* 226; App. *BC* i.55; Plut. *Sulla* 6; Diod. xxxvii.25.

19. Quote: Plut. *Sulla* 6.

20. App. *BC* i.55; Plut. *Mar.* 34; Vell. Pat. ii.18; Livy *Per.* 77.

21. Quotes: Plut. *Sulla* 8, Cic. *Har. Resp.* 41. See also: Plut. *Mar.* 35; Livy *Per.* 76.

22. Quote: Plut. *Sulla* 8. See also: Plut. *Mar.* 35.

23. App. *BC* i.53, 55; Plut. *Sulla* 8; "Cic." *Rhet. Her.* ii.45; Ascon. 64; Livy *Per.* 77.

24. Quote: App. *BC* i.53. See also: Plut. *Sulla* 8; Ascon. 64; Livy *Per.* 77.

25. App. *BC* i.55–56; Plut. *Mar.* 35, *Sulla* 8; Cic. *Amic.* 1–3; Vell. Pat. ii.18; Livy *Per.* 77.

26. App. *BC* i.56; Plut. *Mar.* 35, *Sulla* 8.

27. App. *BC* i.56; Plut. *Mar.* 35, *Sulla* 8; Vell. Pat. ii.18; Flor. ii.9.21; Eutr. v.4; Livy *Per.* 77.

28. Plut. *Sulla* 7; Diod. xxxvii.2; Vell. Pat. ii.18; Eutr. v.4; Oros. v.19.

29. Plut. *Sulla* 8–9; App. *BC* i.57; Oros. v.19.

30. App. *BC* i.57.

31. Plut. *Mar.* 35, *Sulla* 8; Val. Max. vi.7e.1; Oros. v.19.

32. App. *BC* i.57; Plut. *Sulla* 9; Eutr. v.4.

33. Quote: Plut. *Sulla* 6. See also: App. *BC* i.57; Plut. *Sulla* 9.

34. App. *BC* i.57; Plut. *Sulla* 9, *Mar.* 35.

35. Quote: App. *BC* i.57. See also: Plut. *Sulla* 9.

36. App. *BC* i.57; Plut. *Sulla* 9.

37. App. *BC* i.58; Plut. *Sulla* 9.

38. Quote: App. *BC* i.58. See also: Plut. *Mar.* 35, *Sulla* 9; Flor. ii.9.21; Oros. v.19; Eutr. v.4; Livy *Per.* 77.

39. App. *BC* i.58; Plut. *Mar.* 35, *Sulla* 9; Flor. ii.9.21; Vell. Pat. ii.19; Val. Max. viii.6.2; Oros. v.19; Livy *Per.* 77.

40. App. *BC* i.59.

41. App. *BC* i.59; Oros. v.19.

42. App. *BC* i.60; Plut. *Sulla* 10; Cic. *Cat.* iii.24, *Brut.* 168; Flor. ii.9.21; Vell. Pat. ii.19.

43. App. *BC* i.59, 73; Cic. *Phil.* viii.2.7; Livy *Per.* 77.

44. App. *BC* i.59–60; Plut. *Sulla* 10; Vell. Pat. ii.19; Livy *Per.* 77.

45. Quote: Oros. v.19. See also: App. *BC* i.60; Plut. *Sulla* 10; "Cic." *Rhet. Her.* i.25, iv.31, *Orat.* iii.11, *Brut.* 307, *Cat.* iii.24; Vell. Pat. ii.19; Eutr. v.4; Livy *Per.* 77.

46. Plut. *Mar.* 35; Eutr. v.4.

47. Plut. *Mar.* 35–36.

48. Quote: Plut. *Mar.* 36. See also: App. *BC* i.61, 75.

49. Plut. *Mar.* 37.

50. Plut. *Mar.* 37.

51. Quote: Vell. Pat. ii.19. See also: Plut. *Mar.* 38; Cic. *Red. Pop.* 20, *Sest.* 50, *Pis.* 43, *Fin.* ii.105; Sall. *Hist.* i.21; Oros. v.19; Livy *Per.* 77.

52. Quote: App. *BC* i.61. See also: Plut. *Mar.* 38–39; Vell. Pat. ii.19; Val. Max. ii.10.6; Gran. xxxv.15; Oros. v.19; Livy *Per.* 77.

53. Quote: Plut. *Mar.* 39. See also: App. *BC* i.62; Cic. *Sest.* 50, *Planc.* 26; Sall. *Hist.* i.22; Vell. Pat. ii.19; Val. Max. i.5.5; Gran. xxxv.16; Livy *Per.* 77.

54. App. *BC* i.62; Plut. *Mar.* 40.

55. Quotes: Plut. *Mar.* 40, See also: App. *BC* i.62; Cic. *Red. Pop.* 20, *Pis.* 43; Diod. xxxvii.29; Vell. Pat. ii.19; Val. Max. vi.9.6; Oros. v.19; Livy *Per.* 77.

56. App. *Mith.* 22–23; Vell. Pat. ii.18; Plut. *Pomp.* 37; Dio xxx/xxxv.101; Flor. i.40.5; Oros. vi.2; Eutr. v.5; Livy *Per.* 78.

57. App. *Mith.* 22–23, 58, 62; Cic. *Leg. Man.* 7; Vell. Pat. ii.18; Val. Max. ix.2e.3; Dio xxx/xxxv.101, 109; Tac. *Ann.* iv.14; Eutr. v.5; Oros. vi.2; Livy *Per.* 78.

CHAPTER 11: THE SPIKED BOOTS

1. Sall. *Cat.* 11.
2. App. *BC* i.63; Plut. *Sulla* 10.
3. Plut. *Sulla* 10. See also: FC.
4. See Lovano, *The Age of Cinna*, which is an indispensible guide to his life and times.
5. App. *BC* i.60.
6. Plut. *Sulla* 10; Cic. *Planc.* 51; Dio xxx/xxxv.102; Eutr. v.4.
7. Plut. *Sulla* 10.
8. App. *BC* i.63; Vell. Pat. ii.20; Val. Max. ix.7e.2; Livy *Per.* 77.
9. App. *BC* i.64.
10. Plut. *Sulla* 10; Dio xxx/xxxv.102; Eutr. v.4.
11. App. *BC* i.64; Plut. *Mar.* 41; Vell. Pat. ii.20.
12. App. *BC* i.65; Plut. *Mar.* 41, *Sert.* 4; Cic. *Cat.* iii.24, *Phil.* viii.7; Vell. Pat. ii.20; Flor. ii.9.21; Gran. xxxv.15; Livy *Per.* 79.
13. App. *BC* i.65–66; Plut. *Mar.* 41; Vell. Pat. ii.20; Livy *Per.* 79.
14. App. *BC* i.65; Plut. *Sert.* 4; Vell. Pat. ii.20.
15. Quote: App. *BC* i.65. See also: Vell. Pat. ii.20; Livy *Per.* 79.
16. App. *BC* i.66; Vell. Pat. ii.21; Gran. xxxv.19, 21.
17. Quote: Dio xxx/xxxv.102. See also: App. *BC* i.68; Vell. Pat. ii.21; Gran. xxxv.20–21; Dio xxx/xxxv.102; Livy *Per.* 80.
18. Plut. *Sulla* 11; Flor. xl.5.
19. App. *Mith.* 27–28; Plut. *Sulla* 11; Paus. i.20.5; Flor. i.40.5; Eutr. v.6; Livy *Per.* 79.
20. App. *Mith.* 29; Plut. *Sulla* 11.
21. App. *Mith.* 30–32; Plut. *Sulla* 11–12, *Luc.* 2; Paus. ix.7.4; Flor. i.40.5; Eutr. v.6; Livy *Per.* 81.
22. App. *BC* i.67; Plut. *Mar.* 41, *Sert.* 5; Oros. v.19.
23. Quote: Flor. ii.9.21. See also: App. *BC* i.67; Plut. *Mar.* 41, *Sert.* 5; Gran. xxxv.17; Oros. v.19; Livy *Per.* 79.
24. App. *BC* i.67; Plut. *Sert.* 5; Flor. ii.9.21; Val. Max. iv.7.4; Gran. xxxv.17; Oros. v.19; Livy *Per.* 79.
25. App. *BC* i.67; Gran. xxxv.18; Oros. v.19; Livy *Per.* 79.

26. App. *BC* i.67; Plut. *Mar.* 42–43, *Pomp.* 1, 3, *Mor.* 553.b; Vell. Pat. ii.21; Gran. xxxv.18–23; Oros. v.19; Livy *Per.* 80.

27. Quote: Diod. xxxviii.1. See also: App. *BC* i.69–70; Plut. *Mar.* 43; Diod. xxxviii.2–4; Gran. xxxv.23.

28. App. *BC* i.70; Plut. *Mar.* 42; Vell. Pat. ii.21; Dio xxx/xxxv.102; Livy *Per.* 80.

29. Quote: App. *BC* i.70. See also: Plut. *Mar.* 43; Vell. Pat. ii.22; Flor. ii.9.21; Dio xxx/xxxv.102; Val. Max. i.6.10; Ascon. 23; Oros. v.19; Eutr. v.7; Livy *Per.* 80.

30. App. *BC* i.70–71; Plut. *Mar.* 42; Cic. *Tusc.* v.55; Vell. Pat. ii.22; Flor. ii.9.21; Livy *Per.* 80.

31. Quote: App. *BC* i.72. See also: Plut. *Mar.* 44, *Ant.* 1; Cic. *Orat.* iii.10, *Tusc.* v.55, *Brut.* 307, *Fam.*vi.2.2; Flor. ii.9.21; Val. Max. viii.9.2, ix.2.2; Ascon. 25; Livy *Per.* 80.

32. Quotes: Plut. *Mar.* 44, Vell. Pat. ii.22. See also: Cic. *Orat.* iii.9, *Tusc.* v.56, *Brut.* 307, *Nat. Deo.* iii.80; Flor. ii.9.21; Val. Max. ix.12.4–5.

33. Quote: Dio xxx/xxxv.102. See also: App. *BC* i.72–74; Plut. *Mar.* 43, *Cras.* 4; Cic. *Tusc.* v.55, *Cat.* iii.24, *Red. Sen.* 38; Diod. xxxviii.4; Vell. Pat. ii.22; Oros. v.19; Eutr. v.7; Livy *Per.* 80.

34. Quote: Plut. *Mar.* 43. See also: Plut. *Mar.* 44, *Sert.* 5; Dio xxx/xxxv.102; Oros. v.19.

35. Vell. Pat. ii.23; Oros. v.19; Eutr. v.7.

36. Plut. *Sulla* 12, 22.

37. Quote: Plut. *Sulla* 12. See also: Diod. xxxviii.7; Paus. ix.33.6, x.21.6.

38. Quotes: Plut. *Sulla* 13. See also: App. *Mith.* 38–39; Plut. *Sulla* 6, 13–14; Vell. Pat. ii.23; Flor. xl.5; Oros. vi.2; Eutr. v.6; Livy *Per.* 81.

39. Flor. i.40.5; App. *Mith.* 40–41; Plut. *Sulla* 14; Vell. Pat. ii.23–24; Strabo ix.1.15, xiv.2.9; Eutr. v.6.

40. App. *BC* i.75; Plut. *Mar.* 45; Vell. Pat. ii.23; Dio xxx/xxxv.102; Oros. v.19; Livy *Per.* 80.

41. Plut. *Mar.* 45.

42. Plut. *Mar.* 45, *Mor.* 202.b; App. *BC* i.75; Cic. *Tusc.* ii.35, 53, *Nat. Deo.* iii.81; Diod. xxxvii.29; Vell. Pat. ii.23; Flor. ii.9.21; Oros. v.19.

43. Quotes: Livy *Per.* 80, Plut. *Mar.* 45. See also: Plut. *Sulla* 30, *Luc.* 38; Diod. xxxvii.29; Val. Max. ii.2.3, vi.9.14.

44. App. *BC* i.75; Plut. *Sulla* 20; Vell. Pat. ii.23; Livy *Per.* 82.

45. Cic. *Font.* 1; Sall. *Cat.* 33; Vell. Pat. ii.23.

46. Cic. *Leg.* iii.36, *Off.* iii.80–81; Pliny *NH* xxxiii.46, xxxiv.12.

47. App. *Mith.* 42–45; Plut. *Sulla* 15–19, *Luc.* 3, 11; Flor. xl.5; Strabo ix.2.37; Paus. i.20.6, ix.40.7; Eutr. v.6; Oros. vi.2; Livy *Per.* 82.

48. App. *Mith.* 51; Plut. *Sulla* 20.

49. Quote: Plut. *Sulla* 21. See also: App. *Mith.* 49; Plut. *Sulla* 22; Flor. xl.5; Front. ii.3.17, 8.12; Gran. xxxv.24–26; Eutr. v.6; Oros. vi.2; Livy *Per.* 82.

50. App. *Mith.* 52; Plut. *Sulla* 23, *Luc.* 7, 34; Diod. xxxviii.8.1; Vell. Pat. ii.24; Val. Max. 9.11.2; Strabo xiii.1.27; Dio xxx/xxxv.104; Oros. vi.2; Livy *Per.* 82.

51. App. *Mith.* 52; Plut. *Luc.* 3; Diod. xxxviii.8.2–3; Vell. Pat. ii.24; Dio xxx/xxxv.104; Livy *Per.* 83.

52. Plut. *Sulla* 22–23; Gran. xxxv.26–27; Eutr. v.6–7.

53. Quote: Plut. *Sulla* 24. See also: App. *Mith.* 56–58; Plut. *Luc.* 4; Sall. *Hist.* i.27; Vell. Pat. ii.23; Flor. i.40.5; Strabo xiii.1.27–28; Gran. xxxv.27; Eutr. v.7; Livy *Per.* 83.

54. Plut. *Sulla* 24; Flor. i.40.5.

55. App. *Mith.* 59–60; Plut. *Sulla* 25; Diod. xxxviii.8.4; Vell. Pat. ii.24; Oros. vi.2; Livy *Per.* 83.

56. App. *Mith.* 61–63; Plut. *Sulla* 25, *Luc.* 4; Cic. *Flac.* 32; Flor. xl.5; Gran. xxxv.28.

57. Cic. *Brut.* 308.

58. Livy *Per.* 84, 86; Cic. *Phil.* xii.27.

59. App. *BC* i.76; Livy *Per.* 83.

60. App. *BC* i.77.

61. App. *BC* i.76–77; Livy *Per.* 83.

62. App. *BC* i.78; Livy *Per.* 83.

63. App. *BC* i.78.

64. App. *BC* i.78; Plut. *Pomp.* 5, *Sert.* 6; Vell. Pat. ii.24; Dio xlv.47, lii.13; Livy *Per.* 83.

65. Quotes: Cic. *Nat. Deo.* iii.81; Vell. Pat. ii.24.

CHAPTER 12: CIVIL WAR

1. App. *BC* i.60.

2. App. *BC* i.78; Vell. Pat. ii.24; Livy *Per.* 84.

3. Diod. xxxviii.13.

4. App. *BC* i.81.

5. App. *Ill.* 5; Plut. *Cras.* 6, *Numa* 9; Cic. *Verr.* ii.2.5, 5.8; Diod. xxxvii.2, xxxviii.8; Livy *Per.* 84.

6. Quote: Cic. *Brut.* 239. See also: Plut *Pomp.* 1–3, *Mor.* 717.c; App. *BC* i.12; Cic. *Leg. Man.* 28; Vell. Pat. ii.53; Val. Max. v.2.9; Pliny *NH* xxxvii.6; Gran. xxxiii.13; Strabo xiv.1.48.

7. App. *BC* i.82, ii.13–14, iii.46; Plut. *Caes.* 14, *Cato. Min.* 33, *Pomp.* 48, *Cras.* 14; Dio xxxviii.8, xlv.13; Vell. Pat. ii.44; Seut. *Caes.* 14.

8. Quote: App. *BC* i.82. See also: Livy *Per.* 84.
9. Plut. *Sulla* 27; Vell. Pat. ii.24.
10. App. *BC* i.79, 84; Plut. *Sulla* 27; Flor. ii.9.21; Sall. *Hist.* i.28; Vell. Pat. ii.25; Eutr. v.7; Livy *Per.* 85.
11. Plut. *Sulla* 27.
12. App. *BC* i.81.
13. App. *BC* i.80–81; Plut. *Cras.* 6; Dio xxx/xxxv.106; Livy *Per.* 84.
14. App. *BC* i.80.
15. Diod. xxxviii.9; App. *BC* i.80; Plut. *Pomp.* 6–8, *Cras.* 6; Cic. *Phil.* v.43–44, *Leg. Man.* 61; Sall. *Hist.* v.16; Val. Max. v.2.9; Dio xxx/xxxv.107; Livy *Per.* 85.
16. Quote: Plut. *Cras.* 6.
17. App. *BC* i.80; Cic. *Pro. Cons.* 21; Livy *Per.* 85.
18. Plut. *Sulla* 27.
19. App. *BC* i.84; Plut. *Sulla* 27; Vell. Pat. ii.25; Flor. ii.9.21; Oros. v.20; Eutr. v.7; Livy *Per.* 85.
20. App. *BC* i.85; Plut. *Sulla* 28, *Sert.* 6.
21. Quote: App. *BC* i.85. See also: Plut. *Sulla* 28, *Sert.* 6; Cic. *Phil.* xii.27, xiii.1.
22. App. *BC* i.85; Plut. *Sert.* 6.
23. Quote: Plut. *Sulla* 28. See also: App. *BC* i.85–86; Sall. *Hist.* i.29; Diod. xxxviii.16; Vell. Pat. ii.25; Flor. ii.9.21; Eutr. v.7; Livy *Per.* 85.
24. App. *BC* i.86.
25. Quote: Diod. xxxviii.13. See also: App. *BC* i.86; Cic. *Phil.* xii.27.
26. App. *BC* i.86; Plut. *Pomp.* 6; Flor. ii.10.22; Vell. Pat. ii.25.
27. Quote: Diod. xxxviii.10. See also: Plut. *Pomp.* 7.
28. App. *BC* i.86; Plut. *Sert.* 6.
29. App. *BC* i.87; Sall. *Hist.* i.30; Vell. Pat. ii.26; Livy *Per.* 86.
30. App. *BC* i.87.
31. App. *BC* i.87; Diod. xxxviii.12–13.
32. App. *BC* i.87; Plut. *Sulla* 28; Sall. *Hist.* i.30–32; Flor. ii.9.21; Vell. Pat. ii.26; Oros. v.20; Eutr. v.8; Livy *Per.* 87.
33. App. *BC* i.87.
34. App. *BC* i.87–88; Dio xxx/xxxv.108; Livy *Per.* 87.
35. App. *BC* i.88.
36. Diod. xxxviii.17; App. *BC* i.88; Cic. *Brut.* 311, *Nat. Deo.* iii.80, *Fam.* ix.21; Diod. xxxviii.17; Vell. Pat. ii.26; Flor. ii.9.21; Val. Max. ix.2.3; Oros. v.20; Livy *Per.* 87.
37. App. *BC* i.88–89; Eutr. v.8; Livy *Per.* 87.
38. App. *BC* i.89.
39. Quote: Plut. *Sulla* 30.

40. Plut. *Pomp.* 6.
41. App. *BC* i.89; Vell. Pat. ii.28; Pliny *NH* viii.82.
42. App. *BC* i.89–90; Oros. v.20.
43. App. *BC* i.90.
44. Plut. *Sulla* 28.
45. Quote: App. *BC* i.91.
46. Plut. *Sulla* 28; Sall. *Hist.* i.33; Eutr. v.8; Livy *Per.* 88.
47. App. *BC* i.92; Plut. *Sulla* 29.
48. App. *BC* i.92; Plut. *Sulla* 29; Sall. *Hist.* i.34.
49. Quote: Vell. Pat. ii.27. See also: Strabo v.4.11; Livy *Per.* 88.
50. App. *BC* i.93; Plut. *Sulla* 29, *Cras.* 6; Strabo v.4.11; Oros. v.20; Eutr. v.8; Livy *Per.* 88.
51. Quote: App. *BC* i.94. See also: Diod. xxxvii.29, xxxviii.15; Vell. Pat. ii.27; Val. Max. xi.8.2, ix.2.1; Strabo v.3.11; Front. ii.9.3; Livy *Per.* 88.
52. Dio xxx/xxxv.109.

CHAPTER 13: DICTATOR FOR LIFE

1. Seut. *Caes.* 77.
2. Plut. *Sulla* 30; Dio xxx/xxxv.109.
3. Quote: Plut. *Sulla* 30. See also: Dio xxx/xxxv.109; Flor. ii.9.25; Val. Max. ix.2.1; Strabo v.4.11; Oros. v.21.
4. App. *BC* i.95.
5. Quote: Plut. *Sulla* 31. See also: App. *BC* i.95; Livy *Per.* 88.
6. Plut. *Sulla* 31; App. *BC* i.95; Cic. *Leg.* ii.56; Vell. Pat. ii.28; Dio xxx/xxxv.109; Val. Max. ix.2.1; Pliny *NH* vii.54; Gran. xxxvi.33; Seut. *Caes.* 11; Flor. ii.9.25.
7. Plut. *Sulla* 31; App. *BC* i.95; Diod. xxxviii.19; Dio xxx/xxxv.109; Oros. v.21.
8. Plut. *Sulla* 31; App. *BC* i.95; Cic. *Verr.* ii.3.8, *Leg. Agr.* ii.56, *Rosc. Am.* 126; Dio xxx/xxxv.109.
9. Plut. *Sulla* 31, *Cras.* 3, 6; App. *BC* i.96; Dio xxx/xxxv.109.
10. Plut. *Sulla* 32; Sall. *Cat.* 5, 16, 37, *Hist.* i.36–37; Flor. ii.9.25; Val. Max. ix.2.1; Ascon. 84, 90–91; Pliny *NH* xxxiv.12; Oros. v.21; Livy *Per.* 89.
11. Plut. *Sulla* 1; Cic. *Rosc. Am.* 15–32; Dio xxx/xxxv.109; Oros. v.21.
12. Quote: Plut. *Pomp.* 9. See also: Plut. *Sulla* 31; App. *BC* i.95–96; Sall. *Hist.* i.44; Val. Max. v.3.5, vi.2.8, ix.13.2; Eutr. v.8; Oros. v.21; Livy *Per.* 89.
13. Quote: Vell. Pat. ii.22. See also: Dio xxx/xxxv.109; Sall. *Cat.* 37.
14. Quote: Seut. *Caes.* 1. See also: Seut. *Caes.* 74; Plut. *Caes.* 1; Dio xliii.43; Vell. Pat. ii.41, 43.
15. App. *BC* 95, 103; Cic. *Rosc. Am.* 128; Flor. ii.9.25.

294 NOTES

16. Plut. *Sulla* 34 *Mor.* 318.d, 542.f; App. *BC* i.97; Cic. *Phil.* ix13; Diod. xxxviii.15; Vell. Pat. ii.27, 61; Livy xxx.45; Val. Max, xi.4.4, ix.2.1; Pliny *NH* vii.43.

17. Plut. *Sulla* 33, *Pomp.* 9; App. *BC* i.98; Vell. Pat. ii.28; Livy *Per.* 89.

18. App. *BC* i.3, 98; Cic. *Verr.* ii.3.82, *Leg. Agr.* Iii.5–6, 8, *Leg.* i.42; Oros. v.21.

19. Plut. *Sulla* 33.

20. App. *BC* i.98–99.

21. Livy *Per.* 89.

22. App. *BC* i.100, ii.29; Cic. *Verr.* ii.1.155, *Leg.* iii.22; Caes. *BC* i.7; Vell. Pat. ii.30; Ascon. 67, 78; Seut. *Caes.* 5; Livy *Per.* 89.

23. App. *BC* i.100; Cic. *Luc.* ii.1; Tac. *Ann.* 11.

24. Cic. *Fam.* i.9.25, iii.6.3, 6.6, 10.6.

25. App. *BC* i.100; Sall. *Cat.* 37; Livy *Per.* 89.

26. Cic. *Verr.* i.37–38, ii.2.77; Vell. Pat. ii.32; Tac. *Ann.* xi.22.

27. Cic. *Clu.* 151, 154, *Fam.* iii.11.2, *Rab. Post.* 8–9, *Pis.* 50; Just. i.2.2.32, ix.2.5.1, xxix.5.25.1, xlvii.5.23.2, 10.5.1–7, 37, xlviii.2.12.4, 5.33.1, 8.1.17.

28. App. *BC* i.96, 102; Cic. *Leg. Agr.* ii.35, 68–70, 78, 81, iii.7, 12; Gran. xxviii.10; Flor. ii.9.25; Livy *Per.* 89.

29. Gell. ii.24.11; Amm. xvi.5.

30. Plut. *Pomp.* 22, *Mor.* 203.f-204.a; Cic. *Verr.* i.54l; Val. Max. v.9.1. See also Brunt, *Italian Manpower*, ch. 7.

31. Plut. *Sulla* 34; App. *BC* i.103.

32. Plut. *Sulla* 33; App. *BC* i.100; Ascon. 91; Livy *Per.* 89.

33. Quote: App. *BC* i.104. See also: Oros. v.22.

34. Plut. *Sulla* 35–36; App. *BC* i.103–104; Cic. *Planc.* 51; Sall. *Hist.* i.50–53; Val. Max. vi.9.6; Pliny *NH* xxxiii.47.

35. Plut. *Sulla* 37.

36. Quote: Plut. *Sulla* 37. See also: App. *BC* i.105; Pliny vii.43.

37. Quote: Plut. *Sulla* 37. See also: App. *BC* i.105; Dio lii.17; Val. Max. ix.3.8; Pliny *NH* vii.43; Paus. i.20.7, ix.33.6; Livy *Per.* 90.

38. Plut. *Sulla* 38, *Luc.* 43, *Pomp.* 15, 81; App. *BC* i.105–106; Cic. *Leg.* ii.57; Pliny *NH* vii.54; Gran. xxxvi.32–33.

39. Quote: Plut. *Sulla* 38. See also Plut. *Pomp.* 15; App. *BC* i.106.

40. Cic. *Verr.* ii.1.123, *Fam.* xviii.5.2; Dio xliii.50; Vell. Pat. ii.28; Livy *Per.* 88.

41. Tribunes: Cic. *Verr.* i.44, *Leg.* iii.22, 26; Sall. *Cat.* 38; Caes. *BC* i.7; Livy. *Per.* 97; Vell. Pat. ii.30; Ascon. 76; Tac. *Ann.* iii.27; Plut. *Pomp.* 22; App. *BC* ii.29. Juries: Cic. *Verr.* ii.2.174, 3.223, *Clu.* 130, *Phil.* i.20; Livy. *Per.* 97; Vell. Pat. ii.32; Ascon 17, 67, 78; Tac. *Ann.* iii.28; Plut. *Pomp.* 22. Land: Cic. *Leg. Agr.* ii.35, 68–70, 78, 81, iii.7, 12.

42. App. *BC* i.27–30; Plut. *Mar.* 29, *Cras.* 2; Cic. *Leg.* ii.14, *Leg. Agr.* ii.35, 68–70, 78, 81, iii.7, 12; "Caes." *BA* 56; Livy *Per.* 69.

43. Plut. *Cras.* 12, *Cato Min.* 26, *Caes.* 8, *Pomp.* 50; Cic. *Off.* ii.58, *Verr.* ii.3.163, 173, 214–216, ii.5.52, *Scaur.* 3, *Att.* xv.9–12; Dio xxxix.24; Ascon. 48; Sall. *Hist.* ii.44–47, iii.48.

44. See Syme, *Roman Revolution*, ch. 5.

45. Quote: Seut. *Tib.* 32.

46. Quote: Dio lxxviii.9.

47. Plut. *Pomp.* 16–20, *Sert.* 6–27; App. *BC* 108–115; Flor. ii.11; Oros. v.24–25; Livy *Per.* 90–93, 96.

48. Plut. *Cras.* 12, *Pomp.* 23; Seut. *Caes.* 19; Sall. *Hist.* iv.51.

49. Plut. *Caes.* 5; Seut. *Caes.* 6.

50. See most especially: App. *BC* 8–29, *Mith.* 64–113; Plut. *Pomp.* 31–52, *Luc.* 5–42, *Caes.* 14–28, *Cras.* 14–33; Caes. *BC, BG.*

51. Quote: Seut. *Caes.* 77.

52. See most especially: Dio liii.1–33; Seut. *Aug.* 25–31.

THE ANCIENT SOURCES

STANDARD ABBREVIATIONS FOR the ancient sources use the Latin title of the work. For example, the first entry under Appian is "*BC*," which is short for *Bellum Civile*—translated as *The Civil Wars*. Both Varro and Cato the Elder wrote works titled *On Agriculture*, which in Latin is *Re Rustica*, and thus abbreviated *RR*. This reference table moves straight from the Latin abbreviation to the English translation.

The translations of the cited works come from the original editions of the Loeb Classical Library. These editions are now in the public domain and available at several online databases of classical literature. The primary databases utilized were the Perseus Digital Library, LacusCurtius, Livius.org, and Attalus.org. I encourage everyone who is interested in learning more about Roman history to dive headlong into the ancient sources. They are the root of all knowledge.

XII	The Law of the Twelve Tables
1–12	indicates Table
Amm.	Ammianus Marcelinus
RG	*Things Done*
App.	Appian
BC	*The Civil Wars*
Gall.	*The Gallic Wars*
Han.	*The Hannibalic War*
Iber.	*The Wars in Spain*

Ill.	The Illyrian Wars
Isl.	The Wars in Sicily and Other Islands
Mac.	The Macedonian Wars
Mith.	The Mithridatic Wars
Pun.	The Punic Wars
Reg.	The Wars of the Kings
Samn.	The Samnite Wars
Ascon.	Asconius
Orat. Cic.	Commentaries on Five Speeches of Cicero
Athen.	Athenaeus
Dei.	Banquet of Scholars
Caes.	Julius Caesar
BC	Commentaries on the Civil War
BG	Commentaries on the Gallic War
"Caes."	Pseudo-Caesar
BA	The African War
CAH	Cambridge Ancient History
Cato	Cato the Elder
RR	On Agriculture
Cic.	Cicero
Amic.	On Friendship
Arch.	For Archias
Att.	To Atticus
Balb.	For Balbus
Brut.	Brutus
Cael.	For Caelius
Cat.	Cataline Orations
Clu.	For Aulus Cluentius
Deiot.	For King Deiotarus
Div.	On Divination
Div. Caec.	Divinatio Against Quintus Caecilius
Dom.	Speech for His House to the Priests
Fam.	Letters to Friends
Fin.	On the Ends of Good and Evil

Flacc.	*For Flaccus*
Font.	*For Fonto*
Har. Resp.	*On the Responses of the Haruspices*
Leg.	*On the Laws*
Leg. Agr.	*On Agrarian Laws*
Leg. Man.	*For the Manilian Law*
Luc.	*Lucullus*
Milo	*For Milo*
Mur.	*For Lucius Murena*
Nat. Deo.	*On the Nature of the Gods*
Off.	*On Duties*
Orat.	*On the Orator*
Phil.	*Philippics*
Pis.	*Against Piso*
Planc.	*For Planciuso*
Pro. Cons.	*On Consular Provinces*
Quint.	*Letters to/from Quintus*
Rab. Perd.	*Defense of Rabirus for Treason*
Rab. Post.	*For Rabirius Postumus*
Red. Pop.	*Return Address to the People*
Red. Sen.	*Return Address to the Senate*
Rep.	*On the Republic*
Rosc. Am.	*For Sextus Roscius of Ameria*
Scaur.	*For Scaurus*
Sest.	*For Sestius*
Tusc.	*Tusculan Disputations*
Verr.	*Against Verres*

"Cic."	Pseudo-Cicero
Rhet. Her.	*Rhetoric for Herrenius*

CIL	*Corpus Inscriptionum Latinarum*

Dio	Cassius Dio
Hist.	*The Roman Histories*

Diod.	Diodorus Siculus
Bib. Hist.	*Library of Roman History*

Diony.	Dionysius of Halicarnassus
Rom. Ant.	*Roman Antiquities*

| Eur. | Euripides |
| Phoen. | *Phoenissae* |

| Eutr. | Eutropius |
| Brev. | *Abridgement of Roman History* |

| FC | *Fasti Capitolini* |

| Fest. | Festus |
| Brev. | *Summary of the Achievements of the Roman People* |

| Flor. | Florus |
| Epit. | *Epitome of Roman History* |

| Front. | Frontius |
| Strat. | *Strategems* |

| FT | *Fasti Triumphales* |

| Gell. | Aulus Gellius |
| Att. | *Attic Nights* |

| Gran. | Granius Licinianus |
| Hist. | *History of Rome* |

| Hor. | Horace |
| Odes | *Odes* |

| Just. | Justin |
| Phil. | *Philippic Histories* |

| Juv. | Juvenal |
| Sat. | *Satires* |

Livy	Livy
Ab. Urb.	*Books from the Foundation of the City*
Per.	*Periochae*

| Macr. | Macrobius |
| Sat. | *Saturnalia* |

Obseq. Julius Obsequens
Prod. *Book of Prodigies*

ORF *Oratorum Romanorum Fragmenta*

Oros. Orosius
Adv. Pag. *History Against the Pagans*

Paus. Pausanias
Desc. *Description of Greece*

Pliny Pliny the Elder
NH *Natural History*

Pliny Min. Pliny the Younger
Lett. *Letters*

Plut. Plutarch
Aem. Paul. *Aemilius Paullus*
Ant. *Marc Antony*
Caes. *Julius Caesar*
Cam. *Camillus*
Cato Maj. *Cato the Elder*
Cato Min. *Cato the Younger*
CG *Gaius Gracchus*
Cor. *Coriolanus*
Cras. *Crassus*
Dem. *Demetrius*
Fab. Max. *Fabius Maximus*
Flam. *Flaminius*
Luc. *Lucullus*
Mar. *Marius*
Marc. *Lucullus*
Mor. *Roman Questions*
Num. *Numa*
Pomp. *Pompey*
Pub. *Publicola*
Rom. *Romulus*
Sert. *Sertorius*
Sulla *Sulla*
TG *Tiberius Gracchus*

"Plut."	Pseudo-Plutarch
Apoph.	*Sayings of the Romans*
Polyb.	Polybius
Hist.	*Histories*
Sall.	Sallust
Cat.	*Conspiracy of Catiline*
Hist.	*The Histories (Fragments)*
Jug.	*The Jugurthine War*
Seut.	Seutonius
Aug.	*Augustus*
Caes.	*Julius Caesar*
Tib.	*Tiberius*
Strabo	Strabo
Geo.	*Geography*
Tac.	Tacitus
Ann.	*Annals*
Germ.	*Germania*
Hist.	*Histories*
Orat.	*Dialogue on Oratory*
Ulp.	Ulpian
Dig.	*The Digest of Justinian*
Val. Max.	Valerius Maximus
Fact. Dict.	*Memorable Deeds and Sayings*
Varro	Varro
LL	*On the Latin Language*
RR	*On Agriculture*
Vell. Pat.	Velleius Paterculus
Hist.	*The Roman History*
"Vict."	Pseudo–Aurelius Victor
Vir. Ill.	*On Illustrious Men*

SELECT MODERN SOURCES

Astin, A.E. *Scipio Aemilianus*. Oxford: Clarendon Press, 1967.

Badian, Ernst. *Foreign Clientelae, 264–70 B.C.* Oxford: Clarendon Press, (1958) 1984.

———. *Publicans and Sinners: Private Enterprise in the Service of the Roman Republic*. Ithaca, NY: Cornell University Press, 1972.

———. *Roman Imperialism in the Late Republic*. Oxford: Basil Blackwell, 1968.

Baker, G.P. *Sulla the Fortunate*. New York: Barnes & Noble, 1967. First published 1927 by the University of Michigan Press.

Bernstein, Alvin H. *Tiberius Sempronius Gracchus: Tradition and Apostasy*. Ithaca and London: Cornell University Press, 1978.

Botsford, George Willis. *The Roman Assemblies: From Their Origin to the End of the Republic*. New York: MacMillan Company, 1909.

Brunt, P. A. *Italian Manpower 225 BC–AD 14*. Oxford: Clarendon Press, 1971.

———. *Social Conflict in the Roman Republic*. New York and London: W. W. Norton, 1971.

Carney, Thomas. *A Biography of C. Marius*. Assen, Netherlands: Royal VanGorcum, 1961.

Clark, Jessica. *Triumph in Defeat: Military Loss and the Roman Republic*. New York: Oxford University Press, 2014.

Crook, J. A., A. Lintott, & E. Rawson, eds.. *The Cambridge Ancient History Vol. IX*. Cambridge: Cambridge University Press, 1994.

Dart, Christopher. *The Social War, 91–88 BC*. Farnham: Ashgate, 2014.

Earl, D. C. *Political Thought of Sallust*. Cambridge: Cambridge University Press, 1961.

———. *Tiberius Gracchus: A Study in Politics*. Vol. LXIV. Brussels: Collection Latomus, 1963.

Eckstein, Arthur M. *Senate and General: Individual Decision Making and Roman Foreign Relations, 261–194 BC*. Berkeley: University of California Press, 1987.

Evans, Richard. J. *Gaius Marius: A Political Biography*. Pretoria: University of South Africa Press, 1994.

Gabba, Emilio. *Republican Rome: The Army & the Allies*. Berkeley: University of California Press, 1976.

Gargola, Daniel J. *Lands, Laws, & Gods: Magistrates & Ceremony in the Regulation of Public Lands in Republican Rome*. Chapel Hill: University of North Carolina Press, 1995.

Goldsworthy, Adrian. *The Roman Army at War 100 BC–AD 200*. Oxford: Clarendon Press, 1996.

Gruen, Erich. *The Last Generation of the Roman Republic*. Berkeley: University of California Press, 1974.

———. *Roman Politics & the Criminal Courts 149–78 B.C.* Cambridge, MA: Harvard University Press, 1968.

Hildinger, Erik. *Swords Against the Senate: The Rise of the Roman Army and the Fall of the Republic*. Boston: Da Capo Press, 2002.

Hölkeskamp, Karl-Joachim. *Reconstructing the Roman Republic: An Ancient Political Culture and Modern Research*. Woodstock: Princeton University Press, 2010.

Keaveney, Arthur. *The Army in the Roman Revolution*. New York: Routledge, 2007.

———. *Sulla: The Last Republican*, 2nd ed. New York: Routledge, 2005. First published 1982 by Croom Helm.

Lintott, Andrew. *The Constitution of the Roman Republic*. Oxford: Clarendon Press, 1999.

———. *Judicial Reform and Land Reform in the Roman Republic*. Cambridge: Cambridge University Press, 1992.

———. *Violence in Republican Rome*. Oxford: Oxford University Press, 1999.

Lovano, Michael. *The Age of Cinna: Crucible of Late Republican Rome*. Historia: Einzelschriften No. 158. Stuttgart, Ger.: Franz Steiner, 2002.

Mackay, Christopher S. *The Breakdown of the Roman Republic: From Oligarchy to Empire*. New York: Cambridge University Press, 2009.

Mayor, Adrienne. *The Poison King: The Life and Legend of Mithridates*. Princeton: Princeton University Press, 2010.

Millar, Fergus. *The Crowd in Rome in the Late Republic*. Ann Arbor: University of Michigan Press, 1998.

———. *Rome, The Greek World and the East, Vol. 1: The Roman Republic and the Augustan Revolution*. Edited by Hannah M. Cotton and Guy M. Rogers. Chapel Hill and London: University of North Carolina Press, 2002.

Mommsen, Theodor. *The History of Rome: A New Edition*. Merriam Books, 1958.

Mouritsen, Henrik. *Plebs and Politics in the Late Roman Republic*. Cambridge: Cambridge University Press, 2001.

Robinson, O. F. *The Criminal Law of Ancient Rome*. Baltimore: Johns Hopkins University Press, 1995.

Roth, Jonathan P. *The Logistics of the Roman Army at War (264 BC–AD 235)*. Boston: Brill, 1998.

Sampson, Gareth. *The Crisis of Rome: The Jugurthine and Northern Wars and the Rise of Marius*. Barnsley: Pen & Sword, 2010.

Scullard, H. H. *From the Gracchi to Nero: A History of Rome from 133 BC to AD 68*, 5th ed. First published 1982. Reprint, London and New York: Routledge, 2002.

Seager, Robin, ed. *The Crisis of the Roman Republic*. New York: Barnes & Noble, 1969.

Shaw, Brent. *Spartacus and the Slave Wars: A Brief History with Documents*. Boston: Bedford, 2001.

Stockton, David. *The Gracchi*. Oxford: Clarendon Press, 1979.

Syme, Ronald. *Sallust*. Berkeley: University of California Press, 2002. First published 1964 by University of California Press.

———. *Roman Revolution*. Revised Edition. Oxford: Oxford University Press, 2002.

Taylor, Lily Ross. *Party Politics in the Age of Caesar*. Berkeley: University of California Press, 1961.

———. *Roman Voting Assemblies from the Hannibalic War to the Dictatorship of Caesar*. Ann Arbor: University of Michigan Press, 1966.

Vishnia, Rachel Feig. *State, Society and Popular Leaders in Mid-Republican Rome, 241–167 BC*. New York: Routledge, 1996.

Walbank, F.W., A. E. Astin, M. Frederiksen, & R. Ogilvie, eds. *The Cambridge Ancient History Vol. VII* (The Cambridge Ancient History) Cambridge: Cambridge University, 1990.

———. *Polybius*. Berkeley: University of California Press, 1972.

White, Sherwin. *The Roman Citizenship*. Oxford: Clarendon Press, 1973.

Wiseman, T. P. *New Men in the Roman Senate, 139 B.C.–A.D. 14*. Oxford: Oxford University Press, 1971.

INDEX